THE STONYFIELD FARM
YOGURT COOKBOOK

THE STONYFIELD FARM YOGURT COOKBOOK

By Meg Cadoux Hirshberg

SCB

Stonyfield
Cultured
Books

Stonyfield Cultured Books
10 Burton Drive
Londonderry, New Hampshire 03050

First Edition © August 1991 by Meg Cadoux Hirshberg
Second Printing, August 1993

Reprint Edition, August 1995

Library of Congress Cataloging-in-Publication Data

Hirshberg, Meg Cadoux, 1956-
The Stonyfield Farm yogurt cookbook / by Meg Cadoux Hirshberg.
p. cm.
Includes index.
ISBN 0-9646695-0-1 (softcover)
1. Cookery (Yogurt) I. Title
TX759.5Y63H57 1991
641.6'7146 - dc20

Design by Eugenie S. Delaney
Cover and inside photographs by Becky Luigart-Stayner
Photographic assistance by Clare K. Cavanaugh
Food styling by Susan Herr
Illustrations by Susan Melrath

Trade distribution by
CHELSEA GREEN PUBLISHING
205 Gates-Briggs Building
White River Junction, Vermont 05001

Printed and bound in Canada by
D. W. Friesen & Sons, Altona, Manitoba

ACKNOWLEDGMENTS

■

Many thanks to all the recipe testers, who cheerfully sorted out the culinary bombs from the triumphs: Carol Chapman, Pat Collins, Pat Coviello, R. Kent Cummings, Nancy Davis, Mark Evans, Carolyn Gregson, Eileen Kaymen, Louise Kaymen, Diane Koss, Zoe Neal, Jocelyn Secker-Walker, Gretchen Semuskie, Catherine Thibault, Susan White, and Janet Wilson. And bravo to all the recipe submitters! Now your wonderful creations can be enjoyed by all.

Thank you, Sharon Smith, for your expert editing and good humor throughout the process. And many thanks to Sandy Taylor, who believed in this book from the beginning and saw it through to the end.

My gratitude to Betsy Hiser, Camden House nutritionist, who patiently reviewed the introductory material for accuracy. Many thanks to James Lawrence and Rux Martin, also of Camden House, for their early enthusiasm for and attention to this project, despite countless other demands on their time.

Thanks also to Bob Cadoux, Michael Congdon, and Beverly Jacobson, who provided valuable support and advice.

I am indebted to Eugenie Delaney, designer; Becky Luigart-Stayner, photographer; Clare Cavanaugh, photographer's assistant; Susan Herr, food stylist; and Susan Melrath, illustrator; for making this book as attractive and appealing as the recipes it presents.

And finally, thank you, Samuel and Louise Kaymen, partners, neighbors, and friends, for creating the delicious product that made this book possible.

For my beautiful mother, Doris,
nurturer and nourisher; and for Gary, who
makes dreams come true.

Contents

■

The Stonyfield Story 8

Yogurt: The Perfect Food? 10

What Exactly Is Yogurt? 13

A Buyer's Guide to Yogurt 15

A Few Notes for the Cook 16

Breakfasts & Brunches 19

Breads 27

Fresh Fruit & Yogurt 67

Dips, Spreads, Sauces & Dressings 81

Soups 97

Salads & Side Dishes 107

Main Dishes 123

    Poultry 124

    Red Meat 145

    Seafood 156

    Vegetarian 164

Desserts 173

    Cakes & Cookies 174

    Frozen Desserts 187

    Pies, Puddings & Other Desserts 195

Index 218

THE STONYFIELD STORY

∎

It's been almost two hundred years since the original foundation was laid for the main house at Stonyfield Farm. We don't know anything about those hardy folks who first settled this land, but we can be sure that as they cut and hauled trees, lugged rocks for the stone walls, cleared pastures, built the barn, milked the cows, plowed the fields, and thought their thoughts, they could never have dreamed that someday their farm would be the site of a thriving yogurt business.

Today, Stonyfield Farm Yogurt is sold in every major supermarket chain in New England and is rapidly expanding outside that area, as well as into the world of frozen yogurts. But even as recently as the mid-1980s, such an enterprise was not so much as a gleam in founder Samuel Kaymen's eye.

Indeed, Samuel's background and education would not appear to have prepared him for the role of yogurt mogul: trained as a chemist and engineer, he owned a contamination control company in New Jersey, which he sold in 1964 to seek a more rural lifestyle. Samuel, his wife Louise, and their then three children moved to upstate New York, then eventually to a fifty-acre homestead in Cornish, New Hampshire. It was in Cornish that they learned to become self-sufficient, maintaining cows, pigs, sheep, ducks, geese, chickens, huge gardens, fruit trees, berries, grapes, grains, and by then six children.

It was also on this farm that they learned to change the raw milk from "Laurabelle" into delicious yogurt atop their wood stove. Samuel, a diabetic, kept experimenting to find the perfect yogurt: wholesome, sweet, mild, and creamy, requiring no added sugar. By the time they moved to Wilton, New Hampshire, in 1978, they had several Jersey cows to take with them — as well as the recipe for what would become Stonyfield Farm Yogurt.

From Wilton they started selling quarts of plain yogurt to local health food stores. Word spread, demand grew, and soon there were more cows than kids at Stonyfield. But yogurt was still just a sideline for the Kaymens; most of their energy was devoted to a school they had founded in 1979, The Rural Education Center. This was a nonprofit organization devoted to teaching rural and homesteading skills. It attracted students and supporters from all over the world, and at its height had two thousand members and hundreds of students every year. But the Center relied on philanthropy for a large part of its financial support, and in 1981 those funds began to dry up.

Meanwhile, down on Cape Cod, future partner Gary Hirshberg was facing similar problems finding funding for the organization he then directed, the New Alchemy Institute. The Institute is also a nonprofit organization, specializing in developing alternative technologies, including solar greenhouses, organic gardening, and Gary's specialty, the water-pumping windmill. But since funding was becoming a problem at New Alchemy as well, Gary was implementing new programs and mini-enterprises to help the Institute generate its own revenues. Largely because of Gary's business and financial background, Samuel and The Rural Education Center board of trustees recruited him in 1982 to help implement a business strategy.

A seed had been planted. To create a new source of much-needed revenue for the Education Center, why not expand the dairy herd, add value to the farm's very own milk, and make yogurt production a serious financial venture? On April 9, 1983, Stonyfield produced its first fifty-gallon batch of yogurt. In September of that year, Gary left New Alchemy and moved to Wilton with the dream of turning this small-scale yogurt business into a cottage industry that would fund the Education Center. The first hint of just how fast the business would take off came the very next month, when the dairy buyer for a large Massachusetts supermarket chain called Samuel and asked why Stonyfield was being sold to other stores in the buyer's area and not to his chain. Samuel explained that more yogurt meant more cows, and the fledgling business didn't have any more cows. "Well," came the response, "then *get* some more cows!"

But there was no room for more cows. There was also no time to tend them; Samuel, Louise, and Gary were running the farm, milking the cows, making and delivering the yogurt, financing the business, and running the Education Center. Then, suddenly, the enterprise was literally struck by lightning. One November night in 1984 an electrical storm knocked out the power at Stonyfield, and with it the electric milking machine. After a full day of doing their other chores, Samuel, Louise, and Gary were faced with milking all nineteen cows by hand. The cows were even more upset than the people. Unaccustomed to being milked in the dark by human hands, they stomped their feet, mooed, and kicked over buckets. The three milkers looked at one another, recognized the hopelessness of the situation, and realized sadly that the cows just had to go.

Stonyfield began buying pure Jersey milk from local dairy farmers. The old wood boiler that had been used to heat the milk was replaced by an oil-fired boiler; gone were the days of tending wood fires to warm the milk and incubator. The Rural Education Center went into dormancy. Five former bedrooms in the old farmhouse were converted to offices. Wood heat in the offices and a spectacular mountain view belied the fact that Stonyfield had become a modern small business with computers and sophisticated dairy processing equipment.

The addition of a new filling and capping machine in 1985 allowed the company to expand from selling just quarts of plain yogurt to offering individual-serving containers with such flavors as strawberry, raspberry, French vanilla, peach, apricot mango, and cappuccino.

I came into the picture at about this time, when I met Gary at a conference and soon had him making personal weekend deliveries of yogurt to New Jersey, where

I was living. Two years later I joined Gary in New Hampshire when we were married, and we have now added two small yogurt eaters to the population.

A hilltop farm is a great place to raise children, but it's not always the best place to run a business. By the time I joined Gary in 1986, eighteen-wheel tractor trailers were arriving almost daily to pick up and deliver products, and for fully six months of the year they were getting stuck or sliding on the snow, mud, or ice. Full-time yogurt producers became part-time shovelers and rescuers of trucks. And the space for production and storage was cramped and far from ideal.

In the fall of 1988, Stonyfield built a modern, sprawling plant in Londonderry, New Hampshire. The new facility was custom-designed to handle the still-increasing demand for more yogurt as Stonyfield's market area grows and as we introduce new products such as low-fat and nonfat yogurts, and nonfat frozen yogurts.

Much as we loved the farm, we outgrew it. But our origins are there, in that rambling old hilltop farmhouse, and when we left we took with us the nurturing spirit of that place. That is what you are consuming with every cup of Stonyfield Farm Yogurt that you eat! We hope this book conveys this same sense of tradition, of the ancient virtues of yogurt — as well as many creative new ideas for stirring more of yogurt's nutritional wholesomeness into your cooking.

— MCH

. . . .

YOGURT: THE PERFECT FOOD?

■

When my older son was nine months old, he suddenly began to suffer from persistent ear infections. My pediatrician prescribed antibiotics, but after three rounds of different drugs, the infections continued. Finally another physician, recognizing that I had recently weaned the baby from breast milk to cow's milk, suggested that I feed him a sweetened yogurt drink instead of milk. He thought that the foreign protein of cow's milk was causing a mildly allergic reaction and creating mucus, which was becoming fertile territory for the growth of harmful bacteria. Since the fermentation of milk to make yogurt changes the form of the protein, the yogurt would be more digestible. After three days on the yogurt concoction, the ear infection disappeared completely, never to return.

Experiences such as this one have made believers of many faithful yogurt eaters, who credit this remarkable food with treating or preventing everything from dysentery, constipation, and stomach ulcers to arthritis, vaginal infections, and canker sores.

COUNTING CALORIES, CHOLESTEROL & FAT

∎

The fat, cholesterol, and calorie content of yogurt vary widely from one brand to another, and of course depend on the type of product being consumed — whole milk, low fat, or nonfat. Whether yogurt is good for your cholesterol count depends on whether you're using it as a dietary substitute for broiled fish or fresh fruit — which is not appropriate — or in place of mayonnaise, sour cream, or cream cheese, in which case your cardiovascular system will surely benefit. Listed below is a sampling of fat, cholesterol, and calorie content pulled from package labels. (Since calorie counts vary greatly from one brand of yogurt to another, all figures listed for yogurt are based on Stonyfield Farm products.) Figures on labels are based on serving size. For apples-to-apples comparisons, we've converted all numbers to represent the calories, cholesterol, and fat in eight ounces of each food.

· ·

Food	Calories	Cholesterol	Fat	% of Calories from Fat
Mayonnaise	1,600	160 mg.	176 gm.	98%
Salad Dressing	1,120	80 mg.	112 gm.	90%
Light Mayonnaise	800	80 mg.	80 gm.	91%
Cream Cheese	800	240 mg.	80 gm.	90%
Cholesterol-Free Light Salad Dressing	720	0	64 gm.	80%
Sour Cream	480	(not given)	40 gm.	75%
Light Sour Cream	400	80 mg.	32 gm.	72%
Strawberry Yogurt	210	48 mg.	7 gm.	30%
Plain Yogurt	170	54 mg.	9 gm.	48%
Nonfat Strawberry Yogurt	150	0	0	0%
Lowfat Plain Yogurt	120	24 mg.	4 gm.	30%
Nonfat Plain Yogurt	110	0	0	0%

Is all this fact or fable? Controversy continues, as it does in virtually all aspects of human nutrition, but evidence does exist to support many claims concerning yogurt's dietary value.

Yogurt is undoubtedly a nutritious food. It can be an important dietary source of many nutrients, including protein, calcium, riboflavin, phosphorus, and magnesium. An eight-ounce serving of whole-milk yogurt supplies nearly thirty-five percent of the recommended daily allowance (RDA) of calcium for adult men and women over age twenty-five; it contains more than ten times the calcium of an eight-ounce serving of meat, fish, or poultry. It is *not*, however, a fully balanced meal. It is notably deficient in Vitamin C and iron. Nutritionally, yogurt should be considered a substitute for milk—which makes it especially important in the diets of those who are lactose intolerant.

Lactose-intolerant people lack a digestive enzyme—lactase—that is necessary to break down lactose (milk sugar). This category includes three-quarters of the world's adult population; the condition is especially common in Asia and Africa. Drinking abundant amounts of fluid milk can cause gas, abdominal cramps, and diarrhea in the lactose intolerant. This is not an all-or-nothing condition; the degree to which a person suffers depends upon his or her degree of intolerance and the amount of milk consumed.

Yogurt is very low in lactose and allows many lactose-intolerant people to take advantage of milk's beneficial protein, vitamins, and calcium without negative reaction. This is true because the bacteria usually found in yogurt (*Lactobacillus bulgaricus* and *Streptococcus thermophilus*) actually digest some of the milk sugar for you. (It should be noted that lactose intolerance is not the same as an allergy to milk; individuals with milk allergies are sensitive to milk proteins and cannot tolerate yogurt.)

Because these bacteria provide a head start on digestion, it takes only one hour for ninety percent of the yogurt you eat to be assimilated into your body. This compares favorably with the three hours it takes to digest milk, and eight or more hours to digest a doughnut! Quick and easy digestibility is particularly important for the elderly and for infants—given after six months of age, yogurt makes great baby food.

Yogurt may be helpful for people on antibiotics, too. Antibiotics destroy the harmful bacteria that cause infections, but they also kill the beneficial bacteria in the intestines. These beneficial bacteria are vital for good digestion and are particularly efficient producers of vitamins, so when they're destroyed by antibiotics, the result may be constipation, diarrhea, or generally poorer nutrition. If you're on antibiotics, eating yogurt with every meal may help to restore some of these missing microorganisms—and a healthier digestive tract.

Women in particular may benefit from consuming yogurt when on an antibiotic regimen, since destruction of normal body flora can result in vaginal yeast infections. Yogurt containing the bacteria *Lactobacillus acidophilus* in addition to the two bacteria mentioned above may reduce or eliminate the occurrence of these yeast infections. In addition, in a currently ongoing study at Long Island Jewish Medical Center, women *not* taking antibiotics who consume a cup of yogurt containing *L. acidophilus* every day are experiencing a threefold reduction in vaginal yeast infections.

The bacteria found in yogurt also may be beneficial in controlling disease-causing bacteria in the intestines. The powerful beneficial bacteria may kill disease-producing bacteria either outright or by creating an acidic environment that is intolerable to bacteria that cause dysentery, salmonella, and infant diarrhea.

In particular, *L. acidophilus* stands out as having many health-promoting properties. In studies at Tufts University, humans and animals fed *L. acidophilus* were found to have lowered levels of three enzymes that can activate carcinogens. Unlike other yogurt bacteria, *L. acidophilus* is a normal inhabitant of the human gut. Regular intake of acidophilus milk or yogurt (such as Stonyfield) contributes to establishing a healthy environment in the bowel.

Whatever its powers as a curative, there's no question that yogurt provides an outstanding source of calcium and other nutrients found in milk. As a healthy alternative to milk, it's especially valuable for the lactose intolerant. And as a source of variety and good taste in a daily diet—which, after all, is what the recipes in this book are all about—it's a boon to cook and gourmand alike.

. . . .

WHAT EXACTLY IS YOGURT?

■

Yogurt is an old tradition; its use dates back at least four thousand years. According to legend, Abraham was taught how to make this fermented milk product by an angel! Yogurt was probably first used somewhere in the Middle East, where, according to another tale, it was discovered by a hungry nomad who packed some milk away in a goatskin bag while traveling by camel across the desert. When he later opened the bag, he found a thick, tart custard formed by bacteria thriving on milk sugar in the heat of the sun.

In many societies, yogurt is more than just another food. This cultured product is indeed an important part of many cultures, with recipes and bacterial "starters" handed down through the generations. In many societies, yogurt and other cultured milk products (such as kefir) have long been thought to have therapeutic and life-enhancing properties. Persian women felt that yogurt had cosmetic value as well: they applied it to their faces to smooth away wrinkles. Some women still swear by the value of yogurt facials.

Yogurt begins as milk. The raw milk is pasteurized (heated to roughly 190°F) in order to kill off any harmful bacteria, then cooled to incubation temperature and injected with the specific yogurt-making bacteria. These bacteria eagerly feed on the milk sugar, lactose. This produces lactic acid, which gives the milk the tangy taste we associate with yogurt. At the completion of this fermentation, the numbers of beneficial bacteria approach one billion organisms per gram! When the desired thickness and acidity are reached, the yogurt is quickly chilled to stop the fermentation process.

The kind of milk used has tremendous influence on the yogurt made from it. In other parts of the world, yogurt is made from the milk of many animals—goats, cows, sheep, and even yaks, to name the most common. Here in North America we usually consume yogurt made from cow's milk. But even within that species, different breeds produce vastly different milk. Milk from Holstein (black and white) cows is thin in comparison with milk from Jersey (brown) cows, such as Stonyfield uses. The latter is richer and creamier, a result of its higher fat and protein content.

Modern yogurt manufacturers have found ways to produce low-fat and nonfat yogurts, and refinements in the process vary considerably from one brand to another. But in terms of the basic procedure for making yogurt, and the benefits derived from eating the best brands, not much has changed in the last four thousand years!

· ·

A Buyer's Guide to Yogurt

■

1. Always look for yogurt with "live, active cultures" noted on the label. Some manufacturers pasteurize their yogurts *after* the beneficial bacteria have been added, thus prolonging the product's shelf life but killing the bacteria that provide many of yogurt's health benefits.

2. Look for yogurt to which the beneficial *Lactobacillus acidophilus* bacterium has been added. Most yogurts do not contain *L. acidophilus*, but it forms more than half of the bacterial culture used by Stonyfield Farm.

3. Avoid Swiss or pudding-style yogurts. These are fermented in vats and then transferred to the cups in which they are sold. This process breaks the gel, so that artificial binders and stabilizers must be added.

4. Buy yogurt made from unhomogenized milk. Although the process of homogenization, which is practiced by most yogurt manufacturers, is often confused with pasteurization, actually the two have nothing in common. Homogenization involves forcing milk through tiny openings that break up the milk fat (or cream) so that it becomes evenly mixed throughout the product. Yogurt makers who believe that less processing is better usually elect not to homogenize their milk. In their products you'll find a layer of sweet, creamy yogurt on the top of the whole-milk products; in unhomogenized yogurt, the cream simply rises to the top, just as it used to in old-fashioned milk bottles.

5. Read the label to see what sweeteners have been used. Many consumers prefer to avoid sugar or artificial sweeteners and look for yogurt with honey or natural fruit juice as a sweetener.

. . . .

A FEW NOTES FOR THE COOK

■

As the variety of recipes in this book demonstrates, yogurt can add a distinctive taste, a creamy texture, and a wonderful moistness to a wide assortment of dishes. The possibilities range from simple combinations of yogurt and fruit (see pages 67-79) to dishes made with homemade yogurt cheese (see page 87 for instructions). Yogurt cheese is a delicious, unique product that's often used as a lower-calorie alternative to cream cheese; it's full of protein, calcium, and vitamins, and makes a wonderful addition to everything from hors d'oeuvres to desserts.

No matter what food you're making, there are just a few precautions to observe in cooking with yogurt: avoid overheating it, don't heat it too quickly, don't be overly vigorous in stirring it, and don't wait too long to use it.

Heating yogurt to high temperatures destroys the beneficial bacteria. To prevent this, never add yogurt directly to a boiling or extremely hot mixture. Instead, stir a few tablespoons of the hot food into the yogurt, warming it gradually. Then stir the warmed yogurt into the hot mixture. Do this near the end of the cooking process, so the yogurt won't heat for too long. If the temperature of the mixture is higher than 120°F, as it is in baking, you will not get the benefit of the bacteria, but the yogurt will still provide valuable nutrients such as calcium and protein. It should be noted that freezing yogurt, which is called for in many of the dessert recipes included here, does not harm the bacteria.

Heating yogurt too rapidly can cause it to separate into curds and whey. You can avoid this unappetizing prospect by warming the yogurt at least to room temperature before adding it to hot mixtures, and by heating any yogurt mixture slowly, stirring constantly. Another alternative is to add cornstarch to the mixture: allowing 1 to 2 tablespoons of cornstarch per cup of yogurt, dissolve cornstarch in a small amount of cold water. Add this to your yogurt mixture and cook over medium heat, stirring until thickened.

In general, if your warm cooking mixture thins out too much with the addition of yogurt, you can also try adding a little arrowroot or flour (1 or 2 tablespoons per cup of yogurt) mixed with cold water. If adding yogurt to your salad dressing, dip, or cold soup thins it out too much, simply chill the mixture for an hour or two and it will thicken.

Another important rule is to be gentle with yogurt. Ideally, it should be folded into other ingredients and, like James Bond's martini, not beaten or vigorously stirred. Such indecorous action will surely thin it out! You will note exceptions to this rule in some recipes, particularly those for blender products and others where the mixture is meant to be thinner.

As with most cooking ingredients, using the freshest yogurt is always recommended. Yogurt stored unopened in the refrigerator should remain fresh tasting for about ten days after the date stamped on the carton. Once it's opened, however, it is important to keep yogurt tightly covered; it's subject to drying out and to absorbing odors from other foods. If liquid collects on the surface of your yogurt, simply stir it back in. This is the milk whey, which contains many valuable nutrients. A yogurt like Stonyfield will "whey off" rather easily because it contains no artificial binders to keep the yogurt together.

One final note: Virtually all the recipes in this collection were prepared with whole-milk yogurt. Low-fat or nonfat yogurt can be substituted, but the consistency and texture of the final product may be different.

So get ready to dig in! You'll be amazed at the versatility of yogurt, and delighted with the results of cooking with this wonderful food.

· ·

AUTHOR'S NOTE

■

These recipes are brought to you courtesy of roughly three hundred yogurt lovers. They were selected from more than seven hundred submissions to a contest held by Stonyfield Farm in 1987, and to *Harrowsmith Country Life* magazine's call for yogurt recipes in the spring of 1989. All have been carefully tested by experienced home cooks. With pride we present this collection. Enjoy!

BREAKFASTS & BRUNCHES

■

Start your day off right with a tasty yogurt smoothie (see pages 75-79), a yogurt "cream cheese" (page 87) spread on toast, and one of these hearty breakfasts.

In some of the following recipes, yogurt is served up fresh with a mixture of fruit and/or grains for a balanced, wholesome breakfast. In other recipes, yogurt is mixed into pancake or waffle batter, enhancing the moistness and flavor of the final product. At our table, no waffle, pancake, or French toast breakfast is ever served without yogurt. Plain, flavored, or fruited, the yogurt is mixed into the batter, spread on top of the cooked result, or both. With a touch of maple syrup, any one of these creations makes a creamy and delicious treat.

Another wonderful way to use yogurt at the breakfast table is in a simple dish I call "Anniversary Pancakes" because it was first served to my husband and me by friends on our wedding anniversary. They made up a batch of light French pancakes (use your favorite recipe or refer to any basic cookbook) and proceeded to fill them with fruited yogurts and roll them up like blintzes. Then we popped them straight into our mouths! Our hosts could hardly keep the pancakes coming fast enough.

As nutritionists tirelessly point out, breakfast is very important in determining your energy level for the rest of the day. These recipes will provide you with some great-tasting and healthful ways to launch each day.

WILDCAT CAFE BLUEBERRY PANCAKES

■

1 cup unbleached all-purpose flour
1½ cups whole-wheat flour
½ cup oat bran
½ cup sugar
½ teaspoon salt
2 teaspoons baking powder
2 teaspoons baking soda
3 eggs
½ cup butter or margarine, melted
1 cup plain yogurt
1 cup milk
2 cups wild blueberries

Surprisingly moist, light, and fluffy. Excellent with maple syrup and plain or vanilla yogurt.

In a large bowl, whisk together the flours, oat bran, sugar, salt, baking powder, and soda. In a separate bowl, beat the eggs, then add the cooled butter, yogurt, and milk. Stir to combine. Pour the egg mixture into the flour mixture and stir until blended. The batter will be thick. Fold in the blueberries. Spoon the batter onto a preheated, oiled griddle, using ¼ cup batter for each pancake. Batter containing whole wheat tends to brown quickly, leaving the interior uncooked, so cook the pancakes slowly (4 to 6 minutes each) over low heat.

Yield: 6 servings.

Roseann LaPlace
Colinton, Alberta, Canada

. . . .

MUESLI PANCAKES

■

1 cup quick-cooking oats
1 cup skim milk
1 cup plain yogurt
1 medium to large apple, cored, peeled, and grated
3 eggs, beaten
¾ cup whole-wheat flour
¾ cup unbleached all-purpose flour
¾ teaspoon baking soda
¾ teaspoon baking powder
¼ cup butter, melted, or ¼ cup vegetable oil

The full and fruity taste of these pancakes won high marks from our tester.

Stir together the oats, milk, yogurt, and apple in a large mixing bowl. Let sit for 15 minutes. Add the eggs and stir to combine. In another bowl, sift together the flours, soda, and baking powder. Add the flour mixture to the oat mixture and stir well. Add the butter and mix. Drop by large spoonfuls onto a hot, lightly oiled griddle; cook over medium heat until well browned on both sides. Serve with syrup, honey, or jam.

Yield: 10 to 12 pancakes.

Clive Cudmore
Campbellville, Ontario, Canada

. . . .

Yogurt Blender Pancakes

■

1 egg
1 cup plain yogurt
2 tablespoons vegetable oil
1 cup unbleached all-purpose flour
1 tablespoon sugar or maple syrup
1 teaspoon baking powder
½ teaspoon baking soda
¼ teaspoon salt
¼ teaspoon ground cinnamon

BLUEBERRY TOPPING
1 cup plain yogurt
2 tablespoons honey
¼ teaspoon ground cinnamon
½ cup blueberries

Easy, great-tasting pancakes. Wonderful served with blueberry topping or one of the variations listed below.

In a blender, combine the egg, yogurt, and oil. When the mixture is smooth, add the flour, sugar, baking powder, soda, salt, and cinnamon, and mix. Using ¼ cup batter for each pancake, cook the pancakes on a preheated, very hot, oiled griddle until golden.

For the topping, mix together the yogurt, honey, and cinnamon. Fold in the blueberries. Spoon over the pancakes and serve.

Variations: Instead of blueberry topping, serve the pancakes with maple syrup or hot maple butter (1 cup maple syrup heated with ½ cup butter until the butter melts).

Yield: 6 to 8 pancakes.

Rose Strocen
Canora, Saskatchewan, Canada

Maple Wheat & Raisin Pancakes

■

2 cups whole-wheat flour
6 teaspoons baking powder
2 eggs, slightly beaten
2 tablespoons honey
1½ cups milk
¼ cup vegetable oil
1 cup plain or vanilla yogurt
3 tablespoons maple syrup
1 cup golden raisins

Smooth and wholesome—a great way to start the day.

In a large bowl, whisk together the flour and baking powder. Add the eggs, honey, milk, oil, yogurt, and maple syrup to the flour mixture; whisk until just mixed. Stir in the raisins. Using ¼ cup of batter for each pancake, pour the batter onto a preheated and lightly oiled griddle. Cook over medium heat until golden. Butter and serve, accompanied by maple syrup if desired.

Yield: 8 to 10 pancakes.

Suzanne Rak
Nashua, New Hampshire

21

WHOLE-GRAIN WAFFLES

■

⅔ cup whole-wheat flour
⅔ cup brown-rice flour
⅔ cup soy flour
1 teaspoon baking soda
1 teaspoon baking powder
½ teaspoon salt
2 tablespoons wheat germ
1½ cups milk
1 cup plain yogurt
3 tablespoons butter, melted
3 eggs, separated

Exceptionally good waffles for ones made totally with whole-grain flours. Try serving these with syrup, sausage, jams, jellies, or yogurt.

Whisk together the flours, soda, baking powder, salt, and wheat germ in a large bowl. In a smaller bowl, mix together the milk, yogurt, cooled butter, and egg yolks. Add the milk mixture to the dry ingredients and stir until everything is thoroughly blended. In a separate bowl, whip the egg whites until stiff peaks form. Fold the egg whites into the batter. Cook on a hot, oiled waffle iron.

Yield: 10 (8-inch) round waffles.

Christina Renda
Woodbury, Connecticut

. . . .

WHEAT BERRY PORRIDGE

■

1 cup uncooked wheat berries
2 cups water
1 cup plain yogurt
¼ cup fresh lemon juice
1 unpeeled apple, cored and grated
2 bananas, sliced
2 peaches, peeled, pitted, and sliced
1 to 2 cups grapes, halved
¼ teaspoon ground ginger
½ teaspoon ground cinnamon
Dash of ground nutmeg

Very different and very tasty. Wheat berries are the whole grains from which wheat flour is ground; you can find them in most natural-foods stores.

Cook the wheat berries in water over low heat for 4 to 6 hours or until the water is absorbed. (A crock pot is especially useful for this step.) Remove from heat and allow the berries to cool, then mix in the remaining ingredients and chill. Let stand for ½ hour at room temperature before serving.

Yield: 1½ to 2 quarts.

Mario and Laura Geilen
Arlington, Massachusetts

. . . .

✓ YOGURT WAFFLES

∎

1 cup plain yogurt
3 eggs
½ cup whole-wheat flour
⅓ cup oat bran
⅛ teaspoon salt
¼ cup vegetable oil
½ cup milk
1½ teaspoons vanilla
1½ teaspoons ground cinnamon
½ cup chopped nuts (optional)

Great-tasting bran waffles flavored with cinnamon.

Combine all the ingredients in a blender or stir them together until they are well mixed. Cook the waffles on a hot, oiled waffle iron. Serve them hot, topped with more yogurt, fresh or preserved fruit, maple syrup, honey, or peanut butter.

Yield: 4 servings.

Marty and Renata Earles
Grass Valley, California

. . . .

CREAMY PEACH MELBA BREAKFAST BREAD

∎

3 eggs
½ cup light cream or
   half-and-half
1 cup peach yogurt
1 cup raspberry yogurt
1 teaspoon vanilla
1 loaf Italian, French, or
   challah bread, thickly sliced
Fresh peaches or raspberries,
   for garnish
Peach or raspberry yogurt, for
   garnish

An elegant variation of French toast, with a golden-brown crust outside and a sweet custard inside. Start it the night before—it's well worth the wait!

Beat the eggs and combine with the cream, yogurts, and vanilla. Mix well. Pour into one or two shallow rectangular lasagna-type pans. Place the bread in the egg mixture, cover, and let stand overnight, turning once or twice during the standing period to make sure the mixture has soaked through the slices. The next morning, prepare a hot griddle or frying pan with a combination of vegetable oil and butter or margarine. Lightly brown each side of the bread slices, cooking slowly over low heat to firm the custard. Serve immediately with a garnish of fresh peach slices or raspberries and a dollop of peach or raspberry yogurt.

Yield: 4 to 6 servings.

Gloria Sessums
Silver Spring, Maryland

. . . .

WOW! WAFFLES

■

3 eggs, separated
2¼ cups plain yogurt
2 tablespoons nonfat dry milk
½ teaspoon baking soda
1 tablespoon honey
⅓ cup quick-cooking oats
⅓ cup cornmeal
⅓ cup margarine or butter, melted
1 cup unbleached all-purpose flour
1 tablespoon baking powder
⅛ teaspoon salt (optional)
1 to 2 tablespoons milk (optional)

Hearty waffles that freeze beautifully, and a good recipe for a large crowd. See photo, page 49.

Combine the egg yolks, yogurt, dry milk, soda, and honey in a large bowl. Beat with a wire whisk. Stir in the oats and cornmeal, then add the margarine and stir again. Sift in the flour, baking powder, and optional salt. Beat well, then cover the bowl and let the mixture sit for 15 minutes. Beat the egg whites until stiff, then fold them into the mixture. If the batter is too thick, add 1 or 2 tablespoons of milk.

Preheat a waffle iron to the high setting, oil it, and cook the batter. Serve the waffles on warm plates. As accompaniments, you might offer warm maple syrup; fresh, sliced fruit or berries; and yogurt.

To freeze the waffles, cool them on a rack, then place the rack of waffles in the freezer. Store the frozen waffles in tightly sealed plastic bags. To reheat, pop them in the toaster.

Yield: 8 (10-inch) waffles.

Mari Bartlett
Alstead, New Hampshire

• •

BREAKFAST BANANAS FOR TWO

■

2 ripe bananas
1½ cups plain yogurt
½ to 1 cup raisins, to taste
1-inch cube of Cheddar cheese (medium sharp or sharp)
2 tablespoons maple syrup, or to taste

A great-tasting, nutritious, and tasty way to start the day. Endless variations keep it interesting.

Slice the bananas like thick coins into a medium-large bowl. Add the yogurt and stir, then add the raisins and stir again. Cut the cheese into small cubes the size of raisins and add to the mixture. Add the maple syrup. Mix it all up, and share with a friend!

Yield: 2 servings.

Joanne M. Goding
Florence, Massachusetts

• •

NEW ENGLAND BREAKFAST MUESLI

■

¼ teaspoon salt
1 cup rolled oats
1½ cups water
2 cups yogurt
4 to 6 tablespoons maple syrup
  or honey
¼ teaspoon vanilla (optional)
Grated lemon rind (optional)
1 large unpeeled apple, cored
  and chopped
1 banana, sliced
½ cup fresh berries
½ cup raisins
½ cup chopped walnuts or
  toasted slivered almonds

A basic, healthful breakfast, made both sweet and pleasing with honey and fruit. Use whatever berries are in season.

Add the salt and oats to the water. Stir to combine, then leave to soak overnight. In the morning, add the yogurt, maple syrup, and optional vanilla and lemon rind; stir. Add the apple, banana, berries, raisins, and nuts; stir gently to combine all ingredients.

Yield: 4 to 6 servings.

Hannah Rabin
Plainfield, Vermont

. . . .

BOBBIE'S BALANCED BREAKFAST

■

1 large unpeeled apple, cored
  and diced
¾ cup rolled oats
¼ cup maple syrup
½ cup chopped walnuts
1 cup plain yogurt
2 tablespoons wheat germ
Ground cinnamon (optional)
Ground nutmeg (optional)

Crunchy apple and oats in a sweet, creamy, maple sauce—easy, delightful, and delicious.

Stir the apple, oats, maple syrup, and walnuts into the yogurt. Sprinkle with wheat germ. Top with cinnamon and nutmeg if desired.

Yield: 1 to 2 servings.

Roberta Barrett
Beaver Falls, New York

. . . .

BREADS

∎

"Here is bread, which strengthens man's heart, and therefore is called the staff of life." So said Matthew Henry in the seventeenth century. Indeed, there is nothing like a hearty bread to make us feel strong; nothing like the aroma of a yeast bread baking in the oven to make us wistful for the past or for a slower life more connected to natural things.

There's also nothing like a delicious and attractive quick bread to add a special touch to Christmas gift giving, an unusual cornbread to accompany a hearty winter stew, or a fresh batch of muffins to delight the whole family on a weekend morning. The pleasure these treats give to family and friends is far out of proportion to the time involved in creating them.

Yogurt imparts tenderness, moistness, and a savory flavor to baked goods. We bet you've never tasted a bran muffin as moist and flavorful as the Oatmeal Bran Muffins on page 43. They've become a clamored-for classic in our household, as has the Whole-Wheat Raisin Bread (page 28). For a fresh new taste, we've added yogurt to bagels and brown bread, to classic coffee cakes and traditional English scones. The very best of these taste treats are included here.

WHOLE-WHEAT RAISIN BREAD

■

¼ teaspoon honey
½ cup lukewarm water
1 package (¼ ounce) yeast
1 cup milk
¼ cup butter or margarine
2½ cups whole-wheat flour
2 teaspoons salt
3 eggs at room temperature, slightly beaten
1 cup plain yogurt at room temperature
½ cup honey
2 cups raisins
5 to 6 cups unbleached all-purpose flour
¼ cup brown sugar
Ground cinnamon

Fabulous — very moist, with the perfect amount of sweetness. Wonderful both fresh and as toast, and looks beautiful, too. See photo, page 51.

Add ¼ teaspoon honey to the lukewarm water; stir in the yeast. Let the yeast sit for 10 to 15 minutes to proof.

Meanwhile, scald the milk in a medium-size pan. Remove the pan from the heat, add the butter to the hot milk, and set the mixture aside to cool, stirring occasionally to make sure the butter melts.

In a large mixing bowl, combine the whole-wheat flour, proofed yeast, and salt. When the milk mixture feels very warm but not hot, add it to the flour mixture along with the eggs, yogurt, and honey. Stir the batter until it is smooth. Add the raisins and stir again. Add the all-purpose flour gradually, mixing until the dough leaves the sides of the bowl.

Turn the dough out onto a lightly floured board and knead for 8 to 10 minutes or until it is smooth and elastic. Round the dough into a ball and place it in a large, clean, oiled mixing bowl. Lightly oil the surface of the dough and let it rise in a warm place until it has doubled in bulk (about 1½ hours).

Divide the dough into 2 parts. Roll each into a rectangle about 7 by 14 inches. Spread 2 tablespoons of brown sugar evenly over the surface of each rectangle to within 1 inch of the edge. Sprinkle generously with cinnamon. Starting from the short edge, roll each rectangle up tight to form a loaf. Create a seam where you finish rolling by pinching the edge of the dough into the loaf, discarding any raisins that are in the way. Gently pull the ends of the roll down toward the long seam and pinch them closed, once again discarding raisins that are in the way. Place the loaves, seams down, into greased 8x4-inch loaf pans. Discard any raisins that are exposed on the tops of the loaves.

HERB ROLLS

■

½ cup water
2 teaspoons poppy seeds
2 teaspoons caraway seeds
1 teaspoon instant minced onion
2 teaspoons dried chervil or parsley
1 teaspoon dried marjoram
4 tablespoons yeast
1 cup warm water
4 eggs, beaten
1 cup honey, at room temperature
⅔ cup vegetable oil
1½ cups plain yogurt, at room temperature
2 teaspoons salt (optional)
7 to 8 cups whole-wheat flour
2 to 3 cups unbleached all-purpose flour

An exceptionally light roll for one with so much whole-wheat flour; ideal for dinner, snacks, or sandwiches. Delicious the next day as well, or frozen and reheated. The blend of herbs lends a light, mild flavor. If you prefer a stronger herb flavor, add one more teaspoon of each herb.

Heat ½ cup water to the boiling point. Add the poppy seeds, caraway seeds, onion, chervil, and marjoram; set the mixture aside to soak. Dissolve the yeast in 1 cup of warm water.

In a large bowl, mix the eggs, honey, oil, yogurt, and optional salt. Add 5 cups of whole-wheat flour. Beat vigorously. To this mixture add the seeds and herbs with soaking water, 1 cup warm water, and yeast. Add 2 to 3 cups more whole-wheat flour, plus 2 to 3 cups unbleached flour, to make a soft dough. Turn the dough out onto a floured breadboard and knead, adding flour as needed, for about 5 to 10 minutes or until the dough is smooth and elastic.

Return the dough to the cleaned and oiled bowl and let it rise in a warm place for at least 1½ hours or until doubled in bulk. Punch it down. Let it rise again for about 1 hour.

Preheat oven to 350°F. Remove the dough from the bowl and cut it into 6 equal pieces. Roll each piece out into a round about ¼ inch thick and 10 to 12 inches in diameter. Cut each round into 8 pie-shaped wedges. Roll up each wedge, starting at the widest end. If a crescent shape is desired, curl the tips slightly. Place the rolls with seams down on greased cookie sheets; bake for 20 minutes.

Yield: 4 dozen rolls.

Donna Schmidt
Walpole, New Hampshire

QUICK YOGURT YEAST ROLLS

■

4 to 4½ cups unbleached all-purpose flour
2 packages (¼ ounce each) yeast
2 tablespoons sugar
1 teaspoon salt
½ teaspoon baking soda
1½ cups plain yogurt
½ cup water
⅓ cup butter

These rolls are picture-perfect: nicely browned, evenly shaped, and delicious.

In a large bowl, whisk together 1½ cups of the flour with the yeast, sugar, salt, and soda; mix well. Heat the yogurt, water, and butter to 120 to 130°F, but do not simmer. Add the yogurt mixture to the flour mixture and blend well, then beat with an electric mixer at medium speed for 4 minutes. Gradually stir in enough of the remaining flour to make a stiff dough. Knead on a floured surface until the dough is smooth and elastic.

Place the dough in a greased bowl and turn the dough over to grease the top. Cover and let rise in a warm place until doubled in bulk (about 20 to 30 minutes).

Punch down the dough, divide it into 24 pieces, and form the pieces into balls. Place the balls on a greased cookie sheet, cover, and let rise in a warm place for about 20 minutes or until almost doubled in bulk. Bake in a preheated 400°F oven for 20 minutes or until nicely browned. Remove from pan and brush with butter.

Yield: 2 dozen large rolls.

Carol Forcum
Marion, Illinois

• •

BRUNCH BISCUIT

■

1 cup unbleached all-purpose flour
1 cup whole-wheat flour
2 teaspoons baking powder
½ teaspoon baking soda
(continued)

This biscuit gets great reviews for its texture and harmony of flavors.

Preheat oven to 400°F. Sift together flours, baking powder, soda, and optional sugar. Cut in the butter. Add the raisins and caraway seeds; stir to combine. Stir in the yogurt and mix until well blended; the dough will be stiff.

Spread the dough in a greased 9-inch square pan. Use a knife with a serrated edge to cut a decorative "X"

2 tablespoons sugar (optional)
3 tablespoons butter or
  margarine
¾ cup raisins, sprinkled with
  ½ teaspoon flour
2 teaspoons caraway seeds
1 cup plain yogurt at room
  temperature

½ inch deep on the top. Bake for about 30 minutes or until the top is brown and a toothpick inserted in the center comes out clean.

Variation: In place of raisins and caraway seeds, substitute ½ cup chopped walnuts, 1 tablespoon grated orange rind, and 2 teaspoons anise seed.

Yield: About 14 pieces.

Sharon Marshall
Boston, Massachusetts

. . . .

FAST & EASY YOGURT BREAD

■

1½ tablespoons yeast
2 tablespoons honey
2 cups warm water
2 teaspoons salt
1 cup plain yogurt
7½ cups unbleached all-
  purpose flour

A wonderful bread with a great consistency and a subtle hint of honey.

Dissolve the yeast and honey in the warm water and set the mixture aside to proof for 10 minutes. Add the salt and yogurt to the yeast mixture and stir to combine. Sift the flour and add it gradually, stirring it in until you can no longer stir.

Remove the dough to a floured board and knead for 5 to 10 minutes, slowly working in the remaining flour. Divide the dough in half, form 2 loaves, and place each in a greased 8x4-inch loaf pan. Let the dough rise in a warm place for 50 minutes or until it comes to the tops of the pans.

Bake in a preheated oven at 350°F for 40 minutes or until the loaves are browned and sound hollow when tapped. Remove loaves from the pans and cool on a rack. If you want a soft crust, brush the tops of the warm loaves with butter.

Yield: 2 loaves.

Bonnie Heckman Foust
Shannon, Illinois

. . . .

BERRY WALNUT BREAD

■

½ cup butter, softened
½ cup brown sugar
½ cup granulated sugar
2 eggs, beaten
1 teaspoon vanilla
1 cup raspberry yogurt, stirred
  thoroughly
1½ cups unbleached all-
  purpose flour
½ cup whole-wheat flour
1 teaspoon baking soda
¼ teaspoon salt
1 cup chopped walnuts
1 cup fresh blueberries, or
  frozen blueberries, thawed
  and drained

Delicious, moist, and perfect for a dessert or snack. Spread with cream cheese for that extra indulgence.

Preheat oven to 325°F. Butter and flour an 8x4-inch loaf pan. Cream the butter and sugars until light and fluffy. Blend in the eggs and vanilla. Add the yogurt and mix thoroughly. Sift together the flours, soda, and salt and add to the yogurt mixture, stirring with a wooden spoon to just barely incorporate. Mix in the walnuts with a few strokes; fold in the blueberries. Pour into the prepared pan. Bake for 1 hour or until a toothpick inserted in the center of the loaf comes out clean.

Yield: 1 loaf.

Lise Stern
Cambridge, Massachusetts

. . . .

YOGURT HERB QUICK BREAD

■

1 cup unbleached all-purpose
  flour
1 cup whole-wheat flour
1 teaspoon baking powder
½ teaspoon baking soda
½ teaspoon salt
¼ cup butter, melted
2 large eggs, beaten
1 cup plain yogurt
½ cup honey
1 teaspoon dried dill
½ teaspoon dried oregano
½ teaspoon dried thyme
½ teaspoon dried basil
½ teaspoon dried tarragon

Very easy to make, and a perfect companion for a luncheon salad or a hearty stew. Or serve with cream cheese for breakfast, accompanied by fresh fruit or juice.

Preheat oven to 350°F. Sift the flours, baking powder, soda, and salt together into a large bowl. In another bowl, beat the cooled butter, eggs, yogurt, and honey until frothy; add the herbs and beat again. Make a well in the center of the dry ingredients; pour the liquid mixture into the well and stir with a wooden spoon until thoroughly blended. Pour into a lightly greased 8x4-inch bread pan and bake for 40 to 50 minutes.

Yield: 1 loaf.

Trish Abbott
Leduc, Alberta, Canada

. . . .

DRIED FRUIT & YOGURT BROWN BREAD

■

1 cup cornmeal
1 cup unbleached all-purpose
 flour
1 cup whole-wheat flour
1 tablespoon baking powder
½ teaspoon baking soda
½ teaspoon ground allspice
1 large egg
2 cups plain yogurt
¾ cup honey
½ cup chopped pitted dates
¾ cup chopped dried apricots

An easy and unusual bread with a unique texture created by the cornmeal. Very satisfying served warm from the oven with whipped honey butter, and wonderful toasted and spread with cream cheese. Makes a great hostess gift or holiday remembrance.

Preheat oven to 300°F. In a large bowl, whisk together the cornmeal, flours, baking powder, soda, and allspice. In another bowl, stir together the egg, yogurt, and honey, and then add the dates and apricots and stir to combine. Stir the yogurt mixture into the flour mixture until the batter is evenly moistened.

Pour the batter into 2 buttered 8x4-inch loaf pans. Cut 2 sheets of foil slightly larger than the pans. Butter one side of each piece of foil and place the buttered side down on top of the batter in each pan. Press the foil against the rim of the pan. Bake for 1½ hours or until a toothpick inserted in the center comes out clean. Serve warm, at room temperature, or toasted.

Yield: 2 loaves.

Roxanne E. Chan
Albany, California

OAT BRAN, APRICOT & YOGURT BREAD

■

¼ cup butter or margarine, softened
¾ cup honey
2 eggs (or just the whites)
1 teaspoon vanilla
1¼ cups whole-wheat or barley flour
2 teaspoons baking powder
½ teaspoon baking soda
½ teaspoon salt
½ teaspoon ground cinnamon
1 cup oat bran
1 cup plain yogurt
1 cup chopped dried apricots
1 cup chopped pecans, cashews, walnuts, or almonds

When we first sliced into this, it looked suspiciously like fruitcake . . . would that all fruitcakes tasted this good! This bread is dense and nutty, but it is the honey and apricots that give it such a bright and different flavor.

Preheat oven to 350°F. Cream the butter and honey; add the eggs and vanilla and beat until smooth. In a separate bowl, whisk together the flour, baking powder, soda, salt, cinnamon, and oat bran. Stir the flour mixture and the yogurt into the creamed mixture; continue stirring until the mixture is smooth. Stir in the apricots and nuts. Pour into a greased and floured 8x4-inch loaf pan and bake for 45 to 55 minutes or until a toothpick inserted in the center comes out clean.

Yield: 1 loaf.

Marsha Tokareff
Napa, California

. . . .

COUNTRY CORNBREAD

■

1 cup plain yogurt
1 egg, beaten
¼ cup maple syrup
2 tablespoons yogurt cream from top of yogurt (optional)
1½ cups whole-grain cornmeal (try your natural-foods store)
½ cup whole-wheat flour
2 teaspoons baking powder
½ teaspoon baking soda
¼ teaspoon salt

A very satisfying, dense, "corny" bread — a wholesome variation on the traditional recipe.

Preheat oven to 425°F. Beat together the yogurt, egg, maple syrup, and yogurt cream. In another, larger bowl, thoroughly whisk together the cornmeal, flour, baking powder, soda, and salt. Combine the wet and dry mixtures, stirring only enough to combine them thoroughly. Pour into a greased 8-inch square pan and bake for 20 minutes.

Yield: 16 two-inch squares.

Ann Hopkins
Andover, Massachusetts

. . . .

SPICY CORNBREAD

■

¾ cup unbleached all-purpose flour
1 cup cornmeal
2 tablespoons sugar
2 teaspoons baking powder
½ teaspoon baking soda
½ teaspoon salt
½ teaspoon chili powder
⅛ teaspoon curry powder
¼ cup chopped red bell pepper
1 cup plain yogurt
1 egg
3 tablespoons vegetable oil
3 tablespoons chopped green onion

A great spicy flavor but not overly hot; our tester declared this the best cornbread she'd ever tasted. Red pepper adds lively color.

Preheat oven to 400°F. Whisk together the flour, cornmeal, sugar, baking powder, soda, salt, chili powder, and curry powder. Stir in the bell pepper. In a separate bowl, combine the yogurt, egg, oil, and onion. Stir the yogurt mixture into the flour mixture until just combined. Pour into a greased 8-inch square pan. Bake for 20 to 25 minutes or until a toothpick inserted in the center comes out clean. Serve fresh from the oven with butter.

Yield: 9 servings.

*Cathy Malcolmson
Thornhill, Ontario, Canada*

. . . .

YOGURT CORNBREAD

■

2 eggs
¼ cup sugar
1 cup unbleached all-purpose flour
2 teaspoons baking powder
½ teaspoon baking soda
⅔ cup cornmeal
½ teaspoon salt
1 cup plain yogurt
¼ cup butter, melted

A classic, easy cornbread, made extra moist by the addition of yogurt. Serve warm with stews, soups, eggs, or chili. Or simply top with butter and enjoy!

Preheat oven to 400°F. Beat the eggs, add the sugar, and mix well. Whisk the flour, baking powder, soda, cornmeal, and salt together. Add the dry ingredients alternately with the yogurt to the egg-sugar mixture. Stir in the cooled butter. Bake in a greased 10-inch cast-iron skillet for 25 minutes, watching closely after the first 15 minutes to make sure it doesn't burn.

Yield: 8 servings.

*Beatrice McComas Jacobel
Los Altos, California*

. . . .

HEARTY CORNBREAD

■

¼ cup butter or margarine
1 cup cornmeal
1 teaspoon salt
1 teaspoon baking powder
½ teaspoon baking soda
2 eggs, beaten
1 cup plain yogurt
1 cup fresh corn
½ cup minced green onion
½ cup chopped green bell
  pepper
1 cup grated Cheddar cheese
½ cup chopped pepperoni

An exceptional cornbread with a zesty taste and crusty edge. Excellent served with chili.

Preheat oven to 400°F. Place the butter in a 9- or 10-inch ovenproof skillet and leave it in the oven while mixing the other ingredients. In a bowl, whisk together the cornmeal, salt, baking powder, and soda. In a separate, large bowl, stir together the eggs and yogurt. Add the cornmeal mixture to the yogurt mixture and stir to combine. Add the corn, onion, bell pepper, cheese, and pepperoni one at a time, beating thoroughly after each addition.

Remove the skillet from the oven. Pour the hot margarine into the batter; mix quickly, then pour the batter into the hot skillet. Bake for 40 minutes or until golden.

Yield: 6 to 8 pieces.

Julie Ray
Decaturville, Tennessee

. . . .

CURRANT CORN MUFFINS

■

1 cup cornmeal
1 cup unbleached all-purpose
  flour
1 tablespoon baking powder
½ teaspoon baking soda
½ teaspoon salt
3 tablespoons sugar
¼ cup butter or margarine
2 eggs, separated
1 cup plain yogurt
⅓ cup dried currants

Moist, healthful, and relatively easy to prepare. The currants add a nice surprise.

Preheat oven to 400°F. Sift together the cornmeal, flour, baking powder, soda, salt, and sugar. Cut in the butter until the mixture is crumbly. Add the egg yolks and yogurt, and mix just enough to hold the batter together. Add the currants and stir to combine. Beat the egg whites until stiff and fold them into the mixture. Fill the well-greased cups of a muffin tin two-thirds full. Bake for 15 to 20 minutes.

Yield: 10 to 12 muffins.

Mary Jane Jackson
South Hero, Vermont

. . . .

CORN & BARLEY MUFFINS

■

½ cup barley flour
½ cup corn flour (cornmeal ground fine in food processor)
½ cup cornmeal
1 teaspoon baking soda
½ teaspoon salt
¼ cup vegetable oil
¼ cup maple syrup
¼ cup honey
1 teaspoon vanilla
1 cup plain yogurt
¼ cup raisins (optional)

A taste reminiscent of morning on Grandpa's farm. A welcome change from the standard muffin, and ideal for those avoiding wheat or eggs.

Preheat oven to 350°F. Whisk together the flours, cornmeal, soda, and salt. Stir in the oil, maple syrup, honey, vanilla, and yogurt. Add the raisins if desired and stir again. Spoon into lightly greased muffin tins and bake for 25 to 30 minutes.

Yield: 12 muffins.

Peggy DiBlasi
Winchester, Massachusetts

. . . .

HAM & CHEESE MUFFINS

■

2 cups unbleached all-purpose flour
¼ cup sugar
1 tablespoon baking powder
1½ teaspoons baking soda
1 cup plain yogurt
½ cup butter or margarine, melted
2 eggs, beaten
1¼ cups shredded Mozzarella or Cheddar cheese
½ cup chopped cooked ham
1 teaspoon dried basil

A winning combination of flavors. Wonderful for breakfast with any egg dish, or a delicious accompaniment for a dinner stew.

Preheat oven to 400°F. In a large bowl, sift together the flour, sugar, baking powder, and soda. In a separate bowl, combine the yogurt, cooled butter, and eggs; add the yogurt mixture to the dry ingredients and stir. Fold in the cheese, ham, and basil. Spoon into large greased muffin cups and bake for 18 to 20 minutes. Serve warm.

Yield: 12 muffins.

Gwen Klein
Weyburn, Saskatchewan, Canada

. . . .

SALMON MUFFINS

■

1 can (1 pound) salmon
4 carrots, peeled and grated
2 scallions, chopped, or 2 tablespoons chopped chives
1 small green bell pepper, cored, seeded, and chopped
1 stalk celery, chopped
1 cup plain yogurt
1 cup seasoned bread crumbs
½ cup mayonnaise
2 eggs, beaten
Dash of pepper
1 teaspoon dried thyme
Crushed cornflakes or other cereal (optional)

A pleasing variation of salmon croquettes, these are so easy to prepare. They freeze very well and make a lovely buffet dish. Also try baking in mini-muffin tins to serve as hors d'oeuvres.

Preheat oven to 350°F. Grease muffin tins well. Drain the salmon, remove the bones, and break up the salmon. In a separate bowl, mix together the carrots, scallions, bell pepper, and celery. Add the yogurt, bread crumbs, mayonnaise, eggs, pepper, and thyme; stir to combine. Fold in the salmon. Fill the muffin cups and top the batter with crushed cereal, if desired. Bake for 40 to 50 minutes or until brown and a toothpick inserted in the center comes out clean.

Yield: 12 regular-size muffins.

Marilyn Levine
Cranston, Rhode Island

. . . .

BLACK-CURRANT MUFFINS

■

2 cups unbleached all-purpose flour
¼ cup sugar
1 tablespoon baking powder
½ teaspoon salt
¼ cup butter, melted and cooled
1 large egg, lightly beaten
½ teaspoon vanilla
1 cup plain yogurt
¼ cup milk
½ cup black-currant jam

A tasty, moist muffin with a surprise jam filling.

Preheat oven to 425°F. Whisk together the flour, sugar, baking powder, and salt in a large mixing bowl. Pour the butter into a medium-size bowl; stir in the egg and vanilla. Stir the yogurt and milk into the butter mixture. Add the moist mixture to the flour mixture all at once and stir until just blended.

Fill greased muffin tins or paper baking cups one-third full. In each cup, put about 1 teaspoon of jam in the center of the batter; top with the remaining batter. Bake for 15 to 20 minutes.

Yield: 12 muffins.

Jan Gibbs
McBride, British Columbia, Canada

. . . .

CRANBERRY ALMOND MUFFINS

▪

3 cups unbleached all-purpose
    flour
½ cup sugar
2 teaspoons baking powder
1 teaspoon baking soda
⅛ teaspoon salt
2 cups plain yogurt
⅓ cup milk
¼ cup vegetable oil
½ teaspoon almond extract
2 eggs, beaten
1½ cups fresh or frozen
    cranberries, coarsely chopped
2 tablespoons sliced or crushed
    almonds

Pretty, golden-colored cranberry muffins. Not overly sweet.

Grease and flour the muffin tins. Preheat oven to 375°F. In a large bowl, sift together the flour, sugar, baking powder, soda, and salt. In a medium-size bowl, stir the yogurt, milk, oil, almond extract, and eggs until blended. Stir the yogurt mixture into the flour mixture until moistened; the batter will be lumpy. With a rubber scraper and a gentle touch, fold in the cranberries. Spoon the batter into the muffin cups and sprinkle with almonds.

Bake for 30 minutes or until a toothpick inserted in the center comes out clean. Remove the muffins from the pans immediately and cool.

Yield: 12 large or 18 small muffins.

Michelle McIntyre
Jamestown, New York

POPPY-SEED MUFFINS

▪

2 tablespoons butter, softened
¾ cup brown sugar
2 eggs
1 cup plain yogurt
½ cup raisins
½ cup poppy seeds
1 cup unbleached all-purpose
    flour
1 cup whole-wheat flour
½ teaspoon baking powder
2 teaspoons baking soda

A poppy-seed lover's delight! Hearty, filling, and easy to prepare, these are great breakfast muffins. They reheat well, too.

Preheat oven to 400°F. Cream the butter and brown sugar; beat in the eggs. Add the yogurt, raisins, and poppy seeds and mix. Sift together flours, baking powder, and soda and stir into the poppy-seed mixture until just blended. Spoon into greased muffin tins, filling well. Bake for 15 to 18 minutes.

Yield: 12 large muffins.

Clive Cudmore
Campbellville, Ontario, Canada

ZUCCHINI DATE MUFFINS

■

¾ cup bran
¾ cup whole-wheat flour
½ cup sugar
1½ teaspoons ground cinnamon
1 teaspoon baking powder
1 teaspoon baking soda
1 egg, slightly beaten
½ cup plain yogurt
¼ cup vegetable oil
1 cup grated zucchini
½ cup coarsely chopped pitted dates
1 teaspoon grated orange rind

An easy, moist, and chewy muffin, to which the dates add a pleasant sweetness. They keep well enough so you can make them at night to serve the next morning.

Preheat oven to 400°F. In a large bowl, whisk together the bran, flour, sugar, cinnamon, baking powder, and soda. In a separate bowl, stir together the egg, yogurt, and oil; add the zucchini, dates, and orange rind and mix thoroughly. Add the wet mixture to the dry mixture, stirring just until moistened. Fill well-greased muffin cups three-fourths full. Bake for 20 to 25 minutes.

Variations: Try substituting 1 cup of applesauce or mashed banana for the zucchini.

Yield: 12 muffins.

Cora Vanden Bogert
Jordan Station, Ontario, Canada

....

BRAN BLUEBERRY MUFFINS

■

¾ cup bran
¾ cup whole-wheat flour
½ cup wheat germ
½ cup brown sugar
½ teaspoon salt
2 teaspoons baking soda
1 teaspoon grated orange rind
¼ cup vegetable oil
⅔ cup plain yogurt
1 egg, slightly beaten
1 cup blueberries

A very different blueberry muffin—dark and delicious, with a crunchy top.

Preheat oven to 400°F. Whisk together the bran, flour, wheat germ, brown sugar, salt, soda, and orange rind. Add the oil, yogurt, and egg and mix well. Fold in the berries. Spoon into greased muffin tins and bake for 20 minutes.

Yield: 12 muffins.

Susan Brunton
Shelburne, Ontario, Canada

....

VERY BLUEBERRY MUFFINS

■

2 cups unbleached all-purpose
  flour
2 teaspoons baking powder
½ teaspoon salt
1 cup plain yogurt
1 teaspoon baking soda
1 egg
½ cup vegetable oil
½ cup sugar
1 teaspoon vanilla
1 cup blueberries (frozen or
  fresh)

Definitely a hit! Even reheated the next day, these muffins are completely satisfying. See photo, page 51.

Preheat oven to 350°F. Sift together flour, baking powder, and salt. In a separate bowl, combine the yogurt with the soda; set the mixture aside. Beat the egg in a third bowl, then add the oil, sugar, and vanilla, and stir to combine. Add the flour mixture and the yogurt mixture alternately to the egg mixture. Gently fold in the blueberries. Pour into greased muffin tins and bake for 25 to 30 minutes.

Yield: 12 muffins.

Bonnie Freeman
Barriere, British Columbia, Canada

. . . .

OATMEAL BRAN MUFFINS

■

1 cup rolled or quick-cooking
  oats
1 cup boiling water
2 eggs, slightly beaten
½ cup molasses
½ cup vegetable oil
1 cup plain yogurt
1 cup milk
½ cup brown sugar
1½ cups whole-wheat flour
2 teaspoons baking soda
1 teaspoon ground cinnamon
½ teaspoon salt
2 cups bran
1 cup raisins

Absolutely delicious. This has become one of our favorite recipes.

Preheat oven to 375°F. In a small bowl, mix the oats with the boiling water; set aside to cool slightly. In a large bowl, mix together the eggs, molasses, oil, yogurt, and milk. Add the oat mixture and stir until thoroughly combined. In another bowl, thoroughly whisk together the brown sugar, flour, soda, cinnamon, salt, and bran; add this mixture to the wet ingredients and mix thoroughly. Add the raisins and stir again. Spoon the batter into greased muffin tins. Bake for 20 to 30 minutes.

Yield: 18 large or 24 average muffins.

Claire Blake
Belmont, Massachusetts

. . . .

YOGURT BRAN MUFFINS

■

2 eggs
1 cup brown sugar, or less to taste
1 cup vegetable oil
2 cups bran
2 teaspoons vanilla
2 cups plain yogurt
2 teaspoons baking soda
2 cups unbleached all-purpose flour
4 teaspoons baking powder
½ teaspoon salt
2 cups blueberries, raisins, or coconut

Thumbs up! Light and tender, these are eye-catchers from the minute they come out of the oven. Two of our younger samplers declared them "awesome."

Preheat oven to 350°F. In a large bowl, beat together the eggs, brown sugar, and oil. Stir in the bran and vanilla. In a separate bowl, mix together the yogurt and soda; set aside. Sift together the flour, baking powder, and salt and add to the sugar mixture alternately with the yogurt. Fold in the fruit or coconut. Fill lightly greased muffin tins and bake for 20 to 30 minutes.

Yield: 24 muffins.

Laraine Draper
Scarborough, Ontario, Canada

. . . .

APPLE CRANBERRY MUFFINS

■

1 cup rolled oats
1 cup plain yogurt
½ cup vegetable oil
¾ cup brown sugar
1 egg
1 cup unbleached all-purpose flour
½ teaspoon salt
½ teaspoon baking soda
1 teaspoon baking powder
2 teaspoons grated orange rind
¾ cup chopped cranberries
2 tablespoons granulated sugar
1 tart unpeeled apple, cored and chopped

Very flavorful, with an appealing texture and color. A great breakfast or snack for cranberry lovers.

Preheat oven to 375°F. Mix the oats with the yogurt. Add the oil, brown sugar, and egg; stir to combine. Sift in the flour, salt, soda, and baking powder. Add the orange rind and stir. Toss the cranberries with the granulated sugar and stir them into the yogurt mixture. Add the apple and stir. Spoon into greased muffin tins and bake for 15 to 20 minutes.

Yield: 12 muffins.

Edith Shantz
Halifax, Nova Scotia, Canada

. . . .

STRAWBERRY YOGURT MUFFINS

■

2 cups whole-wheat flour
½ cup sugar
1½ teaspoons baking soda
2 eggs
1 cup plain yogurt
¼ cup butter or margarine, melted
1 teaspoon vanilla
1 cup chopped fresh or frozen strawberries

Wet with strawberries. For extra sweetness, dust with cinnamon sugar while still hot.

Preheat oven to 375°F. Grease the muffin tins or line them with paper baking cups. In a large bowl, sift together the flour, sugar, and soda. In another bowl, stir together the eggs, yogurt, cooled butter, and vanilla until blended. Toss the strawberries with the flour mixture. Pour the egg mixture into the flour mixture and stir until the flour is just moistened. (The batter will be lumpy.) Spoon into the muffin cups. Bake for 20 to 25 minutes or until the tops are golden.

Variation: For a lighter muffin, use half whole-wheat flour and half unbleached all-purpose flour.

Yield: 12 muffins.

Doreen Chaput
Milford, New Hampshire

. . . .

CHOCOLATE RASPBERRY MUFFINS

■

2 eggs
½ cup butter, melted and cooled
¼ cup brown sugar, lightly packed
1 cup raspberry yogurt
2 cups unbleached all-purpose flour
¼ cup cocoa
1 teaspoon baking powder
½ teaspoon baking soda
½ cup golden raisins

A delectable, unusual combination of fruit and chocolate. Light, flavorful, and beautiful as well.

In a large bowl, beat together by hand the eggs, butter, and brown sugar. Stir the yogurt gently to blend in the raspberries, then fold into the egg mixture. In a small bowl, sift together the flour, cocoa, baking powder, and soda; add to the egg mixture, stirring just until blended. Gently fold in the raisins.

Heat oven to 375°F; let the mixture sit while the oven heats. Grease muffin tins and spoon in the batter. Mixture will be thick and stiff. Bake for 18 to 20 minutes.

Yield: 12 muffins.

Kathleen F. Casey
Rye, New Hampshire

. . . .

LEMON YOGURT MUFFINS

■

2 cups unbleached all-purpose flour
1 teaspoon baking powder
1 teaspoon baking soda
½ teaspoon salt
¼ cup sugar
2 tablespoons honey
2 eggs, at room temperature
1¼ cups plain yogurt
¼ cup unsalted butter, melted and cooled
1 tablespoon grated lemon rind

LEMON SYRUP
⅓ cup fresh lemon juice
⅓ cup sugar
3 tablespoons water

These muffins have the lightness of old-fashioned popovers. Try them warm with butter and blueberry jam, to accompany fresh fruit topped with vanilla yogurt. What a medley!

Preheat oven to 375°F. Sift together flour, baking powder, soda, and salt. In a separate bowl, mix the sugar, honey, eggs, yogurt, butter, and lemon rind. Add the flour mixture and stir until well combined. Spoon into buttered muffin tins and bake for 15 to 20 minutes.

While the muffins are baking, prepare the lemon syrup by mixing the lemon juice, sugar, and water. When the muffins are fully baked, remove them from the oven and pierce the top of each with a fork. Drizzle lemon syrup over the top of each. Let the muffins cool in the tins for 3 minutes, then remove them to a rack to finish cooling.

Yield: 12 muffins.

Prue Holtman
Wooster, Ohio

....

FRUITY COFFEE CAKE

■

CAKE
1½ cups unbleached all-purpose flour
1 teaspoon baking soda
1 teaspoon baking powder
½ teaspoon salt
½ cup brown sugar
½ cup wheat germ
1 cup plain yogurt
½ cup corn oil or safflower oil
(continued)

A quick and flavorful coffee cake. The wheat germ in the topping gives it a pleasant, nutty flavor.

Preheat oven to 375°F. Oil an 8-inch square pan. In a large bowl, whisk together the flour, soda, baking powder, salt, brown sugar, and wheat germ. In another bowl, stir together the yogurt, oil, egg, vanilla, and mandarin orange juice. Add the liquid mixture to the dry mixture and stir just until moist. Pour the batter into the pan and arrange the mandarin oranges on top.

For the topping, stir together the wheat germ, flour, brown sugar, and cinnamon; cut in the butter until the mixture is crumbly. Sprinkle the topping over the batter. Bake 40 to 45 minutes. Serve warm.

1 egg
1 teaspoon vanilla
1 can (11 ounces) mandarin
   oranges, drained (reserve
   juice)
¼ cup juice from mandarin
   oranges

TOPPING
¼ cup wheat germ
¼ cup whole-wheat flour
¼ cup brown sugar
¼ teaspoon ground cinnamon
¼ cup butter or margarine

Variation: In place of the mandarin oranges, use 2 cans (5¼ ounces each) of pineapple chunks.

Yield: 4 to 6 servings.

R. M. Norrie
Sidney, British Columbia, Canada

. . . .

Yummy Honey & Yogurt Coffee Cake

■

CAKE
1 cup butter, softened
2 heaping tablespoons honey
2 tablespoons brown sugar
2 eggs
2 cups plain yogurt
1 teaspoon vanilla
2 cups whole-wheat flour
2 tablespoons baking powder
Pinch of salt

FILLING
2 cups chopped walnuts
2 tablespoons brown sugar
2 teaspoons ground cinnamon

Not overly sweet, this is an unusual coffee cake because it's made entirely with whole-wheat flour. Especially delicious when served warm.

Preheat oven to 350°F. In a large bowl, cream the butter with the honey and brown sugar until well blended. Beat the eggs and stir them into the butter mixture. Add the yogurt and vanilla and blend well. In a separate bowl, sift together the flour, baking powder, and salt. Stir the flour mixture into the butter mixture.

Stir together all the filling ingredients until well combined. Butter a 10-inch Bundt pan. Spread half the cake mixture on the bottom, then half the filling. Add the remaining cake batter, then top with the rest of the filling. Bake for 50 minutes or until the cake springs back when touched. Cool for 10 minutes before removing from pan.

Yield: 10 to 12 servings.

Buddy Kring
New York, New York

. . . .

47

APPLE & YOGURT COFFEE CAKE

■

CAKE
¾ cup butter or margarine, softened
½ cup brown sugar
½ cup granulated sugar
½ teaspoon vanilla
2 eggs
2 cups unbleached all-purpose flour
¾ teaspoon baking powder
¾ teaspoon baking soda
½ teaspoon ground cinnamon
¼ teaspoon ground nutmeg
3 apples, peeled, cored, and coarsely chopped
1 cup raisins
½ cup chopped walnuts
1 cup plain or vanilla yogurt

TOPPING
¼ cup brown sugar
2 tablespoons unbleached all-purpose flour
½ teaspoon ground cinnamon
2 tablespoons chopped walnuts

A wonderful coffee cake—moist and just sweet enough. Our tester's family voted: Be sure to bake this one again!

Preheat oven to 325°F. In a large bowl, cream the butter and sugars; add the vanilla and eggs and beat together. In another bowl, sift together flour, baking powder, soda, cinnamon, and nutmeg. Add the apples, raisins, and walnuts to the flour mixture and toss lightly to coat. Add the flour mixture to the butter mixture and blend thoroughly. Gently fold in the yogurt until evenly mixed. Pour the batter into a greased 9x13-inch pan.

Mix all the topping ingredients together; sprinkle the topping over the batter. Bake for 30 to 40 minutes or until a toothpick inserted in the center comes out clean. Do not underbake.

Variation: Instead of using the brown sugar topping, bake the batter without topping. After the cake has cooled, mix together ½ cup confectioners' sugar, 1 tablespoon plain or vanilla yogurt, and ¼ teaspoon vanilla; spread over the cooled cake.

Yield: 14 to 16 pieces.

Elizabeth Crosbie
Southington, Connecticut

. . . .

Wow! Waffles (page 24).

Peach Colada (page 78).

Yogurt Streusel Coffee Cake (page 58), Whole-Wheat Raisin Bread (page 28),
Fresh Fruit with Yogurt Dressing (page 72), Very Blueberry Muffins (page 43).

Mandarin Chicken Salad (page 125).

Yogurt Cheese Parfait (page 212).

Artichoke Chicken (page 138).

Roasted Pepper & Yogurt Soup (page 98).

Frozen Raspberry Yogurt Cream (page 188).

HONEY ALMOND COFFEE CAKE

■

CAKE
½ cup butter, softened
½ cup honey
1 teaspoon vanilla
¼ teaspoon almond extract
2 eggs
2 cups unbleached all-purpose
  flour
1 teaspoon baking powder
1 teaspoon baking soda
1 cup plain yogurt
¼ cup milk

FILLING
¼ cup honey
⅓ cup raisins
1 cup sliced almonds
1 teaspoon ground cinnamon
¼ teaspoon ground nutmeg
1 tablespoon butter, melted

A honey lover's dream of a coffee cake—tasty but with no refined sugar. The almond extract adds a delicate flavor.

Preheat oven to 350°F. In a large bowl, cream together the butter and honey. Add the vanilla and almond extract and stir. Add the eggs and mix until smooth. In a medium-size bowl, sift together the flour, baking powder, and soda. Add the yogurt and the flour mixture alternately to the creamed butter mixture, stirring after each addition. Add the milk and mix until smooth. Do not overbeat.

For the filling, combine the honey, raisins, almonds, cinnamon, and nutmeg in a small bowl. Stir until the raisins and almonds are evenly coated. Add the butter and again stir until everything is well blended.

Spoon half the cake batter into a well-buttered 10-inch Bundt pan. Sprinkle half the filling mixture over the batter. Spoon the remaining batter over that and top with the rest of the filling. Bake for about 45 minutes or until a toothpick inserted in the center comes out clean. Serve this cake either side up— though of course only one side will show the filling.

Yield: One 10-inch Bundt cake.

Andrea Muraida
Brookline, Massachusetts

. . . .

PECAN ORANGE COFFEE CAKE

■

⅔ cup butter or margarine, softened
¾ cup sugar
2 eggs
1 cup plain yogurt
1 teaspoon grated orange rind
1 teaspoon vanilla
½ teaspoon ground cinnamon
¼ cup sugar
1 cup whole-wheat flour
1 cup unbleached all-purpose flour
1½ teaspoons baking powder
½ teaspoon baking soda
½ teaspoon salt
1 cup pecans, chopped

GLAZE
½ cup confectioners' sugar
Juice of one orange

A crumbly, moist, and delicious coffee cake that's perfect for a brunch. Try serving it with a layer of mandarin oranges on top.

Preheat oven to 350°F. In a large bowl, cream the butter with ¾ cup sugar. Beat in the eggs. Add the yogurt, orange rind, and vanilla and stir to combine. In a separate, small bowl, combine the cinnamon with ¼ cup sugar and set aside. Whisk together the flours, baking powder, soda, and salt, add to the creamed mixture, and stir to combine.

Pour half the batter into a well-buttered 10-inch Bundt pan and sprinkle with half the pecans and half the cinnamon-sugar mix. Add the rest of the batter; top with the remaining nuts and cinnamon-sugar. Bake for 40 to 50 minutes. Cool 10 minutes, then remove from the pan. While the cake is still warm, combine the confectioners' sugar and orange juice for the glaze; drizzle over the top of the cake and serve.

Yield: 12 servings.

Helen Campbell
Loughborough Inlet, British Columbia, Canada

. . . .

YOGURT STREUSEL COFFEE CAKE

■

CAKE
½ cup butter or margarine, softened
1 cup sugar
2 eggs
1 cup vanilla yogurt
(continued)

This has become one of our favorite coffee cakes — great to wake up to, and good for packing in lunch boxes, too. Virtually any yogurt, nut, and flavoring combination works well in this recipe. See photo, page 51.

Preheat oven to 350°F. In a large mixing bowl, cream the butter and sugar. Add the eggs and mix well. Add the yogurt and vanilla; stir to combine. In a separate bowl, sift together the flour, soda, baking powder, and salt. Add to the butter mixture and mix well.

To make the streusel, mix the brown sugar, flour, cinnamon, and butter until all the ingredients

1 teaspoon vanilla
2 cups unbleached all-purpose
  flour
½ teaspoon baking soda
1 teaspoon baking powder
½ teaspoon salt

STREUSEL
½ cup light brown sugar
2 tablespoons unbleached all-
  purpose flour
2 teaspoons ground cinnamon
2 tablespoons butter or
  margarine, melted
½ cup chopped pecans

are combined and damp. Stir in the pecans.

Grease and flour a 10-inch Bundt pan or tube cake pan. Put half the cake batter in the pan. Spread this with half the streusel mixture. Add the rest of the cake batter, then sprinkle the remaining streusel on top. Bake for 40 minutes. Let the cake cool in the pan for 10 minutes before turning it out onto a rack to cool.

Variations: Let your imagination go. Try plain yogurt with rum flavoring and walnuts, or plain yogurt with Angostura bitters and peanuts. Fruited yogurt works well, too.

Yield: 10 to 12 servings.

Sandra Webster
Yarmouth Port, Massachusetts

. . . .

Yogurt Spice Coffee Cake

■

2½ cups unbleached all-
  purpose flour
1 cup sugar
1½ teaspoons baking soda
1 teaspoon baking powder
1 teaspoon ground cinnamon
½ teaspoon ground cloves
⅓ cup sliced almonds
  (optional)
½ cup butter, melted
1½ cups plain yogurt

So easy to prepare and perfect with afternoon tea. The almonds are a great addition.

Preheat oven to 350°F. In a large bowl, sift together the flour, sugar, soda, baking powder, cinnamon, and cloves. Stir in the almonds if desired. Add the butter and blend; add the yogurt and mix thoroughly until smooth.

Grease a tube cake pan or 10-inch Bundt pan and dust it lightly with granulated sugar. Pour in the batter and bake for 1 hour or until a toothpick inserted in the center comes out clean. Cool and remove from the pan. Serve in thin slices.

Yield: 12 pieces.

Katharine Kulmala
Carlisle, Massachusetts

. . . .

CRANBERRY PECAN COFFEE CAKE

■

1½ cups fresh or frozen
  cranberries
¼ cup light corn syrup
¾ cup margarine or butter,
  softened
1¼ cups sugar
2 eggs, beaten
1 cup plain yogurt
2 cups unbleached all-purpose
  flour
1 teaspoon baking powder
1 teaspoon baking soda
¼ teaspoon salt
1 teaspoon vanilla
½ cup chopped pecans
1 tablespoon sugar

A great coffee cake for a special brunch. For a homey touch, serve it directly from a cast-iron skillet placed right on the table.

Preheat oven to 350°F. In a saucepan, combine the cranberries and corn syrup and cook over medium heat, stirring occasionally, until the berries pop. Remove the cranberries with a slotted spoon and drain on paper towels.

In a large bowl, cream the margarine and 1¼ cups sugar. In a separate bowl, stir together the eggs and yogurt, then set the mixture aside. Sift together the flour, baking powder, soda, and salt. Add the dry ingredients to the creamed mixture alternately with the yogurt mixture, stirring after each addition. Add the vanilla and stir. Reserving ¼ cup of the drained cranberries, fold the remaining berries into the cake mixture.

Pour into a greased 10-inch iron skillet or a buttered and floured 9x13-inch baking dish. Top with the reserved cranberries, chopped nuts, and 1 tablespoon sugar. Bake for 40 to 50 minutes.

Yield: 6 to 8 servings.

Lorraine Carr
Rochester, Massachusetts

. . . .

GERMAN APPLE CAKE

■

CAKE
1 cup milk, scalded
2 teaspoons yeast
¼ cup butter or margarine,
  softened
(continued)

A sweet crust with a tasty yogurt custard topping and delightful cinnamon aroma. Delicious warm from the oven, it becomes even more moist over time.

Pour ⅓ cup of the scalded milk into a large bowl. Sprinkle the yeast over the milk when the milk is lukewarm; allow the mixture to stand for 10 minutes.

Cream together the butter, sugar, and salt; stir in the remaining milk. Add the sugar mixture to the yeast mixture. Mix well. Add the egg yolk, and mix again.

⅓ cup sugar, generously
   measured
½ teaspoon salt
1 egg yolk
3 to 3½ cups unbleached all-
   purpose flour

TOPPING
6 cups peeled, cored, thinly
   sliced apples
⅓ cup sugar
1 cup plain yogurt
1 egg
Milk (optional)
Ground cinnamon

Add the flour gradually, mixing well after each addition. Knead the dough until it is smooth and elastic. Sprinkle with a little additional flour, cover, and let rise in a warm place for about 2 hours or until doubled in bulk. After the dough has risen, punch it down and spread it to fit a lightly greased 10x15-inch cookie sheet or jelly roll pan.

Preheat oven to 350°F. Arrange the apple slices in rows on the surface of the dough, overlapping the slices slightly. Allow the dough and apples to rest for a few minutes.

Mix the sugar, yogurt, and egg together. The mixture should be runny; if it's too thick, thin it with a bit of milk. Just before putting the cake in the oven, drizzle the yogurt mixture over the apples and spread the mixture with a spoon to achieve a fairly even coating. Sprinkle generously with cinnamon. Bake for 30 to 35 minutes or until the crust is well browned and the apples are somewhat soft.

Variation: The apple version is a family favorite, but in-season peaches, cherries, and blueberries also work very well. When using very juicy fruit, add flour, arrowroot, or cornstarch to the yogurt topping as a thickening agent.

Note: Because the custard may boil over, it's a good idea to place an extra pan under the cake in the oven to catch any spills.

Yield: About 24 servings.

Karen Kappel
Summerland, British Columbia, Canada

. . . .

HONEY WHOLE-WHEAT ENGLISH MUFFINS

■

¼ cup honey
1½ cups warm water
2 tablespoons yeast
1½ cups yogurt
½ cup water
1 teaspoon salt
1 teaspoon baking soda
7 to 8 cups whole-wheat flour
½ cup cornmeal

Sweet, tender muffins that freeze very well. The cinnamon-raisin variation is especially delicious. Be sure to test the griddle with a trimmed piece of dough to prevent scorching a whole panful.

In a tall glass, dissolve the honey in the warm water. Sprinkle the yeast on top of the warm water and honey; stir to dissolve. Set the yeast and water mixture aside to proof for about 20 minutes or until the yeast begins to bubble and multiply.

Combine the yogurt with ½ cup water and warm slightly to remove any chill. Pour the yeast-water mixture into a large mixing bowl and add the yogurt-water mixture, salt, and soda. Beat in as much of the flour as possible, 1 cup at a time, until the dough is stiff.

Turn the dough onto a floured board and knead in more flour, a little at a time, until the dough is no longer sticky. Form the dough into a ball. Cover the dough with a bowl and allow it to rise at room temperature for about 1 hour.

Punch down the dough and roll it out to a thickness of ¼ to ½ inch. Cut the dough into rounds (an empty, washed tuna can works perfectly for this). Sprinkle several cookie sheets with cornmeal and place the cut-out rounds on top of the cornmeal. Sprinkle the tops with additional cornmeal and cover the rounds with waxed paper or a clean towel. Allow them to rise for about 45 minutes.

In the meantime, lightly grease an electric skillet and preheat it to 300°F. (If you don't have an electric skillet, use a cast-iron skillet over medium heat on top of the stove.) Cook about 6 or 8 muffins at a time, covered, for about 8 minutes on a side or until golden brown. Allow them to cool on racks before storing in plastic bags. Fork-split the muffins before serving.

Variation I: Before allowing the dough to rise under the bowl, divide it in two. Add 1 teaspoon ground cinnamon and ½ to 1 cup raisins to one portion, knead, and place under a separate bowl on a floured surface. Continue with the recipe as above.

Variation II: For lighter muffins, use unbleached all-purpose flour in place of half the whole-wheat flour.

Yield: 24 to 36 muffins depending on size.

Carol Vanier
Georgetown, Massachusetts

. . . .

SCONES

■

½ cup raisins
2 tablespoons boiling water
2½ cups unbleached all-purpose flour
2 teaspoons baking powder
1 teaspoon baking soda
2 tablespoons sugar, or less to taste
¼ cup margarine
1 egg, lightly beaten
1 cup plain yogurt

A classic English tea-time or breakfast treat, these moist scones are a welcome change from the standard snack bread or muffin. They're at their best while still warm.

Preheat oven to 425°F. Add the raisins to the boiling water and set them aside to soak. Sift the flour with the baking powder and soda. Mix in the sugar. Cut in the margarine until the mixture resembles coarse meal. Add the raisins and water, egg, and yogurt. Mix well but gently. The batter will be sticky and soft.

Make balls of batter the size of a large egg and arrange them on a lightly greased cookie sheet. Pat them down to ½-inch thickness. Or roll out the dough to ½-inch thickness on a floured surface with a floured rolling pin and then cut out the scones. Bake for 10 minutes or until lightly browned. Split and spread with butter or jam.

Yield: 16 three-inch scones.

Audrey Reeves
Hornby Island, British Columbia, Canada

. . . .

YOGURT & OAT BRAN BAGELS

■

¾ cup lukewarm water (about 95°F)

½ cup plain yogurt

1 tablespoon molasses

1 tablespoon quick-rising instant yeast

2½ cups unbleached all-purpose flour

½ cup whole-wheat pastry flour

1 teaspoon salt

2 tablespoons oat bran

Cornmeal

¼ cup milk

2 teaspoons sugar

Bagels are fun to make. These are quite tasty and suitably chewy with a coarse, open texture.

In a large bowl, combine the warm water, yogurt, molasses, and yeast. Whisk vigorously until smooth. Add 1 cup of the all-purpose flour, all of the whole-wheat flour, and the salt. Beat. Gradually add the rest of the all-purpose flour and the oat bran. Turn out onto a floured surface and knead for 8 to 10 minutes, sprinkling with flour to eliminate any excess stickiness but being careful not to add too much. Return the dough to a clean, oiled bowl and let rise in a warm place for at least 1 hour, or until doubled in size.

Sprinkle the top of the dough lightly with flour. Punch it down and place it on a floured surface. Form a rectangle about 8 inches wide and ¾ inch thick; divide the rectangle into 16 eight-inch strips. Roll each piece into a rope about 8 inches long with tapered ends. Join the ends of each rope to make a circle. Let the bagels rest while a large pot of water is brought to a boil.

Drop several bagels at a time into the boiling water. Be careful not to crowd them; they will expand. After the bagels have come to the surface, allow them to boil for 1 or 2 minutes, then turn them and boil for 2 to 3 minutes more. Remove the bagels, using a slotted spoon, and let them drain.

Preheat oven to 400°F. Oil a cookie sheet and dust it with cornmeal; place the bagels on the cookie sheet. Mix the milk with the sugar, stirring until the sugar has dissolved; brush the milk mixture over the bagels. Bake for 25 to 30 minutes or until brown.

Yield: 16 bagels.

Helen Shepherd
Lyndhurst, Ontario, Canada

YOGURT SCONES WITH LEMON

■

2½ cups unbleached all-purpose flour
2 teaspoons baking powder
1 teaspoon baking soda
½ teaspoon salt
¼ cup sugar
6 tablespoons cold butter
1 cup plain yogurt
1 egg, beaten
Grated rind of 1 lemon
¾ cup currants

GLAZE
1 tablespoon plain yogurt
1 teaspoon sugar

Light scones with a lemon twist.

Preheat oven to 425°F. In a mixing bowl, sift together the flour, baking powder, soda, and salt; stir in the sugar. Cut in the butter until the mixture is crumbly. In a small bowl, stir the yogurt into the egg; add to the crumbly mixture. Add the lemon rind and currants; mix lightly.

Turn out onto a floured surface. Pat into a circle ½ inch thick, using only the flour necessary to keep the dough from sticking to the surface. (The dough will be very soft.) Grease a knife and a large cookie sheet. Cut the dough in half, then cut each semicircle into 6 wedges. Lift the wedges carefully onto the greased cookie sheet.

To make the glaze, mix the yogurt and sugar together; brush over the scones. Bake for 10 to 12 minutes or until lightly browned. Serve warm.

Yield: 12 large scones.

Margaret Pope
Windsor, Ontario, Canada

FRESH FRUIT
& YOGURT

■

Of all the ways to prepare yogurt, you can't get much fresher, or much simpler, than fresh fruit and yogurt. I personally am addicted to a sunflower-seed- or walnut-topped salad of nothing but whatever fruit we happen to have, drenched in a sea of vanilla yogurt. It's simple, it's fresh, and it's wonderful.

Another variation on this theme is the yogurt smoothie, in which fresh fruit and yogurt are blended together into a cool and creamy version of a traditional milkshake. On hot summer days especially, a yogurt smoothie can make the perfect breakfast, lunch, or snack: filling and hearty, but light. Smoothies are also virtually foolproof — just about any combination of yogurt and fruit makes a delectable treat. Yogurt smoothies are so delicious that they can quickly lure your children away from less healthful sweets, and so easy that often the kids themselves can prepare them. In our household, not a day passes when we don't find ourselves mixing up some yogurt concoction in the blender.

The preparation and presentation in the following recipes vary from quite simple to very dressed up and elegant. In virtually all cases, however, the yogurt is not heated or altered, so it retains all its nutritional goodness. Try these many ways to combine fresh fruit and yogurt, and use them as a springboard for inventing other easy, low-calorie ways to incorporate yogurt into your diet.

STRAWBERRIES IN YOGURT

■

1 quart fresh strawberries, washed, hulled, and sliced
1 cup plain yogurt
1 teaspoon vanilla
½ teaspoon almond extract
¼ cup brown sugar, or to taste

Quick and easy, this is an elegant way to prepare fresh berries.

Place the berries in a large bowl. Stir together the yogurt, vanilla, almond extract, and brown sugar and gently fold into the berries. Cover and refrigerate for about 1 hour to blend the flavors before serving.

Variations: Substitute other fruit or fruit combinations for the strawberries, or use 2 tablespoons of honey in place of the brown sugar.

Yield: About 4 cups.

Michele Henry
Hamburg, New Jersey

. . . .

GRAND MARNIER FRUIT SALAD

■

2 apples
2 oranges
2 bananas
2 peaches
2 pears
1 cup grapes
½ cup cantaloupe (or any other fresh fruit)
¾ cup dark raisins
½ cup chopped walnuts or sunflower seeds
¼ cup finely shredded coconut
1 cup plain yogurt
¼ cup honey at room temperature
¼ cup Grand Marnier

Coconut, honey, and Grand Marnier add the perfect touches to this very special dish.

Peel all the fruit, remove the seeds and cores, and cut into small pieces. Place the fruit in a large bowl and add the raisins, walnuts, and coconut. In a separate bowl, mix together the yogurt, honey, and Grand Marnier. Pour the yogurt mixture over the fruit mixture and stir to combine thoroughly. Refrigerate or serve immediately.

Yield: 6 to 8 servings.

Micheline Bell
Brackendale, British Columbia, Canada

. . . .

FRESH FRUIT & YOGURT DELIGHT

■

2 small fresh pineapples
1 pint fresh strawberries
2 cups vanilla yogurt
¼ cup shredded coconut
   (preferably unsweetened)
½ cup sliced almonds

Simple but flavorful, and extremely attractive. Be sure to handle the pineapple shells with care; they become your serving dish.

Cut each pineapple down the center, lengthwise. Remove the fruit from the shell, cutting to within ½ inch of the shell at all points. Set the shell halves aside. Remove the core and cut the pineapple fruit into ¾-inch chunks. Place in a medium-size bowl and set aside.

Wash the strawberries and set aside 4 with stems. Hull and slice the remaining berries and add them to the pineapple chunks. In a smaller bowl, combine the yogurt and coconut. Add to the fruit and gently mix. Spoon the yogurt-fruit mixture into the 4 pineapple shells. Sprinkle with almonds and garnish with a whole strawberry on top of each serving.

Variation: Try plain or strawberry yogurt in place of vanilla.

Yield: 4 servings.

Pat Sprankle
Nashua, New Hampshire

SCRUMPTIOUS SUNDAE

■

1 cup plain or vanilla yogurt
1 banana
Wheat germ, toasted or
   untoasted
½ cup chopped walnuts
Honey or maple syrup, to taste
1 large, fresh strawberry with
   stem

Easy and nourishing.

Spoon the yogurt into an individual serving bowl. Slice the banana into rounds and drop over the yogurt. Sprinkle with wheat germ. Cover with chopped walnuts. Drizzle honey over all. Top with the strawberry and serve.

Yield: 1 serving.

Lois Picard
Hope Valley, Rhode Island

PINEAPPLE YOGURT AMBROSIA

■

Lemon juice
2 large bananas, sliced
1 or 2 unpeeled apples, cored
  and diced
1 unpeeled pear, cored and
  diced
2 oranges, peeled and sectioned
1 cup fresh pineapple chunks
1⅓ cups flaked coconut
1 cup plain or vanilla yogurt

Coconut and pineapple are the surprises in this colorful fruit salad.

Sprinkle lemon juice over the bananas, apple, and pear to prevent them from darkening. Drain. Combine with the orange sections and pineapple chunks in a glass bowl. Chill for 1 hour. Fold in the coconut and yogurt, and serve.

Yield: 2 to 3 servings.

Mrs. Kit Rollins
Cedarburg, Wisconsin

. . . .

FANTASTIC FRUIT SALAD

■

¼ cup sunflower seeds, toasted
1 apple, peeled, cored, and
  diced
2 oranges, peeled and cut up
1 unpeeled pear, cored and
  diced
2 tablespoons pitted and
  chopped dates
2 tablespoons raisins
2 tablespoons wheat germ
2 tablespoons chopped walnuts
2 tablespoons slivered almonds
⅔ cup plain yogurt
1 tablespoon tahini (sesame-seed
  paste, available in natural-
  foods stores)
1 tablespoon liqueur (Grand
  Marnier, kirsch, or amaretto)

A nice blend of fruit and nut flavors, brought together by the hint of tahini. Excellent with ham, lamb, chicken, or beef, or served alone as a light dessert.

In a large bowl, combine the sunflower seeds, apple, oranges, pear, dates, raisins, wheat germ, walnuts, and almonds. In a separate bowl, mix the yogurt with the tahini and liqueur. Fold all the ingredients together and serve.

Yield: 4 servings.

Helen Shepherd
Lyndhurst, Ontario, Canada

. . . .

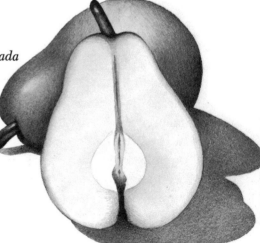

70

LAYERED FRUIT SALAD

■

3 cups shredded lettuce
1 honeydew melon, cubed
1 can (20 ounces) pineapple chunks, unsweetened or in light syrup, drained
1 pint fresh strawberries, hulled and halved
1 large banana, sliced in rounds
1 cup lemon or vanilla yogurt
½ cup shredded Swiss cheese

A simple dish that, served with rolls or bread, makes a perfect light lunch during the dog days of summer. Best eaten right away so the lettuce doesn't get soggy.

Place half the lettuce in a large salad bowl. Top with layers of melon, pineapple, berries, and banana; then add the remaining lettuce. Spread the yogurt on top and sprinkle with cheese. Cover and chill for 2 to 3 hours. Toss gently before serving.

Yield: 12 servings.

Diane B. Johnson
State College, Pennsylvania

. . . .

EMERALD SALAD WITH YOGURT DRESSING

■

3 large unpeeled apples, cored and cubed
2 cups honeydew melon balls
2 cups seedless green grapes, halved
2 kiwifruit, peeled and thinly sliced
¼ cup orange juice

YOGURT DRESSING
2 cups plain yogurt
3 tablespoons confectioners' sugar
2 tablespoons orange juice
½ teaspoon grated orange rind
¼ teaspoon ground cinnamon
⅛ teaspoon ground mace

An attractive presentation, with the creamy dressing setting off the emerald-colored fruits. Just a hint of sweetness and spice.

Combine the apples, melon balls, grapes, and kiwi with the orange juice in a large bowl. Cover and chill. Combine the dressing ingredients in a small bowl and mix well. Spoon the dressing over the chilled fruit salad and serve.

Yield: 8 servings.

Rose Strocen
Canora, Saskatchewan, Canada

. . . .

SUNFLOWER SEED & STRAWBERRY SALAD

∎

1 medium unpeeled apple, cored and chopped
1 cup halved seedless green grapes
1 cup sliced strawberries
½ cup sliced celery
¼ cup raisins
¾ cup lemon yogurt
2 tablespoons sunflower seeds
Lettuce

Colorful, fresh, and flavorful. The sunflower seeds provide an unusual and appealing crunch.

In a bowl, combine the apple, grapes, strawberries, celery, and raisins. Toss gently. Fold in the yogurt. Cover and chill for 2 to 3 hours. Just before serving, stir in the sunflower seeds. Serve each portion on a lettuce leaf.

Yield: 6 servings.

Mrs. Kit Rollins
Cedarburg, Wisconsin

· ·

FRESH FRUIT WITH YOGURT DRESSING

∎

Grated zest of ½ orange
1 tablespoon sugar (or less, to taste)
¼ cup plain yogurt
2 teaspoons raspberry vinegar
1 teaspoon frozen orange juice concentrate
1 teaspoon poppy seeds
2 to 3 cups fresh green grapes; peeled and sliced nectarines, kiwifruit, oranges, or bananas; or hulled and sliced strawberries

Most unusual and tasty, with a tang from the vinegar. Equally good with a single fruit or a combination of your favorites. A food processor is not essential here, but it is useful. See photo, page 51.

In a food processor, use the steel blade to blend the zest with the sugar. Add the yogurt, raspberry vinegar, orange juice concentrate, and poppy seeds; mix well. Transfer the mixture to a sauceboat.

Place the sliced fruit in a serving bowl and offer the dressing on the side, or combine the fruit and the dressing, toss lightly, and serve.

Yield: 2 servings.

Alice Weir
Boulder, Colorado

· ·

SIMPLE, CREAMY YOGURT SAUCE

■

Blueberries, pears, apples, bananas, mangoes, or your favorite fruit combination
1 cup plain yogurt
1½ tablespoons honey
¼ teaspoon ground nutmeg
¼ teaspoon ground cinnamon
⅛ teaspoon ground ginger

Light and delicious, with just the right blend of spices. Fresh fruit is best, but frozen unsweetened kinds are good, too.

Peel and cut up all fruits except berries. Mix together the yogurt, honey, nutmeg, cinnamon, and ginger. Pour over the fruit and serve.

Yield: 1 generous cup of sauce.

Susan Kahn
Framingham, Massachusetts

. . . .

CREAMY FRUIT TOPPING

■

4 ounces cream cheese, softened
2 tablespoons sugar
1 cup strawberry yogurt

Tastes like fruit-topped cheesecake.

Whip the cream cheese with an electric mixer until light and fluffy. Add the sugar; mix well. Add the yogurt and mix. Spoon over fresh fruit or berries.

Yield: 1½ cups of topping.

Mrs. Kit Rollins
Cedarburg, Wisconsin

. . . .

WALNUT RAISIN YOGURT

■

1 cup plain yogurt
1 teaspoon ground cinnamon
½ teaspoon ground nutmeg
2 tablespoons raisins
1 tablespoon chopped walnuts

Enjoy this as a healthy topping for cereal, or eat it alone for a flavorful snack.

Mix all the ingredients together and enjoy.

Yield: About 1½ cups.

Jonathan Steiner
Durham, New Hampshire

. . . .

FRUIT CREAM

■

1 cup whipping cream
1 cup plain yogurt
1 cup sour cream
½ cup sugar
1 tablespoon Grand Marnier or kirsch
Assorted fresh fruits such as blueberries, blackberries, or peaches

An unusual and creamy fruit sauce with a delicate flavor. Try it as a refreshing fruit dip, too.

Whip the cream until soft peaks form. Fold in the yogurt, sour cream, sugar, and Grand Marnier. Chill until ready to serve.

Clean and pick over the berries; peel the other fruits, remove pits, and chop into small pieces. Spoon the cream over the fruit and serve.

Yield: 4 cups.

Helen Campbell
Loughborough Inlet, British Columbia, Canada

YOGURT WITH CURRIED FRUIT

■

½ cup butter
2 tablespoons curry powder, preferably Madras style (if not Madras, add 1 teaspoon ground cinnamon)
3 tablespoons lemon juice
½ cup fresh or canned apricot or pineapple juice
2 cups sliced apricots, unpeeled
2 cups sliced peaches, unpeeled
2 cups sliced pears, unpeeled
2 cups pineapple chunks
1 mango, peeled and cut in chunks
2 cups yellow raisins
2 bananas, sliced in rounds
1 quart plain yogurt
1 cup chopped walnuts

A fine side dish or a satisfying light dessert in summer. Any combination of fruit, fresh or canned, is satisfactory, but always include bananas—they really complement the sauce. If using canned fruits, be sure to drain them before measuring, and reserve the juice to use in place of the fresh apricot juice.

Preheat oven to 325°F. Melt the butter in a small pan. Whisk in the curry powder and lemon juice. Add the fruit juice and whisk again. Arrange the fruit in a medium-size casserole and pour the butter mixture over the top. Bake, uncovered, for 1 hour. Serve warm, or cool overnight to enhance the flavor. Top each portion with a generous scoop of yogurt and a sprinkle of chopped nuts.

Variation: Add 1 tablespoon of brown sugar to the fruit juice.

Yield: 6 servings.

Roxanna Whitney Wolfe
Exeter, New Hampshire

SUMMER FRUIT DELIGHT

■

2 quarts plain yogurt
1 can (16 ounces) pineapple
  chunks
4 oranges, peeled, sectioned,
  and cut into pieces
Orange juice, preferably freshly
  squeezed
Honey, to taste (optional)
Toasted coconut

Refreshing and very easy to prepare, this makes a great ending for a summer meal. Prepare the yogurt cheese the day before you plan to serve the dish.

Drain the yogurt for 8 to 10 hours to make yogurt cheese (see directions on page 87). You should have approximately 2¾ cups of yogurt cheese.

The next day, drain the pineapple chunks and set aside the juice. Combine the pineapple chunks and orange pieces. Chill. Thin the yogurt cheese with orange juice and pineapple juice to taste and stir in the honey if desired. Top the fruit with the sweetened yogurt cheese; sprinkle toasted coconut over all.

Yield: 4 servings.

Sharon L. Marshall
Boston, Massachusetts

. . . .

STRAWBERRY YOGURT SHAKE

■

2 bananas, peeled, wrapped in
  plastic wrap, and frozen
2 to 3 cups fresh strawberries,
  hulled
1 quart plain yogurt
1 tablespoon vanilla
2 tablespoons maple syrup
4 strawberries with stems for
  garnish

Creamy and healthful, and the strawberries give it an appealing pink color. Tastes just like a milkshake.

Combine the bananas, 2 to 3 cups strawberries, yogurt, vanilla, and maple syrup in a blender; mix until all ingredients are thoroughly combined. Pour into 4 drinking glasses, or use parfait glasses for an elegant touch. Garnish each glass with a whole strawberry.

Variation: Substitute other berries or cantaloupe for the strawberries. Garnish with strawberries, if available.

Yield: 4 servings.

Marcia Appleton
North Conway, New Hampshire

. . . .

FRUIT SMOOTHIE

■

2 ripe bananas, peeled,
  wrapped in plastic wrap, and
  frozen
½ cup apple juice
1 cup plain yogurt
2 or 3 ice cubes

Freezing the bananas the night before makes this an especially refreshing treat.

Blend all the ingredients together at high speed in a blender. Pour into glasses and serve cold.

Variation: Replace the apple juice with 1 orange, peeled and with seeds removed, plus ¼ cup orange juice.

Yield: 2 servings.

Cheryl Veitch
Quesnel, British Columbia, Canada

. . . .

STRAWBERRY FRUIT FRAPPE

■

1 cup fresh strawberries
1 cup plain yogurt
1 cup apple-strawberry juice
  (try Winter Hill or After The
  Fall brand)

Rich, delicious, and so easy to make. For a thicker frappe, use more yogurt.

Reserve a few strawberries for garnish. In a blender, combine the yogurt, juice, and remaining strawberries. Blend until smooth. Pour into glasses, garnish each with a fresh strawberry, and serve cold.

Yield: 1 to 2 servings.

Martha E. Moore
Arlington, Massachusetts

. . . .

BASIC NUTRITIOUS FRAPPE

■

1 cup plain yogurt
8 to 10 ounces orange juice
1 banana

We tested this recipe with 15 kindergartners, and they loved it! All begged for seconds.

Combine all the ingredients in a blender, using high speed. Pour into glasses and serve.

Yield: 3 cups (about 2 servings).

John Dupuis
Leominster, Massachusetts

. . . .

TROPICAL FRUIT FRAPPE

■

1 ripe banana
1 cup plain yogurt
1 cup piña colada juice, chilled
  (try Winter Hill brand)
Fresh fruit, for garnish
  (optional)

This delicious, nutritious frappe will send you straight into a tropical fantasy. It also freezes to make great popsicles or ices.

In a blender, combine the banana, yogurt, and juice; process until smooth. Pour into glasses and serve cold, garnished with pieces of fresh fruit if desired. For a thicker frappe, use more yogurt or blend in fresh fruit.

Yield: 1 to 2 servings.

Martha Moore
Arlington, Massachusetts

. . . .

FROSTY SHAKE

■

1 ripe banana
1 cup strawberry or raspberry
  yogurt
1 cup red raspberry sherbet
1 cup milk

Sweet, creamy, and attractive. Kids love the flavor, and it's so easy they can make it themselves. Wonderful frozen, too.

Put all the ingredients in a blender and process on liquefy for 10 seconds. Pour into 2 tall glasses. For an extra treat, float a scoop of sherbet on top of each.

Yield: 2 servings.

Linda Gerry
Haverhill, Massachusetts

. . . .

BEST-EVER SHAKE

■

2 bananas
½ cantaloupe
1 papaya
1 cup applesauce
½ cup grated coconut, fresh or
    packaged
1 cup plain or vanilla yogurt
Dash of ground cinnamon
Sprigs of mint

We like the thick texture and great taste of this smoothie. It's a healthful treat, too, especially if the coconut and applesauce are unsweetened.

Remove all rinds, peels, and seeds from the fruit and cut into large chunks. Purée the bananas, cantaloupe, papaya, applesauce, and coconut in a blender or food processor until smooth. Pulse in the yogurt, cinnamon, and mint until fully blended. Pour into glasses and serve cold.

Yield: About 6 cups (4 servings).

Rose Donato
Somerset, New Jersey

. . . .

PEACH COLADA

■

2 fresh or frozen peaches,
    peeled and pitted
¾ cup plain yogurt
3 to 5 tablespoons peach jam,
    to taste
12 to 15 ice cubes
4 ounces white rum
1 tablespoon chopped almonds
    or coconut

Creamy, cool, and refreshing. Perfect for a summer or early fall garden party. See photo, page 50.

Place all the ingredients in a blender and mix on high until the ice is crushed fine. Pour into glasses and serve immediately.

Variation: For a delicious change of flavor, substitute fresh strawberries for the peaches and use strawberry rather than peach jam.

Yield: 4 servings.

Sandra Ausma
Guelph, Ontario, Canada

. . . .

HAWAIIAN PAPAYA COOLER

∎

2 cups plain yogurt
1 cup milk
2 ripe papayas, peeled and
    seeded
2 ripe bananas
Dash of Angostura bitters
½ cup sugar
2 ounces peach liqueur
2 ounces light rum
1 cup cracked ice
Ground nutmeg, for garnish

Easy to make, and so flavorful it can be served as a dessert. If papayas are not available, substitute fresh peaches for equally delicious results.

Mix the yogurt and milk. Mash the papayas and bananas and add to the yogurt and milk. Add the bitters, sugar, peach liqueur, rum, and cracked ice. Combine in a blender or shake thoroughly in a tight container. Pour into glasses, top each with a sprinkle of nutmeg, and serve.

Yield: 6 to 8 servings.

Helen Shepherd
Lyndhurst, Ontario, Canada

. . . .

ORANGE YOGURT COOLER

∎

1 cup plain yogurt
2 cups orange juice
1 pint orange sherbet
Fresh strawberries, pineapple
    chunks, or other fruit, for
    garnish

Everyone in our tester's family enjoyed this drink, but the children were especially crazy about it. They loved it for breakfast and as a fast cool-down on summer afternoons.

Mix the yogurt, orange juice, and sherbet together in a blender. Serve in tall glasses with lots of ice, garnished with fresh fruit.

Yield: 2 to 3 servings.

Martha Giammusso
Andover, Massachusetts

. . . .

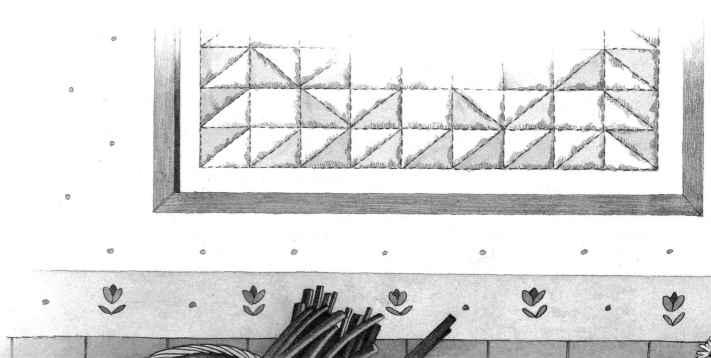

DIPS, SPREADS, SAUCES & DRESSINGS

∎

Traditionally, when we've used dips, spreads, sauces, and dressings to add flavor to our diet, we've added lots of calories as well. These items will rarely, if ever, be low-calorie parts of any menu, but in most of the recipes included here, you will find that yogurt is being substituted for all or part of something much more fattening—usually sour cream, mayonnaise, or cream cheese. Yogurt dips, spreads, sauces, and dressings provide not only a more healthful alternative for you and those you nourish, but an alternative that's delicious as well.

There are simple ways to incorporate yogurt into these foods. You can add plain yogurt to pan drippings to make gravy. Or simply substitute yogurt for half the mayonnaise or sour cream called for in other recipes you enjoy. Carol Chapman, one of our testers and a dedicated Stonyfield employee, got us hooked on mixing plain yogurt in with hot salsa for a chip dip. The yogurt adds a wonderfully refreshing and cooling balance to the hot-pepper bite.

So dip into these recipes! You'll find yourself going back for more.

AUSTRIAN ALPS YOGURT DIP

■

1½ cups plain yogurt
6 anchovies
½ onion, cut into large chunks
1 tablespoon capers
4 ounces cream cheese, softened
¼ cup butter, softened
1 teaspoon paprika
1 tablespoon caraway seeds
1 teaspoon powdered mustard
1 teaspoon Worcestershire sauce
⅛ teaspoon Tabasco
1 teaspoon dried thyme

A lively, piquant blend of flavors that's a delight for the palate. Good with raw vegetables or crackers — or serve on top of baked potatoes, steak, or hamburgers. For best results, refrigerate for one day before serving.

Drain the yogurt in several layers of cheesecloth for at least ½ hour or until it's the desired consistency — up to 1 hour for a thicker dip. In a blender or food processor, mince the anchovies, onion, and capers. Add the drained yogurt, cream cheese, butter, paprika, caraway seeds, mustard, Worcestershire sauce, Tabasco, and thyme; blend thoroughly. Refrigerate before serving.

Yield: About 2 cups.

Jeanne Bird
Cambridge, Massachusetts

. . . .

YOGURT VEGETABLE DIP

■

1 medium carrot, peeled and
  cut in large chunks
1 medium-size green bell
  pepper, cored, seeded, and
  cut in large chunks
½ small onion
¼ cup vinegar
1 pound Cheddar cheese, grated
1 cup mayonnaise
1 cup plain yogurt
2 teaspoons celery seeds

A fresh-tasting and unusual dip. Prepare the night before serving; refrigeration enhances the flavor and allows the dip to thicken.

Purée the carrot, bell pepper, onion, and vinegar in a blender or food processor. Add the cheese and mayonnaise and blend again. Fold in the yogurt and celery seeds. Refrigerate for 24 hours, then serve in a hollowed red cabbage, accompanied by sliced raw vegetables for dipping.

Yield: 1 generous quart.

Terry Lynn Clark
Elbridge, New York

. . . .

GUACAMOLE

■

6 ripe avocados, peeled, seeded,
and quartered
Juice of 2 lemons
2 cloves garlic
1 medium onion, coarsely
chopped
1 green bell pepper, cored,
seeded, and diced
1 cup plain yogurt
1 teaspoon chili powder
2 teaspoons salt

Chili powder adds a sparkle to this lemony guacamole. Serve as a salad on lettuce leaves, as a dip with tortillas, or as a garnish on chili.

Blend all the ingredients together in a blender or food processor. Chill before serving.

Yield: 1 quart.

Katherine MacKenzie
Allston, Massachusetts

. . . .

CREAMY CUCUMBER DIP

■

¾ cup peeled, shredded
cucumber
2 cups plain yogurt
1 teaspoon salt
2 cloves garlic, crushed
1 tablespoon olive oil

Served with wedges of Syrian bread, a smooth and refreshing dip for a party or a snack.

Press liquid out of the shredded cucumber. Mix the yogurt, salt, garlic, and olive oil in a large bowl, blend in the cucumber, and serve.

Yield: 3 cups.

Lisa Mellian
Taunton, Massachusetts

. . . .

YOGURT DIP

■

1½ cups plain yogurt
1 cup mayonnaise
2 teaspoons dried dill
1 teaspoon celery salt
1 small clove garlic, crushed
1½ teaspoons lemon juice

Smooth, easy to make, and very versatile. Try it over baked potatoes or avocados, as a salad dressing, or as a dip for raw vegetables.

Combine all the ingredients and enjoy.

Yield: 3½ cups.

Shirley Vandor
Ormotown, Quebec, Canada

. . . .

83

HUMMUS WITH A DIFFERENCE

■

⅓ cup tahini (sesame-seed
  paste)
¼ cup lemon juice
2 to 3 cloves garlic, crushed
¼ cup plain yogurt
1 can (19 ounces) chickpeas,
  drained
¾ cup plain yogurt
⅛ teaspoon ground cumin
Salt and pepper, to taste
Chopped parsley, for garnish
Paprika, for garnish

A very pleasing hummus, with an appealing blend of spices. If you prefer to use this as a spread rather than a dip, simply add more chickpeas.

Combine the tahini, lemon juice, garlic, and ¼ cup yogurt in a blender until smooth. Add the chickpeas, ¾ cup yogurt, cumin, and salt and pepper; again blend until smooth. Spoon into serving dish, and garnish with chopped parsley and paprika. Serve as a dip with Syrian bread.

Yield: 3 cups.

Lauren O'Reilly
Bartlett, New Hampshire

BLUE CHEESE DUNK

■

1 cup plain nonfat yogurt
⅓ cup low-fat cottage cheese
¼ cup crumbled blue cheese
2 teaspoons thinly sliced green-
  onion tops
½ teaspoon Worcestershire
  sauce
⅛ teaspoon salt
Pinch of pepper

A good, chunky blue-cheese dip. It doesn't have quite the full flavor of the standard cream-cheese or sour-cream variety, but it's quite good and has far fewer calories.

Line the filter cone of a drip coffee maker with a paper filter, or line a sieve with a double layer of paper towels. Suspend the cone over a 4-cup glass measure or narrow container. Spoon the yogurt into the filter and let it drain for 30 minutes. Set aside the drained-off liquid for another purpose; spoon the drained yogurt into a medium-size bowl. Stir in all the remaining ingredients. Cover and refrigerate for at least 1 hour to blend the flavors before serving.

Yield: 1½ cups.

Lucia M. Cyre
Logan Lake, British Columbia, Canada

ZUCCHINI CORIANDER DIP

■

1¾ cups plain yogurt
2 tablespoons olive oil
2 cloves garlic, finely chopped
2 small firm zucchini, trimmed, rinsed, and shredded (about 1 cup)
1 to 2 teaspoons white wine vinegar
3 tablespoons chopped fresh coriander leaves
Salt, to taste

A creamy, zesty, and attractive dip with a distinctive coriander and garlic flavor. Good with corn chips, pita bread, or fresh vegetables; with empanadas; or as a piquant sauce for fish or lamb.

Whisk the yogurt, oil, and garlic in a bowl until thoroughly combined. Stir in the zucchini, vinegar, coriander, and salt. Cover and refrigerate for 2 hours. Serve chilled.

Yield: 2½ cups.

Cheryl Veitch
Quesnel, British Columbia, Canada

. . . .

GREEK CUCUMBER DIP

■

2 large cucumbers, peeled and coarsely grated
1 cup plain yogurt
1 cup sour cream
1 small clove garlic, minced
1 teaspoon salt
¼ teaspoon pepper
Paprika (optional)
Small rounds of pita bread

Refreshing and nicely tangy — a great way to use up those extra summer cucumbers.

Wrap about one-fourth of the grated cucumbers in the corner of a clean dish towel and wring the towel to remove as much moisture as possible. Place the drained cucumbers in a bowl. Repeat the process with the remaining cucumbers, working with a portion of them at a time. Stir the yogurt, sour cream, garlic, salt, and pepper into the cucumbers. Sprinkle the mixture lightly with paprika, if desired.

Preheat oven to 325°F. Split each round of pita bread in half with scissors, forming 2 thin rounds. Cut the rounds into wedge-shaped quarters. Place them on an ungreased cookie sheet and bake for 7 to 10 minutes or until crisp and lightly browned. Serve the dip with the pita crisps.

Yield: 3 cups.

Bonnie Heckman Foust
Shannon, Illinois

. . . .

CURRY DIP

■

1 cup plain yogurt
1 cup mayonnaise
1 tablespoon ketchup
2 teaspoons chopped green
  onions
½ to 1 teaspoon curry powder
⅛ teaspoon garlic powder
¼ teaspoon Worcestershire
  sauce

A mild, creamy dip lightly flavored with curry. Easy to prepare and attractive, too.

Combine all the ingredients. Cover and refrigerate for several hours. Serve with raw vegetables.

Yield: 2¼ cups.

Gwen Klein
Weyburn, Saskatchewan, Canada

. . . .

BABA GHANOOJ

■

2 large eggplants
4 or 5 cloves garlic, crushed
1 cup tahini (sesame-seed paste)
Juice of 3 lemons
1 to 1½ cups plain yogurt, to
  taste
Chopped parsley, for garnish
Olive oil

A smooth dip or spread, quite pungent with the fresh garlic and tart from the lemon and yogurt. The name means "Daddy Laughed."

Preheat oven to 400°F. Pierce the eggplants in several places with a fork. Place them on foil in a pan and bake for 1 hour or until extremely soft. Cool them to room temperature.

When cool, scrape the eggplant pulp from the peel and place the pulp in a large bowl. Mash it well with a potato masher or pastry blender. Add the garlic, tahini, and lemon juice. Mix well. Carefully fold in the yogurt. Serve at room temperature, garnished with parsley and drizzled with olive oil, accompanied by pita bread and crackers. Store any leftovers in the refrigerator.

Yield: 3 cups.

Zana M. Lutfiyya
Syracuse, New York

. . . .

YOGURT CHEESE

■

Yogurt cheese is, of course, not cheese at all, but merely yogurt thickened to a soft cream-cheese-like consistency. Delicious and versatile, it is a lower-calorie substitute for cream cheese; one cup of yogurt cheese has about 250 calories, whereas one cup of cream cheese has about 800 calories. It picks up the flavors of the ingredients it's mixed with and makes a wonderful dip, spread, or pie or parfait filling.

To make yogurt cheese, simply line a bowl with a moist white cloth napkin or approximately eight layers of cheesecloth. Pour in the yogurt. (Allow 1 cup of yogurt for every ⅓ cup of yogurt cheese called for in a recipe; about half to two-thirds of the yogurt will be lost in the cheese-making process.) Tie the ends of the cloth together and suspend the whole thing from a faucet or kitchen cabinet. Make sure that the whey that drips through is watery, not thick. If it seems as though the yogurt itself is draining, then you don't have sufficient layers of cheesecloth.

Allow the yogurt to drain for 8 to 10 hours, or up to 12 hours if you want the cheese very thick. Although it does not need to be refrigerated while draining, you should store the finished product in the refrigerator, where it will keep for about a week.

Although all the yogurt cheese recipes in this book call for plain yogurt, you can make the cheese from flavored yogurt, too, as long as it contains no fruit or gelatin. If you use a cream-topped yogurt like Stonyfield, it is best to mix the cream in before making the cheese; otherwise the creamy layer can become a barrier next to the cheesecloth and prevent the whey from dripping through.

(Incidentally, don't discard the whey; it contains valuable nutrients, and you can use it as a substitute for milk or water in many bread and muffin recipes. And don't discard the cheesecloth; it can be machine-washed with mild soap and re-used. The weave will be looser, however, and more layers of cheesecloth may be necessary when it is next used.)

When making a dip or spread with yogurt cheese, combine the ingredients gently, using a fork or spoon. Avoid vigorous beating and mixing and never put the cheese in a food processor.

The culinary possibilities of yogurt cheese are as delightful as they are endless. Let your imagination go! Sometimes we like to keep it simple and make a tasty spread with garlic and dill. Sometimes we just can't resist whipping up a special parfait (see page 212). It seems as though no matter what we do with yogurt cheese, the end result is delicious.

SMOKED BLUEFISH SPREAD

■

1½ quarts plain yogurt
¼ pound smoked bluefish
1 teaspoon chopped fresh dill
1 tablespoon finely chopped
 sweet onion
Fresh dill, for garnish

Simply wonderful — tastes like a gourmet dip prepared by a caterer! Much richer tasting than the ingredients would suggest.

The day before serving, drain the yogurt for 8 to 10 hours to make yogurt cheese (see directions on page 87).

Mash the smoked bluefish and mix with 2 cups of the yogurt cheese, plus the dill and onion. Mound on a plate and garnish with fresh dill. Serve with thin rye crackers or as a spread on pumpernickel or caraway bagels.

Yield: 2 cups.

Marcy Ruppel
Newton Highlands, Massachusetts

. . . .

SALMON SPREAD

■

1½ quarts plain yogurt
4 ounces nova lox bits
Pinch of salt

A creamy, flavorful spread. Delicious also as an omelet filling with a dollop of sour cream on top.

Two days before serving, drain the yogurt for 8 to 10 hours to make yogurt cheese (see directions on page 87).

The day before serving, mix 2 cups of yogurt cheese, lox, and salt together. Refrigerate for 1 day. Serve with water biscuits or thin crispbread.

Yield: 2 generous cups.

Sharon L. Marshall
Boston, Massachusetts

. . . .

YOGURT CHEESE HORS D'OEUVRES

■

1½ quarts plain yogurt
½ cup extra virgin olive oil
2 cloves garlic, crushed
½ teaspoon crushed dried thyme
½ teaspoon crushed dried rosemary
½ teaspoon crushed dried basil
1 tablespoon chopped fresh dill

A superb spread. The combination of garlic, olive oil, herbs, and creamy yogurt cheese makes you feel you're in Greece.

Two days before serving, drain the yogurt for 8 to 10 hours to make yogurt cheese (see directions on page 87).

The day before serving, combine the olive oil with the garlic and herbs and mix well. Divide 2 cups of the yogurt cheese into four portions, shaping them into patties with your hands. Place the patties in a wide, shallow bowl and pour the oil mixture over them. Let sit at room temperature for half an hour; then cover and refrigerate overnight. Remove from the refrigerator about half an hour before serving.

Serve with French bread and crackers. For a special treat, slice the French bread into rounds, butter, and broil briefly before serving.

Yield: 2 cups.

Lise Stern
Cambridge, Massachusetts

. . . .

GREEN SAUCE

■

½ packed cup mixed greens and herbs of your choice (e.g., chives, sorrel, spinach, dandelion, parsley, curly endive)
1 tablespoon finely chopped shallot
1 cup plain yogurt

A simpler, healthier alternative to a classic green sauce. Use as a spread or dip, or as a creamy sauce for a hot vegetable dish. Or mix with the flesh of a hot baked potato for a delicious stuffed potato.

Combine all the ingredients in a blender or food processor and mix to the desired consistency.

Yield: 1 cup.

Ellen Ogden
Londonderry, Vermont

. . . .

STEVEN'S SIMPLE SENSATIONAL SAUCE

■

2 cups plain yogurt
1 teaspoon grated fresh ginger
2 tablespoons honey
2 teaspoons vanilla
1 tablespoon lemon juice

A lively ginger sauce that's great mixed with fresh fruit for dessert, poured over hot or cold asparagus, or served with any number of other dishes for a special added spark.

Mix all the ingredients together and serve.

Note: For super chicken salad, mix the sauce with 2 to 3 pounds of cold chopped chicken, plus chopped celery, pineapple chunks, garlic salt, and caraway seeds to taste. Allow to set overnight to bring out the flavor.

Yield: 2 cups.

Steven C. Sawyer
Kittery, Maine

. . . .

SESAME YOGURT SAUCE

■

1 onion, diced
1 green bell pepper, cored, seeded, and diced
2 tablespoons vegetable oil
2 tablespoons sesame seeds
3 cloves garlic, minced
¼ cup peeled and chopped green chili peppers
1 cup plain yogurt
½ teaspoon salt
¼ teaspoon ground cumin

An easy, unusual, and distinctive mixture that's a delight for fans of Mexican food. Serve hot over rice as a side dish, or cold with corn chips as a dip. See photo, page 132.

In a medium-size skillet, sauté the onion and bell pepper in oil over medium-high heat for 5 to 7 minutes or until soft. In a small dry skillet, sauté the sesame seeds until they are golden. Add the garlic and green chili peppers to the onion mixture and cook several minutes more, stirring constantly. Add the sesame seeds and stir. Remove from heat and stir in the yogurt, salt, and cumin. Serve hot over cooked grains, pasta, or vegetables.

Yield: 1½ cups.

Nanette J. Blanchard
Mancos, Colorado

. . . .

CITRUS YOGURT SAUCE

■

1 cup plain yogurt
1 teaspoon grated orange rind
2 tablespoons brown sugar, or
   to taste
½ teaspoon vanilla

Pleasant, smooth, and a wonderful complement to fresh fruit. Try it as a fruit dessert dip, too. Or serve as a tasty topping for waffles and pancakes, and turn any breakfast into a special occasion.

Stir all the ingredients together and refrigerate for at least 1 hour. Pour the sauce over sliced fruit and serve.

Yield: 1 cup.

Cathy Malcolmson
Thornhill, Ontario, Canada

. . . .

CRUNCHY CURRIED YOGURT SAUCE

■

1 cup plain yogurt
¾ teaspoon curry powder
1½ teaspoons honey
1 teaspoon finely chopped
   chives
2 teaspoons seasoned bread
   crumbs
Salt and pepper, to taste

Delicious on cooked asparagus, carrots, or greens. Also great on baked potatoes. Best served well chilled.

Mix all the ingredients well. Refrigerate for 6 to 8 hours to strengthen and enhance the flavor.

Yield: 1 generous cup.

Karen Paradies
Sudbury, Massachusetts

. . . .

MOCK SOUR CREAM

■

⅔ cup low-fat plain yogurt
⅓ cup low-fat cottage cheese
Dash of lemon juice

A low-calorie substitute for sour cream.

Mix all the ingredients in a blender until smooth. Chill before serving.

Yield: 1 cup.

Diane B. Johnson
State College, Pennsylvania

. . . .

YOGURT CREAM TOPPING

■

1 cup heavy cream or whipping cream
2 tablespoons brown sugar
2 cups plain or flavored yogurt
Finely chopped toasted almonds, for garnish (optional)
Finely chopped coconut, for garnish (optional)

A wonderful topping for fresh fruit or desserts, and easily varied by using different flavors of yogurt. We used one cup of plain and one cup of vanilla and got a smooth and delightful result.

Whip the cream until peaks form. In a separate bowl, combine the brown sugar and yogurt; fold in the whipped cream. For an elegant touch and a slightly crunchy texture, top with toasted almonds and coconut.

Yield: 3 cups.

Kathy Card
Manchester, New Hampshire

. . . .

YOGURT DIJON SALAD DRESSING

■

3 tablespoons Dijon mustard
½ cup plain yogurt
½ teaspoon salt
Pinch of freshly ground pepper
3 tablespoons lemon juice
1 teaspoon sugar
1 clove garlic, finely chopped
1 tablespoon capers, drained

A spicy dressing that's the perfect complement to a summer salad of tomatoes, lettuce, hard-boiled eggs, green beans, and cold potato slices. See photo, page 135.

Combine the mustard, yogurt, salt, pepper, lemon juice, sugar, and garlic in a small bowl; beat well. Stir in the capers and serve.

Yield: 1 cup.

Connie Dingman
Hannon, Ontario, Canada

. . . .

NATURAL GARLIC DRESSING

■

2 cups plain yogurt
(continued)

If you love garlic and chives, this dressing is for you! Extra versatile, it can be used over crisp, fresh greens or in potato or macaroni salads.

Blend all the ingredients together in a blender for 2 minutes. Store in the refrigerator for up to a week or until ready to serve.

Yield: 2½ cups.

¼ cup milk
10 cloves garlic
25 stalks fresh chives (or a good handful)
1 medium green bell pepper, cored, seeded, and quartered

Ellie Hebert
Southbury, Connecticut

• •

√Healthy Salad Dressing with Yogurt

∎

1 cup plain yogurt
1 tablespoon Dijon mustard
¼ teaspoon black pepper
½ teaspoon salt (optional)
¼ cup chopped fresh parsley
1 clove garlic, minced
2 fresh scallions, chopped
½ cup wine vinegar (or ⅓ cup if you like less vinegar)
10 green olives with pimientos (optional)

Healthful, simple, and spicy — a great salad dressing.

Blend together the yogurt, mustard, black pepper, optional salt, parsley, garlic, scallions, and vinegar. Stir in the optional olives. Pour over your favorite green salad.

Yield: 2½ cups.

Nana Katsiff
New York, New York

• •

Creamy Mustard Salad Dressing

∎

1 cup plain yogurt
3 tablespoons Dijon mustard
2 tablespoons balsamic vinegar
1 tablespoon honey
½ teaspoon ground coriander
¼ teaspoon salt

Piquant with mustard and a hint of coriander. Recommended over a salad of Romaine lettuce, avocado, sweet red pepper, Bermuda onion, and fresh red grapefruit sections.

Combine all the ingredients in a quart jar and shake vigorously, or stir until blended. Pour over salad and serve.

Yield: 1¼ cups.

Marc Kotz
Hartford, Connecticut

• •

YOGURT, RADISH & MINT SALAD DRESSING

■

1 cup plain yogurt
1 clove garlic, minced
1 teaspoon sugar or honey
1 tablespoon fresh lemon juice
½ teaspoon salt
¼ cup chopped radishes
1 heaping tablespoon chopped
   mint
Freshly ground pepper

A smooth, creamy, and attractive dressing with a tang from the lemon, radishes, and garlic. Nicely complemented by the addition of mint.

Combine all the ingredients in a blender until the radishes and mint are finely chopped. Pour over salad and serve.

Yield: About 1 cup.

Elaine Park
Williston, Vermont

. . . .

CUCUMBER & BLUE CHEESE DRESSING

■

1 pickling cucumber, peeled,
   seeded, and cut in chunks
¼ cup chopped fresh dill
¼ cup diced red bell pepper
1 cup plain yogurt
Salt and white pepper, to taste
4 ounces blue cheese (preferably
   imported), crumbled

A pretty pale-green sauce with great flavor. Try it as a dip or as a sauce for cold poached salmon.

In a food processor fitted with the steel blade, chop the cucumber until it is reduced to fine pieces. Transfer to a strainer set over a bowl. Let drain for 30 minutes, occasionally pressing down on the cucumber to extract the maximum amount of juice. After the cucumber has drained, combine with the remaining ingredients. Chill for at least 2 hours before serving.

Yield: 1½ cups.

Anne Dehman
Sharon, Massachusetts

. . . .

✓ # EASY NIFTY DRESSING

■

Creamy, light, and delicate. Try it on salads, cooked fish, or tuna fish sandwiches.

Place the vinegar, salt, sugar, and ¼ cup oil in a blender and mix on high speed for 5 seconds. Switch the blender to its lowest speed; add the remaining oil

⅓ cup vinegar
1 teaspoon salt
1 teaspoon sugar
1 cup vegetable oil
1 cup plain yogurt
¼ cup country-style mustard
 (such as Dijon)

slowly while continuing to mix. Pour the mixture into a bowl and fold in the yogurt and mustard. Store in a glass container in the refrigerator until ready to serve. Will keep, refrigerated, for 10 to 14 days.

Yield: 3 cups.

Elizabeth Lessard
Bedford, New Hampshire

• •

BLUE CHEESE SALAD DRESSING

■

1 cup plain yogurt
½ cup vegetable oil
2 tablespoons vinegar
1 teaspoon Worcestershire sauce
1 teaspoon dried basil
1 teaspoon garlic powder
1 teaspoon dried thyme
1 teaspoon dried oregano
½ teaspoon salt
6 ounces blue cheese, crumbled

A dressing that's thick, as blue cheese should be, with a strong and full flavor.

Combine all ingredients but blue cheese in blender and blend until smooth. Fold in blue cheese and serve.

Yield: 2½ cups.

Cheryl Veitch
Quesnel, British Columbia, Canada

• •

AVOCADO SALAD DRESSING

■

1 avocado, peeled, seeded, and
 mashed
½ cup plain yogurt
2 tablespoons vegetable oil
2 cloves garlic, minced
¼ teaspoon salt
½ teaspoon ground cumin
¼ teaspoon hot-pepper sauce
 (optional)

Tastes like liquid avocado, with a subtle bite from the garlic and hot-pepper sauce (which, though optional, is strongly advised). Try this drizzled over a Mexican tortilla salad in lieu of guacamole.

Combine all the ingredients in a blender or food processor and blend until smooth. Add more yogurt to thin the dressing to desired consistency before serving.

Yield: 1 cup.

Nanette J. Blanchard
Mancos, Colorado

• •

SOUPS

■

Yogurt provides a versatile soup base any time of year, but many of the recipes included here are especially appealing soups for summertime: instantly refreshing, often quick and easy to make, and perfect for using up that extra garden produce or the bounty of the berry patch. Whether served as a light lunch or an appetizer before dinner, any of these soups will please both family and guests.

This chapter offers four variations on a summer cucumber soup theme—all similar in their basic ingredients but remarkably different in their results. Try each one over the course of the season, both to enjoy the pleasing variations and to find a delicious use for all those fresh garden cucumbers!

Come back to this chapter in winter, too, on those freezing days when hot soup becomes a "comfort food" and yogurt adds a thick and luxurious touch that's hard to resist. When hours of shoveling leave you chilled to the bone, try our favorite Yogurt Carrot Soup for an aroma that warms you even before the first spoonful.

ROASTED PEPPER & YOGURT SOUP

■

1¾ pounds red bell peppers
1¼ pounds yellow bell peppers
2 cups plain yogurt
1 cup chicken stock
1 tablespoon chopped fresh chervil
1 tablespoon chopped fresh tarragon
1 tablespoon chopped fresh basil
½ teaspoon salt, or to taste
White pepper, to taste
1 tablespoon balsamic vinegar
1 pound tiny salad shrimp, peeled, deveined, and poached; or 1 pound small scallops, poached

GARNISH

Julienned red and yellow bell peppers
Yogurt mixed with more chervil, tarragon, and basil

Excellent and unusual hot-weather fare, with a delightful combination of flavors. It's a bit time consuming to prepare, but worth every moment. Our tester declares this the best recipe she's ever tested! See photo, page 55.

Preheat the broiler and place the broiler rack as close to the heat as possible. Use aluminum foil to line a cookie sheet with sides. Place washed and dried peppers on the foil and broil them, turning them with tongs every few minutes until they are charred all over. Be careful not to break the skins. Remove the charred peppers to a large bowl or bowls and let them cool.

When the peppers are cool, place a colander over a large bowl. Peel the peppers, catching the peeled peppers in the colander and the juices in the bowl. Discard the seeds and blackened skins.

Transfer the peppers and their juices to the bowl of a food processor fitted with a steel blade. Purée until smooth, then strain the purée through a sieve. Return the strained mixture to the food processor with the steel blade in place. Add the yogurt, chicken stock, chopped herbs, salt, pepper, and vinegar. Process until blended. Chill.

Serve very cold, poured over the poached shrimp or scallops in individual soup bowls. Garnish with julienned peppers and yogurt mixed with chervil, tarragon, and basil.

Yield: 6 generous portions.

Anne S. Dehman
Sharon, Massachusetts

· ·

STRAWBERRY SOUP

∎

1 package (10 ounces) frozen
   unsweetened strawberries,
   thawed
2 teaspoons sugar
Juice of ½ lemon
½ teaspoon almond extract
1 cup strawberry yogurt
8 ounces champagne

Served with a sprig of mint, this is the very essence of freshness.

Purée the strawberries in a blender or food processor. Add the sugar, lemon juice, and almond extract, then the yogurt and champagne. Blend until very smooth. Chill for at least 3 hours. Serve cold in small dessert dishes or cups with saucers.

Note: For a thicker soup, use 2 cups of yogurt.

Yield: 4 to 6 servings.

Mary Branscombe
Goffstown, New Hampshire

. . . .

CREAMY BLUEBERRY BISQUE

∎

2 cups blueberries
2 cups water
⅓ cup granulated sugar
1 tablespoon brown sugar
1 cinnamon stick
1 lemon, thinly sliced
2 cups plain yogurt
1 cup apple juice
Plain yogurt for garnish

An easy, refreshing fruit soup, best made with fresh (not frozen) blueberries. It has a beautiful color and a pleasant tang.

Reserve a few blueberries for garnish. Place the remaining berries, water, sugars, cinnamon, and lemon in a saucepan. Simmer, uncovered, for 15 minutes, then drain through a sieve. Chill the sieved liquid. Just before serving, whisk in the yogurt and apple juice. Garnish each serving with a spoonful of yogurt and a few berries.

Yield: 4 to 6 servings.

Lorraine Carr
Rochester, Massachusetts

. . . .

COLD TOMATO DILL SOUP

■

2 tablespoons olive oil
2 to 3 medium onions, chopped
2 to 4 cloves garlic, crushed
6 to 8 tomatoes, peeled and chopped
2 cups chicken stock (homemade is best)
½ teaspoon white pepper
3 tablespoons finely chopped fresh dill, or 1½ teaspoons dried dill
1 teaspoon sugar
2 cups plain yogurt
1 cup buttermilk or skim milk
Plain yogurt for garnish
Chopped dill or chives, for garnish

A satisfying soup for July or August. It's important to wait until the yogurt has been added before adjusting the seasonings.

Heat the olive oil in a skillet over medium heat. Add the onions and garlic and sauté until soft but not brown. Add the tomatoes, chicken stock, white pepper, and dill. Cover and simmer for 15 minutes.

Cool the cooked mixture slightly, then process in a blender or food processor in batches. Add the sugar, yogurt, and milk to the tomato mixture. Blend well. Chill. Adjust seasonings, pour into individual bowls, and garnish each with a dollop of yogurt sprinkled with chopped dill or chives. Serve very cold.

Note: Can be frozen before adding the sugar, yogurt, and milk. After thawing, proceed with the recipe.

Yield: 6 to 8 servings.

Hugh and Dolores Johnston
Bracebridge, Ontario, Canada

CUCUMBER SOUP

■

4 cucumbers
1 quart plain yogurt
½ cup water
¼ teaspoon salt
1 clove garlic, crushed
1 tablespoon dry mint

Chunky, tasty, and so easy to make.

Peel the cucumbers. Cut into quarters lengthwise, and slice crosswise into ¼-inch-thick pieces. Stir the yogurt in a bowl until it is smooth. Add the water and blend. Add the cucumbers, salt, garlic, and mint. Stir, then chill before serving.

Yield: 4 servings.

Dorothy Parker
Holden, Massachusetts

CUCUMBER YOGURT SOUP

■

4 medium to large cucumbers, peeled
Sprigs of fresh mint
2 cups milk
2 cups plain yogurt
1 to 2 tablespoons honey
1 teaspoon chopped fresh dill
2 to 3 scallions, chopped
Salt and pepper, to taste

An easy and rewarding cold soup, with a beautiful pale-green color. Serve as a refreshing summer appetizer.

Reserve a few cucumber slices and whole mint leaves for garnish. Chop remaining cucumber into large pieces, then purée with the remaining mint and all the other ingredients in a blender or food processor. Chill for several hours. Serve cold, garnished with reserved mint leaves and cucumber slices.

Yield: 6 servings.

Mario and Laura Geilen
Arlington, Massachusetts

PERSIAN YOGURT SOUP

■

2 long European cucumbers, peeled
4 cups plain yogurt
2 cups mineral (seltzer) water
Salt, to taste
1 teaspoon sugar
1 teaspoon celery salt
White pepper, to taste
2 tablespoons chopped fresh dill, or to taste
½ cup raisins
½ cup grapes (red and green mixed or one variety)
½ cup walnut pieces
Fresh dill sprigs for garnish

Full flavored from the grapes, raisins, and walnuts—and wonderfully refreshing on a hot day.

Grate and drain the cucumbers, squeezing out excess liquid; set aside. Mix the yogurt with the mineral water. Stir in the salt, sugar, celery salt, and pepper. Let sit in the refrigerator for about 2 hours.

Before serving, stir in the drained cucumbers, dill, raisins, grapes, and walnut pieces. Pour into individual bowls, garnish each with a fresh dill sprig, and serve with warm pita bread.

Yield: 5 to 6 servings.

Siga Rastonis
East Sandwich, Massachusetts

SUMMER YOGURT SOUP

∎

1 quart fresh orange juice
1 quart plain yogurt
1 tablespoon honey (or more to taste)
2 tablespoons fresh lemon juice
Dash of ground cinnamon
Dash of ground nutmeg
1½ pints fresh strawberries, raspberries, or blueberries
Fresh mint sprigs for garnish

Simple and delightful. Serve as a light first course or refreshing dessert.

Whisk together the orange juice, yogurt, honey, lemon juice, cinnamon, and nutmeg. Hull the strawberries and slice any large ones; otherwise, berries should be left whole. Divide the berries equally among individual serving dishes and ladle the soup on top. Garnish with fresh mint.

Yield: 4 to 6 servings.

Deborah Jean Ham
Springfield, Massachusetts

. . . .

CREAMY YOGURT BEET SOUP

∎

1 medium onion (preferably Vidalia), sliced
1 tablespoon butter or vegetable oil
1 can (16 ounces, not drained) or 2 cups cooked fresh beets
2 cups chicken stock, canned or homemade
2 cups plain yogurt
1 cup sour cream
1 tablespoon red or white wine vinegar
1 tablespoon fresh lemon juice
Salt and pepper, to taste
Additional sour cream or yogurt, for garnish
Fresh dill, coriander, or pepper, for garnish

Tasty and easy to prepare, this is an ideal light lunch or appetizer on a hot day. Serve with crusty dark bread.

In a small skillet, sauté the onion in butter until soft. In a food processor, combine the beets, beet liquid (only if using canned beets), chicken stock, and onion. Puree until smooth, in batches if necessary.

If the soup is to be served cold, simply whisk in the yogurt, sour cream, vinegar, lemon juice, and salt and pepper, then chill. To serve it warm, stir the beet mixture constantly while heating it on top of the stove. When the mixture is hot but not boiling, slowly stir in the yogurt, sour cream, vinegar, lemon juice, and salt and pepper. Do not boil or the yogurt will curdle. Soup may be garnished with a dollop of sour cream or yogurt and topped with fresh, chopped herbs or pepper.

Yield: 6 cups.

Stephen R. Sozanski
Topsfield, Massachusetts

. . . .

ARABIC COLD YOGURT SOUP

■

½ cup raisins
1 cup cold water
2½ cups plain yogurt
½ cup light cream
1 hard-boiled egg, chopped
6 ice cubes
1 cucumber, peeled and
    chopped
¼ cup chopped green onion
2 teaspoons salt
½ teaspoon white pepper
1 tablespoon chopped parsley
1 tablespoon chopped fresh dill

Great taste and consistency. The hard-boiled egg and raisins add an unusual touch.

Soak the raisins in cold water for 5 minutes. Combine the yogurt, cream, egg, ice cubes, cucumber, onion, salt, and pepper in a mixing bowl. Add the raisins and water; stir. Chill for 2 to 3 hours. Garnish with parsley and dill, and serve.

Yield: 6 servings.

Siga Rastonis
East Sandwich, Massachusetts

. . . .

CUCUMBER MINT SOUP

■

2 medium cucumbers, peeled
    and finely shredded
¼ teaspoon salt
2 cloves garlic
2 cups low-fat plain yogurt
2 tablespoons finely chopped
    fresh mint or 1½ teaspoons
    crumbled dry mint
White pepper, to taste
Sprigs of fresh mint, for garnish

Very thick, with a wonderful fresh taste.

Toss the shredded cucumbers with salt, place in a colander, and set aside to drain for 10 minutes. Chop the garlic or squeeze it through a press; mix the garlic with the yogurt. Press the last of the juice out of the draining cucumbers and mix the cucumbers with the yogurt and garlic. Add the chopped mint and the pepper, then stir. Cover and chill. Serve in cold individual bowls, garnished with sprigs of fresh mint.

Note: If this soup is too thick for your taste, thin it with a bit of skim milk.

Yield: 4 servings.

Mary Jane Jackson
South Hero, Vermont

. . . .

YOGURT CARROT SOUP

∎

¼ cup butter
1 onion, chopped
2 cloves garlic, minced
½ teaspoon mustard seeds
½ teaspoon ground turmeric
½ teaspoon ground ginger
¼ teaspoon cayenne pepper
½ teaspoon salt
½ teaspoon ground cinnamon
½ teaspoon ground cumin
1 pound carrots, peeled and
  thinly sliced
1 tablespoon lemon juice
3½ cups water
2 cups plain yogurt
1 tablespoon honey
Black pepper (optional)
Chopped fresh parsley, for
  garnish

This recipe has been floating around Stonyfield Farm for many years, creator unknown! Aromatic while cooking, it produces a sensational creamy result. Be very careful not to overheat once the yogurt is added.

Melt the butter in a skillet and sauté the onion and garlic until they are golden. Add the mustard seeds, turmeric, ginger, cayenne, salt, cinnamon, and cumin and sauté for several minutes, stirring constantly. Add the carrots and lemon juice, stir to combine, and continue cooking for several more minutes. Add 2 cups of water. Cover and simmer for at least ½ hour or until the carrots are tender.

Purée the carrot mixture in a blender with the remaining 1½ cups of water. Pour the purée into a soup pot and stir in the yogurt with a whisk. Add the honey and heat the soup gently; don't let it boil. Sprinkle with black pepper, if desired. Serve hot, garnished with parsley.

Yield: 3 to 4 servings.

TURKISH YOGURT SOUP

∎

½ cup barley
1 cup water
3 cups chicken stock
2 medium onions, chopped
2 tablespoons butter
¼ cup chopped fresh mint (or
  1 tablespoon dried mint)
½ cup chopped fresh parsley
1 teaspoon salt, or to taste
Pinch of white pepper
2 cups plain yogurt

A tangy, lively, warm soup, definitely meant for those who love yogurt and don't want the flavor hidden! Easy to prepare, nutritious, and very inexpensive.

Soak the barley in water overnight. Drain well. Boil the barley in the chicken stock for about 10 minutes or until tender. Meanwhile, cook the onions in the butter until soft. Stir the onions into the barley and stock. Add the mint, parsley, salt, and pepper. Cover and simmer for 1 hour. Fold in the yogurt, heat through (do not boil), and serve.

Yield: 4 hearty bowls.

Siga Rastonis
East Sandwich, Massachusetts

CREAM OF ASPARAGUS SOUP

■

1 pound fresh asparagus, cut into 1-inch pieces
1 cup water
½ cup chopped onion
1 tablespoon butter
4 cups chicken stock
1 tablespoon butter
1 tablespoon unbleached all-purpose flour
2 cups plain yogurt
Cayenne pepper, to taste

This smooth, creamy, hot soup has a fine asparagus flavor.

Separate the asparagus tips from the stalks. Simmer the tips in water for 5 minutes, then drain and reserve. Sauté the onion in 1 tablespoon of butter. Add the asparagus stalks and sauté briefly. Add the chicken stock, bring to a boil, and simmer for 5 to 8 minutes, or until the asparagus is tender. Purée the vegetable mixture in a blender, then return it to the pan.

In a separate pan, melt the remaining 1 tablespoon butter and blend in the flour; gradually blend in ½ cup of the hot stock. Add this mixture to the puréed vegetables and mix thoroughly. Simmer for 1 minute. Add the reserved asparagus tips. Stir in the yogurt and add cayenne pepper. Serve immediately. Do not boil after adding the yogurt or the mixture will curdle.

Yield: 6 servings.

Prue Holtman
Wooster, Ohio

SALADS &
SIDE DISHES

•

In many of these recipes, yogurt has been suc-
cessfully substituted for mayonnaise or sour
cream, reducing the calorie count of the dish. But
more than simply a calorie-cutting substitute, yogurt
adds its own distinctive flavor and delight. In these
pages you'll find plenty of enticing yogurt-based
variations on old favorites, as well as some unique
and tasty new inventions.

Ten of these recipes are for what are loosely
known as "raitas." A raita (the word comes from
India) is a simple yogurt dish touched up with spice
and a featured fruit or vegetable. These refreshing
salads are often used as mouth-cooling complements
to hot and spicy dishes such as curries. But we find
we can't wait for the excuse of a spicy meal to enjoy these delicious salads!

For menu-planning purposes, it's helpful to
know that the salads in this chapter are usually served
as side dishes. You'll find other yogurt-based salads,
more appropriate for main dishes, on pages 124-26.

EGG SALAD WITH YOGURT DRESSING

■

SALAD

1 head red leaf lettuce
1 bunch radishes, washed and sliced
3 hard-boiled eggs, chopped
½ cup diced celery
½ cup diced green bell pepper
½ cup diced red bell pepper

DRESSING

1 cup plain yogurt
¼ cup frozen apple juice concentrate, thawed
¼ cup minced fresh chives
¼ cup minced fresh parsley
Black pepper, to taste

A colorful and simple salad. The creamy dressing uses fresh herbs for an outstanding accent.

Wash the lettuce and dry thoroughly. Tear the lettuce into bite-size pieces and place in a salad bowl. Add the radishes, eggs, celery, and bell peppers. Blend the dressing ingredients together and toss the salad with the dressing.

Yield: 4 servings.

Doris Rice
North Hampton, New Hampshire

. . . .

FRUIT & NUT SLAW

■

2½ cups finely shredded cabbage
½ cup thinly sliced celery
⅓ cup raisins
1 tablespoon lemon juice
⅛ teaspoon salt
1 cup peach yogurt
1 unpeeled, medium-size tart apple, cored and chopped
¼ cup chopped walnuts
½ teaspoon poppy seeds

Simply delicious! All the ingredients of a Waldorf salad, but with an unusual yogurt twist. Would be especially pretty served with mandarin oranges on the side.

Mix together the cabbage, celery, and raisins. Combine the lemon juice, salt, and yogurt; pour over the cabbage mixture. Add the apple and walnuts and mix gently. Transfer to a serving dish; sprinkle the poppy seeds on top. Chill for at least 2 hours before serving.

Yield: 4 servings.

Alice Weir
Boulder, Colorado

. . . .

TANGY CABBAGE SALAD

■

1 cup plain yogurt
¼ cup mayonnaise
1 teaspoon honey
3 tablespoons cider vinegar
1 teaspoon dried basil
½ large cabbage, shredded
1 large carrot, peeled and
  shredded
Raisins (optional)

A tasty and unusual cole slaw, and extremely easy to prepare.

In a blender, mix together the yogurt, mayonnaise, honey, vinegar, and basil until all are combined. Stir the dressing into the shredded cabbage and carrot. Add raisins if desired.

Yield: 4 servings.

Christine L. Blake
Greenland, New Hampshire

. . . .

GRANDMOTHER'S CARROT SALAD

■

SALAD
1½ pounds carrots, peeled and
  grated
2 unpeeled Granny Smith apples,
  cored and diced
½ cup raisins
½ cup chopped walnuts

DRESSING
1 teaspoon Dijon mustard
1 teaspoon brown sugar
2 tablespoons lemon juice
2 tablespoons orange juice (freshly
  squeezed, if possible)
1 cup plain yogurt
Salt and pepper, to taste

A sweet, tasty, and healthful variation on the usual carrot salad. Attractive and easy to make, too.

Stir together the carrots, apples, raisins, and walnuts in a large bowl. In a separate bowl, mix the dressing ingredients with a wire whisk until well blended. Add the dressing to the carrot mixture and toss.

Yield: 8 generous servings.

Brigitte Carter
Belmont, Massachusetts

. . . .

POTATO SALAD WITH YOGURT

■

20 small red potatoes
2 cups plain yogurt
3 hard-boiled eggs, chopped
3 scallions, chopped
1 large red or green bell
   pepper, cored, seeded, and
   chopped
1 tablespoon black pepper
1 teaspoon salt
5 slices cooked bacon, broken
   into pieces (optional)
½ cup white wine vinegar
2 tablespoons chopped fresh dill

An attractive and healthy alternative to traditional potato salad. In summer, serve with thickly sliced garden-fresh tomatoes on the side.

Boil the potatoes in their skins for about 45 minutes or until tender. Do not remove the skins. Let the potatoes cool, then cut them into 1½-inch cubes.

In a large bowl, combine all the other ingredients and mix well. Add the potatoes, stir together to mix all ingredients, cover, and let marinate in the refrigerator for several hours. Serve at room temperature with crusty, fresh-baked whole-wheat bread.

Yield: 8 to 10 servings.

Nana Katsiff
New York, New York

. . . .

ZESTY POTATO SALAD

■

6 to 8 medium potatoes, or
   enough to make 6 cups cubed
1 cup plain yogurt
3 tablespoons chopped fresh
   parsley
2 tablespoons capers
¾ cup shredded Parmesan
   cheese (powder-fine texture
   not recommended)
2 teaspoons dried thyme
2 shakes hot-pepper sauce
1½ teaspoons paprika
Salt and freshly ground pepper,
   to taste
Fresh parsley, for garnish
   (optional)
Lettuce

As the name suggests, the capers and hot-pepper sauce make this a lively dish. A good choice for a picnic or potluck supper.

Boil the potatoes, cool them, and then skin and cut into 1½-inch cubes. Place the cubed potatoes in a large bowl. Add the yogurt, mix well, and then add the parsley, capers, cheese, thyme, hot-pepper sauce, paprika, and salt and pepper. Mix well. Garnish with parsley, if desired, and serve on a bed of garden-fresh lettuce.

Yield: 4 to 6 servings.

Martie Holmer
Boston, Massachusetts

. . . .

BERRY PATCH POTATO SALAD

■

5 cups peeled, cubed raw
  potatoes
4 slices bacon
3 cups thickly sliced fresh
  mushrooms
⅔ cup sliced celery
⅔ cup chopped onion
¼ teaspoon garlic powder
1 cup strawberry yogurt
Salt and pepper, to taste
Hulled and sliced fresh
  strawberries, for garnish
Sliced mushrooms, for garnish
Fresh parsley, for garnish

*An unusual and attractive combination of ingredients
that's also unusually delicious. Kids like it, too.*

Cook the cubed potatoes in lightly salted boiling
water until tender. While the potatoes are cooking,
sauté the bacon in a large skillet over medium heat
until crisp. Drain on paper towels; crumble and
reserve.

Drain the bacon grease from the skillet; add the
mushrooms, celery, onion, and garlic powder to the
skillet; cook over medium-high heat for 2 minutes,
stirring frequently.

When the potatoes are done, drain them, then shake
them in their pan over the burner for a few seconds
to remove excess moisture. Add the potatoes to the
skillet and stir to combine. Stir the yogurt into the
skillet mixture. Cook until just heated through, then
remove from heat and let stand for 5 minutes.

Add the salt and pepper. Spoon the potato salad into
a shallow serving dish and sprinkle with the crumbled
bacon. Garnish with strawberries, mushrooms, and
parsley.

Yield: 6 to 8 servings.

*Marjorie Fortier
West Redding, Connecticut*

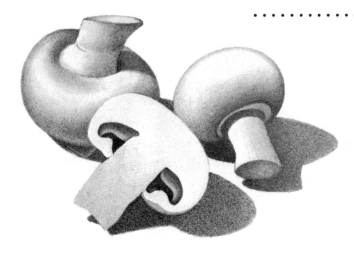

CUCUMBERS & FENNEL

■

2 large cucumbers
1 small fennel bulb (2 cups sliced)
1 cup plain yogurt
½ cup finely chopped onion
1 teaspoon finely minced garlic
2 tablespoons white vinegar
1½ tablespoons sugar
1 tablespoon olive oil
2 tablespoons finely chopped fresh dill

A wonderful side dish for fennel-lovers.

Peel the cucumbers and cut them in half lengthwise. Scrape out the seeds. Cut the cucumbers crosswise into thin half-moon slices and place in a bowl. Trim the fennel bulb. Cut it in half and then crosswise into thin slices. Add the fennel and all the remaining ingredients to the cucumbers. Blend well. Chill for at least 1 hour before serving.

Yield: 8 cups (about 8 servings).

Mrs. Kit Rollins
Cedarburg, Wisconsin

• •

YOGURT COCONUT RICE

■

3 cups plain boiled basmati rice (available in most natural-foods stores)
1 tablespoon unsalted butter
3 cups plain yogurt
1 teaspoon salt
1 tablespoon grated fresh ginger
1 cup grated fresh coconut
1 tablespoon unsalted butter or vegetable oil
1 teaspoon black mustard seeds
Chopped fresh coriander leaves

A creamy, sweet, nutty rice with a pudding-like texture. Serve as a refreshing complement to a strong, spicy entrée.

Immediately after cooking the rice, and before it cools, add to it 1 tablespoon of butter. Mix well and set aside to cool. When the rice has cooled, add the yogurt, salt, ginger, and coconut; mix well and set aside.

In a heavy, stainless-steel skillet, heat 1 tablespoon of butter. When the butter is hot, add the black mustard seeds. The seeds will crackle, pop, and scatter, so it's best to keep the pan covered. When all the seeds have popped, pour them over the rice mixture and stir. Serve immediately or chilled. Just before serving, mix in the chopped coriander.

Yield: 6 cups (10 to 12 servings).

K. I. Loppedrayer
Milverton, Ontario, Canada

• •

SUPER SLIM SALAD

■

2 large red bell peppers, cored and seeded
2 cucumbers, peeled
2 medium onions
1 cup plain yogurt
2 teaspoons Dijon mustard
2 to 3 dashes hot-pepper sauce
2 tablespoons chopped chives

A colorful salad with a hot/tart touch. Try serving it with hamburgers or steak.

Cut the bell peppers into thin strips. Thinly slice the cucumbers and onions. Stir together the yogurt, mustard, and hot-pepper sauce. Place the vegetables in a large bowl, pour the yogurt sauce over them, and toss to coat evenly. Sprinkle with chives.

Yield: 6 servings.

Kim Boucher
Danbury, Connecticut

. . . .

YOGURT-DILL MARINATED CUCUMBER RAITA

■

4 medium cucumbers, peeled and sliced very thin
2 to 3 teaspoons salt (to taste)
1 tablespoon chopped *fresh* dill
1 teaspoon dry dill
Juice of 1 or 2 limes (¼ cup)
2 tablespoons maple syrup
1 cup plain yogurt

Much tastier than the usual sour cream–cucumber salad, this recipe got rave reviews from our testers. The lime is well balanced by just the right amount of sweet maple syrup.

Sprinkle the cucumber slices with 1½ to 2 teaspoons salt to wilt them and prepare them to absorb the marinade. Layer the cucumber slices in a bowl with the remaining salt, being sure to get salt on all surfaces. Chill for 2 hours.

Combine the dill, lime juice, maple syrup, and yogurt, and refrigerate. When the cucumbers have chilled, rinse and drain them thoroughly. Add the dill marinade and chill for another 1 to 1½ hours before serving.

Yield: 6 to 8 servings.

Sandra Labarge-Newmann
Nashua, New Hampshire

. . . .

MASTO-KHIAR RAITA

■

1 large or 2 small cucumbers
1 to 2 cups plain yogurt
2 tablespoons honey
¼ cup raisins
½ cup chopped walnuts
1 small onion, grated (optional)
1 tablespoon crushed dried mint
    leaves
Salt and pepper, to taste

An Iranian recipe, with a subtle but refreshing mint flavor.

Peel and grate the cucumbers. Squeeze the cucumbers in a towel to remove excess liquid, then mix well with the yogurt and honey. Add the raisins, walnuts, optional onion, mint, and salt and pepper; mix well. Chill before serving.

Yield: 6 servings.

Shirley White
Dubuque, Iowa

LOUISE'S CUCUMBER & YOGURT RAITA

■

3 cups plain yogurt
1 teaspoon salt
1 teaspoon black pepper, or to
    taste
2 cloves garlic, crushed
½ teaspoon curry powder
½ teaspoon cayenne pepper, or
    to taste
2 tablespoons chopped fresh dill
1 medium-size sweet red onion,
    thinly sliced (optional)
2 to 3 large cucumbers, peeled
    and thinly sliced

A perfect summer salad: cool yet lively with flavor.

Combine the yogurt, salt, black pepper, garlic, curry powder, cayenne pepper, dill, and optional red onion; mix well. Pour over the cucumbers, blend well, and serve.

Yield: 6 cups (about 10 to 12 servings).

Louise Kaymen
Wilton, New Hampshire

GREEK RAITA

∎

1 or 2 cloves garlic, minced
Pinch of salt
1 teaspoon red wine vinegar
1 tablespoon olive oil
1½ cups plain yogurt
1 tablespoon chopped fresh dill
1 medium cucumber, unpeeled,
　cut into large chunks

A classic version of the simple yogurt-cucumber dish. Especially good as a dip for mini pita breads or Greek-style pork or lamb. See photo, page 131.

Combine the garlic, salt, vinegar, oil, yogurt, and dill. Chill for 2 hours. Half an hour before serving, grate the cucumber in a food processor. Squeeze out as much liquid as possible from the grated cucumber, then add the cucumber to the yogurt mixture and stir to combine. Chill briefly before serving.

Yield: 2 cups.

Cathy Malcolmson
Thornhill, Ontario, Canada

. . . .

SPICED YOGURT & ZUCCHINI RAITA

∎

2 small zucchini, sliced
2 cups plain yogurt
½ cup grated coconut
½ teaspoon salt
White pepper, to taste
2 tablespoons vegetable oil
1 teaspoon mustard seeds
1 hot chili pepper, seeded and
　chopped
1¼ cups chopped onion
1 teaspoon ground cumin

The coconut and spices give this dish a complex and unusual flavor.

Steam the zucchini and set it aside to cool. Blend the yogurt, coconut, salt, and pepper in a bowl. Add the cooled zucchini and toss gently to combine; set aside.

Heat the oil in a frying pan and fry the mustard seeds and hot chili until the mustard seeds start to pop. Add the onion and sauté until golden. Add the cumin and cook for 2 minutes more. Pour the onion mixture into the yogurt and zucchini mixture. Chill. Serve as an accompaniment to rice or East Indian cuisine.

Yield: 7 cups (about 8 to 10 servings).

Hilda Cowan
Ottawa, Ontario, Canada

. . . .

CARROT RAITA

■

¾ cup plain yogurt
⅛ teaspoon cayenne pepper
¼ teaspoon ground cumin
2 cups peeled and coarsely
  shredded carrots
2 tablespoons dry-roasted
  peanuts

A colorful and spicy way to serve fresh carrots with a Mexican twist. Great served at a barbecue.

Combine the yogurt, pepper, and cumin; mix well. Add the carrots and peanuts and mix to moisten all ingredients. Refrigerate before serving.

Yield: 3 cups (about 4 servings).

Elizabeth Hanson
Osceola, Wisconsin

. . . .

CUCUMBER & TOMATO RAITA

■

1 medium cucumber, peeled
1 tablespoon finely chopped
  onion
2 teaspoons salt
1 small tomato, cut into 1-inch
  cubes
1 tablespoon finely chopped
  fresh coriander
1 teaspoon ground cumin
1 cup plain yogurt

An easy, refreshing, colorful raita with great flavor. A cool complement to any spicy entrée.

Dice the cucumber into ½-inch cubes. Combine the cucumber with the onion and salt. Let stand for 5 minutes, then squeeze out as much liquid as possible. Place the cucumber mixture in a bowl and add the tomato and coriander.

Toast the cumin in an ungreased skillet for 30 seconds over medium-low heat. Add the cumin and yogurt to the cucumber mixture; toss and serve.

Yield: 2 cups (about 4 servings).

Cynthia R. Topliss
St. Stanislas de Kostka, Quebec, Canada

. . . .

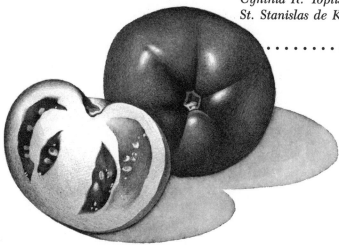

MINT, ONION & HOT-CHILI RAITA

■

3 tablespoons minced fresh mint
3 tablespoons finely chopped
　onion
½ teaspoon finely chopped
　green chili
½ teaspoon salt
⅛ teaspoon chili powder
1 cup plain yogurt

A simple raita with great flavor and color, this can be used as a sauce or a side dish. It is best left to chill overnight, to properly blend the spices.

In a small bowl, combine the mint, onion, green chili, salt, and chili powder. Stir in the yogurt. Cover and chill thoroughly before serving.

Yield: 1 generous cup (about 3 servings).

Cynthia R. Topliss
St. Stanislas de Kostka, Quebec, Canada

• •

BANANA & COCONUT RAITA

■

2 tablespoons vegetable oil
1 teaspoon mustard seeds
½ cup grated fresh coconut or
　coconut cream
1 cup plain yogurt
1 teaspoon salt
1 medium-size ripe banana,
　sliced into ¼-inch-thick
　rounds
1 teaspoon finely chopped fresh
　coriander, or ¼ teaspoon
　dried coriander

A surprising side dish with well-balanced flavor. Less sweet and fruity than you might expect, this provides a refreshing balance to hot, spicy entrées.

In a small skillet, heat the oil and add the mustard seeds; cook until the seeds pop. Add the coconut, stir, and remove from heat. Add 2 tablespoons of yogurt. Place the remaining yogurt in a bowl; add the skillet mixture, salt, banana, and coriander and mix well. Serve immediately or, for a stronger fruit flavor, cover and chill before serving.

Yield: 2 cups (about 4 servings).

Cynthia R. Topliss
St. Stanislas de Kostka, Quebec, Canada

• •

BANANA RAITA

■

1 teaspoon butter
1½ teaspoons cumin seeds
¼ teaspoon cardamom seeds
¼ teaspoon ground coriander
¼ teaspoon cayenne pepper
2 cups mashed ripe bananas
2 cups plain yogurt

This tasty, sweet-and-spicy raita can be served with everything from a curry to your morning oatmeal. Fun to make, and well worth the little extra effort.

Melt the butter in a skillet. Lightly crush the cumin, cardamom, coriander, and cayenne in a mortar (they should not be pulverized), then add them to the butter. Stir the spices for 2 to 3 minutes, quickly add the mashed bananas, and stir again over medium-low heat. Remove from heat, stir in the yogurt, and transfer to a serving dish. Chill well before serving.

Yield: 6 servings.

Cheryl Veitch
Quesnel, British Columbia, Canada

BEET KOSHUMBIR

■

3 to 4 medium beets
2 cups plain yogurt
Fresh dill and/or parsley, for garnish

Very simple, very beautiful, and very good. Serve on greens for a special summer salad — or purée it for excellent baby food.

Boil the beets for 20 to 30 minutes or until cooked. Cool, peel, and chop beets into small cubes. Gently fold the beets into the yogurt. Place in a serving bowl and garnish with dill and/or parsley.

Yield: 4 to 6 servings.

Kamala Diwan
North Windham, Connecticut

EGGPLANT SALAD WITH CHILI BITES

■

SALAD

1 medium eggplant, unpeeled
    but cubed
1 teaspoon mustard seeds
1 teaspoon cumin seeds
¼ teaspoon fenugreek seeds
    (optional)
2 tablespoons olive oil
1 small onion, chopped
1 large clove garlic, finely
    chopped
¼ teaspoon crushed dried
    chilies
2 tablespoons lemon juice

YOGURT DRESSING

1 cup plain yogurt
½ ripe banana, mashed
1 tomato, chopped
1 tablespoon chopped fresh
    mint leaves

CHILI BITES

½ cup unbleached all-purpose
    flour
½ teaspoon baking powder
¼ teaspoon salt
¼ teaspoon crushed dried
    chilies
¼ to ½ teaspoon crushed black
    pepper
¼ cup plain yogurt
Oil for shallow frying
¼ teaspoon ground cumin

This dish involves a bit of work, but the exotic result is worth it.

To make the salad, soak the eggplant cubes in lightly salted water. Cook the mustard, cumin, and optional fenugreek seeds in a deep, ungreased pot over medium heat until they pop. Add oil and heat again. Add the onion, garlic, and chilies; cook over medium heat until softened. Drain the eggplant and add to the mixture. Cover the pot and reduce the heat. Continue cooking, stirring occasionally and adding small amounts of water as needed. When the eggplant is fork tender, remove the pot from the heat and stir in the lemon juice.

Whisk all the dressing ingredients together, mix the dressing with the salad, and chill for at least 1 hour.

To make the chili bites, sift the flour, baking powder, and salt together, then add the chilies and black pepper. Mix in the yogurt to make a thick batter. Form small balls the size of the eggplant cubes and fry them in oil until crispy. Sprinkle with cumin while hot.

At serving time, remove the salad from the refrigerator and fold in the chili bites or use them for decoration.

Yield: 4 to 6 servings.

Lesley-Anne Paveling
Lumsden, Saskatchewan, Canada

. . . .

INDIAN POTATOES, CABBAGE & GREEN PEPPERS

■

2 tablespoons vegetable oil
3 medium unpeeled potatoes, cut french-fry style
1 medium onion, chopped
1 green bell pepper, cored, seeded, and cut into strips
½ teaspoon mustard seeds
½ teaspoon caraway seeds
¾ cup water
½ teaspoon curry powder
½ teaspoon ground turmeric
Pinch of ginger or ½ teaspoon chopped fresh ginger
1½ teaspoons salt
¼ teaspoon pepper
2 cups chopped cabbage
1 cup plain yogurt

This dish is as tasty as it is beautiful. While not overwhelming, the flavor does make a statement, so avoid serving this with a spicy entrée. Lamb kebab would be a perfect complement.

Heat the oil in a skillet and add the potatoes, onion, bell pepper, mustard seeds, and caraway seeds. Fry for about 5 minutes, stirring frequently. Add the water, curry powder, turmeric, ginger, salt, and pepper and cook over medium heat for 10 minutes more. Add the cabbage and cook until limp. Remove from heat and stir in the yogurt before serving.

Yield: 4 to 6 servings.

Renee Martin
Calgary, Alberta, Canada

. . . .

REFRESHING SPINACH

■

1 medium-size sweet onion, chopped
2 tablespoons olive oil
2 pounds fresh spinach, cleaned and chopped
½ teaspoon salt
1½ cups plain yogurt
Grated fresh nutmeg (optional)

Barely wilted spinach topped with a thinned yogurt dressing makes a simple but delicious side dish.

In a large skillet, sauté the onion in oil until soft. Add the spinach. Stir and cook over medium heat until the spinach is done. Sprinkle with salt. Place on individual serving plates; top each with a healthy portion of yogurt and freshly grated nutmeg, if desired.

Yield: 4 servings.

Sheri Clemen
Eugene, Oregon

. . . .

RICE CURRY

■

1 unpeeled apple, cored and
  diced
1 medium onion, diced
½ pound fresh mushrooms,
  sliced
1 stalk celery, sliced
½ cup sliced green bell pepper
2 tablespoons olive oil
3 cups cooked brown rice
2 teaspoons curry powder
2 tablespoons soy sauce
1 cup plain yogurt
½ cup raisins
½ cup halved seedless grapes
  (optional)

*Smooth and moist, with a moderate curry flavor.
Serve with lamb curry or any barbecued meat.*

Preheat oven to 350°F. Sauté the apple, onion,
mushrooms, celery, and bell pepper in oil. Remove
from heat and add the rice, curry powder, soy sauce,
yogurt, and raisins. Mix well and pour into a
medium-size greased casserole. Bake for 25 minutes,
stir in the grapes if desired, and bake for 5 minutes
more.

Yield: 4 servings.

Ann Lutz
Black Mountain, North Carolina

. . . .

STUFFED BAKED POTATOES

■

6 baking potatoes
2 tablespoons chopped chives
Salt and pepper, to taste
½ teaspoon dried dill or 1
  tablespoon chopped fresh dill
2 tablespoons butter (optional)
1 cup plain yogurt, generously
  measured
Grated Cheddar cheese, for
  topping

*A delicious way to serve baked potatoes, and much
healthier than the sour-cream version. Smooth and
creamy even without the butter.*

Bake the potatoes. Let them cool slightly, then split
them lengthwise. Scoop out the flesh and combine
with the chives, salt and pepper, dill, optional butter, and yogurt. Whip with an electric mixer to a thick
consistency. Refill the 12 potato cases and top with
grated cheese. Bake at 350°F for about 3 to 5 minutes
or until the cheese topping browns.

Yield: 4 to 6 servings.

Renee Martin
Calgary, Alberta, Canada

. . . .

MAIN DISHES

■

Whether used as a tenderizing marinade for meat, as a source of succulence and piquancy for fish or vegetarian dishes, or as the basis for a delicious cream sauce in a poultry recipe, yogurt provides great taste and appearance without lots of extra work. Some of these dishes take extra time to prepare, but many are quickly put together after a hard day's work or just in time to impress those last-minute dinner guests.

One of the most common uses of yogurt in main dishes is as a substitute for milk or cream in making sauces. In these recipes, try to avoid heating the yogurt too high too rapidly. Rapidly heated yogurt may separate into curds and whey, and heat extremes kill the potentially beneficial bacteria. For these reasons, yogurt is often added just before serving, and it is just heated through rather than allowed to simmer or boil. However, even when the yogurt does reach high temperatures, it still can be an important source of calcium and other valuable nutrients — in addition to adding great taste to your meal.

Enjoy the multitude of ways that you can tastefully add yogurt to your main meals. If the variety of these recipes is any indication, the sky (or the bottom of your yogurt container) is the limit.

POULTRY

MEDITERRANEAN CHICKEN SALAD

■

1 cup mayonnaise
½ cup washed fresh basil leaves
Juice of ½ lemon
1 cup nonfat plain yogurt
2 cups cubed poached chicken
   breast
1 cup cubed cooked potatoes
1 red bell pepper, cored, seeded,
   and finely diced
1 green bell pepper, cored, seeded,
   and finely diced
1 yellow bell pepper, cored,
   seeded, and finely diced
½ cup Greek (black) olives
¼ cup rinsed capers
¼ cup finely chopped red onion
Salt and pepper, to taste
Basil sprigs, for garnish

The peppers provide color, the capers and olives add a pleasant sharpness, and the basil-yogurt-mayonnaise dressing makes this salad especially fresh tasting. A good summer dish, but even on a very cold and snowy January day, it received rave reviews from the folks at our tester's town hall.

Purée the mayonnaise and basil in a blender. Add the lemon juice. Place in a large bowl, stir in the yogurt, and mix well. Fold in the chicken, potatoes, bell peppers, olives, capers, and onion; season with salt and pepper. Cover and chill for at least 3 hours to allow flavors to mellow. Garnish with basil sprigs just before serving.

Yield: 4 to 6 servings.

Mary Jane Jackson
South Hero, Vermont

MANDARIN CHICKEN SALAD

■

SALAD

3 cups cubed or shredded
  cooked chicken
3 stalks celery, sliced diagonally
1 can (11 ounces) mandarin
  oranges, well drained
½ cup drained and sliced water
  chestnuts
½ cup finely sliced scallions
  (white and green parts)
1 small red bell pepper, cored,
  seeded, and minced
¼ cup sliced almonds, toasted

DRESSING

½ inch fresh ginger, minced
2 cloves garlic, minced
3 tablespoons minced fresh
  parsley
2 tablespoons soy sauce
¼ cup tahini (sesame-seed paste)
2 tablespoons fresh lemon juice
1 tablespoon sesame oil
1 cup plain yogurt
1 tablespoon white or rice wine
  vinegar
1 tablespoon brown sugar
¼ cup safflower oil
¾ teaspoon ground coriander
Salt and pepper, to taste

GARNISH
Toasted sesame seeds

A truly delectable blend of tastes, textures, and colors — well worth the small extra effort. See photo, page 52.

Mix all the salad ingredients in a large bowl. Blend the dressing ingredients, drizzle over the salad, and mix. Serve over lettuce or other greens, in tomato halves, or on toast points. Sprinkle toasted sesame seeds on top for added flavor. Cover and refrigerate at least 1 hour, or up to 2 days, before serving.

Yield: 4 to 6 servings.

Nancy Settle
Boxborough, Massachusetts

CHICKEN & BARLEY SALAD

∎

1 cup barley
2 cups water
2 cups cubed cooked chicken breast
2 stalks celery, thinly sliced
½ cup thinly sliced water chestnuts
½ cup finely chopped red onion
1 cup plain yogurt
1 tablespoon lemon juice
2 tablespoons soy sauce
¼ teaspoon black pepper

Unusual, spicy, and filling enough to be served as a main course. The soy sauce and water chestnuts complement each other.

Soak the barley in water for several hours, then bring the barley and water to a boil in a large saucepan. Reduce heat and simmer, almost completely covered, over low heat for 25 minutes. Drain and allow to cool.

In a bowl, mix the cooled barley with the chicken, celery, water chestnuts, and onion. In another bowl, mix together the yogurt, lemon juice, soy sauce, and pepper; pour the yogurt mixture over the chicken and barley mixture, stir together, and serve.

Yield: 6 generous servings.

Karin Beebe
Great Barrington, Massachusetts

COLD CHICKEN CURRY

∎

2 teaspoons curry powder
1 tablespoon vegetable oil
1 cup plain yogurt
½ teaspoon grated fresh ginger
2 cups chopped cooked chicken
1 cup raisins
½ cup salted cashews
1 cup chopped zucchini
1 cup diced mango
½ cup chopped celery
Salt and pepper, to taste

A quick and easy meal for company or family. Serve on crisp lettuce leaves for a wonderfully cool summer supper.

Mix the curry powder and oil together. Add the yogurt, then pour the mixture into a saucepan. Add the grated ginger and cook over low heat, stirring frequently, until heated through. Make sure the mixture doesn't overheat or it will curdle.

Combine the chicken, raisins, cashews, zucchini, mango, and celery in a bowl. Fold in the curry-yogurt mixture. Season to taste with salt and pepper and chill before serving.

Yield: 4 to 6 servings.

Shirley M. Weber
Richfield, Connecticut

SUMMER CHICKEN CURRY

■

1 cup plain yogurt
¼ cup mayonnaise
1 tablespoon curry powder
2 whole chicken breasts,
    poached, skinned, boned, and
    cut into 1-inch chunks (or 4
    cups leftover cooked chicken)
⅓ cup finely chopped scallions,
    green included
2 cups seedless green grapes,
    halved lengthwise
¾ cup slivered almonds, toasted

A cold, creamy curry, terrific for sandwiches or a salad plate.

In a large bowl, blend the yogurt, mayonnaise, and curry powder. Add the chicken, scallions, grapes, and almonds. Toss together to coat. Serve chilled, with pita bread triangles, assorted crudités, and chutney.

Yield: 4 to 6 servings.

Elizabeth March
Concord, New Hampshire

. . . .

INDIAN CHICKEN

■

2 large onions, sliced (not diced)
4 carrots, sliced in rounds
2 tablespoons butter
2 cloves garlic, crushed
1 tablespoon curry powder
3 tablespoons soy sauce
1 tablespoon honey
½ cup orange juice
½ cup water
1 fresh green chili pepper (hot
    or very hot, to taste), seeded
    and chopped
¼ cup raisins (optional)
1 cup plain yogurt
6 chicken thighs

Highly rated by everyone who tried it. "Hotness" can be adjusted by the type of chili pepper you use.

Preheat oven to 350°F. Sauté the onions and carrots in the butter for 2 minutes. Add the garlic and curry powder and cook for 5 minutes more. Add the soy sauce, honey, orange juice, water, chili, and optional raisins and simmer for 10 minutes. Remove from heat and stir the yogurt into the sauce.

Place the chicken thighs in an ungreased 2½- or 3-quart casserole. Pour the sauce over the chicken, cover, and bake for 45 minutes. Remove the cover and bake for 15 minutes more or until tender. Serve over rice.

Yield: 6 servings.

Peggy A. Bailey
Durham, New Hampshire

. . . .

CHICKEN KARMA

■

2 whole chicken breasts, split, skinned, and boned
1½ tablespoons vegetable oil
2 apples, peeled, cored, and cubed
¼ cup sherry
1 cup fruited yogurt (any flavor)
2 tablespoons curry powder
2 tablespoons raisins
½ cup (2 ounces) cashews
1 tablespoon mango chutney

A truly delectable American-style chicken curry. A yogurt raita (see pages 113-18) makes a good accompaniment.

Slice the chicken into strips about ½ inch wide. Heat the oil in a heavy skillet. Add the chicken and sauté, on medium-high heat, for about 2 to 3 minutes. Add the apples and sherry, stir to combine, and continue cooking for another 1 to 2 minutes.

Reduce heat to medium. Add the yogurt and blend. Add the curry powder, raisins, cashews, and chutney; stir to combine. Simmer for about 3 to 4 minutes. Serve with rice and additional chutney.

Yield: 3 to 4 servings.

Emile Ferrara
Bristol, Rhode Island

. . . .

LOW-CAL YOGURT BAKED CHICKEN

■

2 cups low-fat plain yogurt
6 tablespoons Dijon mustard
6 cloves garlic, chopped or crushed
2 teaspoons ground ginger
Salt and pepper, to taste
1 chicken, cleaned, washed, and ready for baking (preferably skinned and cut up)

Low in calories but high in taste appeal, this has a slightly oriental flavor from the ginger and garlic.

Mix together the yogurt, mustard, garlic, ginger, and salt and pepper. Spread the mixture on the chicken, rubbing it in. Place in an ovenproof dish, cover, and let marinate for at least 2 hours (preferably overnight).

Preheat oven to 375°F. Bake the chicken, uncovered, for 1 hour or until it is brown. Baste often.

Yield: 4 servings.

Dominic DiNardo
West Bridgewater, Massachusetts

. . . .

Curried Shrimp & Baby Vegetables (page 161).

129

Blender Salmon Mousse with Tangy Yogurt Dill Sauce (page 160).

Armenian Shish Kebab (page 145), Greek Raita (page 115).

131

Sesame Yogurt Sauce (page 90) on millet.

Pears Eleganza (page 214).

Yogurt Cream Mold with Raspberry Sauce (page 216).

Shepherd's Fall Vegetable Pie (page 167), Yogurt Dijon Salad Dressing (page 92).

Chocolate Yogurt Cheesecake (page 182).

SITOO (GRANDMOTHER'S) CHICKEN

∎

3 whole chicken breasts, split, skinned, and boned
⅔ cup plain yogurt
2 cups crumbs from fresh whole-wheat bread
½ teaspoon salt
½ teaspoon pepper
½ teaspoon ground cinnamon
½ teaspoon ground allspice
2 tablespoons dried crushed mint
3 tablespoons butter
⅓ cup plain yogurt
¼ cup minced fresh parsley
¼ cup toasted pine nuts or chopped walnuts (optional)

A refreshing and unusual way to prepare chicken. A very lively dish, it dances on your tongue! Make the bread crumbs by toasting the bread, then breaking up the toast in the food processor.

Cover the chicken thoroughly with ⅔ cup yogurt; marinate for ½ to 1 hour. Mix the bread crumbs with the salt, pepper, cinnamon, allspice, and mint. Place the crumb mixture in a wide bowl and pat crumbs over the yogurt-covered chicken pieces, covering all of the chicken thoroughly.

Grease a 9x13-inch baking dish with 1 tablespoon of the butter. Place the crumb-coated chicken in the dish and, to set the coating, refrigerate uncovered for at least 30 minutes or until ready to bake. The dish can be prepared up to this point earlier in the day.

Preheat oven to 375°F. Melt the remaining 2 tablespoons of butter and drizzle it over the chicken pieces. Bake the chicken, uncovered, for about 40 to 45 minutes or until done; remove from the oven. Just before serving, spoon the remaining yogurt on the chicken and sprinkle with parsley and toasted nuts, if desired. Serve with tabouli and pita bread.

Yield: 4 servings.

Norma Ouellette
Bedford, New Hampshire

. . . .

CHICKEN IN CURRIED YOGURT

■

2 pounds chicken pieces (with bones)
1 teaspoon salt, or to taste
Dash of pepper
2 to 4 celery stalks
4 cups plain yogurt
1 egg, slightly beaten
1 onion, minced
1 teaspoon salt
½ to 1 teaspoon each: pepper, ground allspice, and curry powder (or to taste)
1 tablespoon unbleached all-purpose flour
3 tablespoons butter

Allspice is the secret behind this delicious, wonderfully aromatic dish. Makes a hearty but delicate meal.

Place the chicken pieces in a large pot and cover with cold water. Add the salt, pepper, and celery stalks and bring to a boil. Reduce heat to a simmer, skim foam from the top, and cook, covered, for up to 1 hour, skimming as needed. When done, remove the chicken from the broth with a slotted spoon, remove the skin and bones from the chicken, and cut the chicken into generous pieces. Set aside the chicken; discard the broth or reserve it for another purpose.

In a double boiler or heavy pot, combine the yogurt, egg, onion, salt, pepper, allspice, and curry powder; cook over low heat. Be careful not to overheat or the yogurt will curdle. Carefully stir in the flour and continue to cook over low heat until the mixture thickens. Add the butter, then the chicken, and cook for 5 minutes or until the mixture is well heated and fragrant. Serve over rice.

Yield: 4 servings.

Eleni Goltsis
Cambridge, Massachusetts

. . . .

ARTICHOKE CHICKEN

■

2 tablespoons butter
12 ounces mushrooms, sliced
1 can (13¾ ounces) chicken broth
1 jar (6 ounces) marinated artichoke hearts
3 chicken breasts, split, skinned, and boned
1 cup plain yogurt

Moist chicken served in a savory sauce — elegant enough for company, but very easy to prepare. The marinated artichokes give the dish an interesting, slightly herb-flavored bite. See photo, page 54.

In a medium-size frying pan, melt the butter. Add the mushrooms and sauté until wilted. In a large skillet, mix the chicken broth with the juice from the artichoke hearts; bring to a boil. Add the chicken, cover, and poach for 20 minutes, turning the chicken occasionally.

Remove the chicken from the pan and place it in a covered dish to keep it warm. Reduce the liquid in the pan by half. Add the artichoke hearts and mushrooms and stir. Reduce heat and add the yogurt, mixing gently. Pour over the chicken. Serve with rice pilaf.

Yield: 4 servings.

Corinne J. Konstantinakos
North Andover, Massachusetts

. . . .

BARBECUED SPICY CHICKEN

■

5 cloves garlic
2-inch piece of fresh ginger, chopped
1 fresh hot pepper
1 large onion, cut up
Juice of 1 lemon
⅔ cup vegetable oil
¼ cup dry white wine
1 cup plain yogurt
1¼ teaspoons cumin seeds
1¼ teaspoons coriander powder
1½ teaspoons freshly ground black pepper
4 cardamom seeds (outer shell included), or 1 teaspoon ground cardamom
2 teaspoons salt
4 whole chicken breasts, split and skinned

Moist, tender chicken breasts in a hot and zesty barbecue sauce.

Blend all the ingredients except the chicken in a food processor or blender. The mixture should be creamy. Pierce each piece of chicken with a fork. Place the chicken in a container and pour the yogurt mixture over it, thoroughly coating the chicken. Cover the container and refrigerate for 6 to 24 hours.

Using an outdoor barbecue grill, line the grill rack with aluminum foil. Place the chicken on the rack and grill on medium-high heat, with the lid of the grill down, for 15 to 20 minutes on each side. Chicken should be browned.

Yield: 6 to 8 servings.

Rosanne Kiley
Hudson, New Hampshire

. . . .

CHICKEN LIVERS STROGANOFF WITH SNOW PEAS

■

¼ pound fresh snow peas
½ pound chicken livers
1 tablespoon soy sauce
1 tablespoon sherry
1 teaspoon cornstarch
2 cups thinly sliced onions
¼ cup butter
¼ pound mushrooms, sliced
1½ cups plain yogurt

An excellent and unusual way to prepare chicken livers. Our tester reports that she plans to use this recipe frequently.

Drop the snow peas in boiling water and cook for 1 minute. Drain, chill with cold water, blot dry, and set aside. Wash the chicken livers with cold water and blot dry. Cut them into slices. Combine the soy sauce, sherry, and cornstarch. Toss the livers in the cornstarch mixture.

Cook the onions in the butter until tender. Add the livers and mushrooms and cook for 3 to 4 minutes or until lightly browned. Add the snow peas and yogurt and heat through. Serve over rice or noodles.

Yield: 2 to 3 servings.

Ruth Dawes
Lincoln, Massachusetts

. . . .

CHICKEN ENCHILADAS

■

SAUCE
2 cups finely chopped onions
1 clove garlic, crushed
2 to 4 tablespoons margarine or butter
1 jar (7½ ounces) mild chilies
1 can (14½ ounces) tomatoes
Salt and pepper, to taste

FILLING
3 cups chopped cooked chicken
2 cups plain yogurt
1 cup shredded Monterey Jack cheese
Salt and pepper, to taste

Mexican lasagna! The corn tortillas provide a chewy contrast to the creamy, cheesy chicken filling.

Sauté the onions and garlic in margarine until the onions are transparent. Drain the chilies and remove the seeds; chop the chilies and add them to the onions. Chop the tomatoes, if whole; add the tomatoes and their juice to the onion-chilies mixture. Simmer for 30 minutes. Season with salt and pepper, to taste.

Preheat oven to 325°F. Prepare the filling by gently mixing the chicken, yogurt, cheese, and salt and pepper.

Pour the oil into a medium-size frying pan to a depth of ¼ inch; heat until hot but not spitting. Quickly dip each tortilla into hot oil to soften, then briefly allow excess oil to drip off. Place filling in a line down the center of each softened tortilla, roll the tortilla around the filling, and place the filled tortilla in a

TORTILLAS & TOPPING
Vegetable oil
12 corn tortillas
**½ cup shredded Monterey Jack
cheese**

greased 12x14-inch baking dish. Repeat with remaining tortillas until all filling has been used. Pour the sauce over the tortillas. Bake for 20 minutes.

Sprinkle the remaining cheese over the top of the tortillas and return to the oven just until the cheese begins to bubble. Serve with hot salsa and a dollop of sour cream on each portion.

Yield: 6 servings.

*Linda Giesecke
Philadelphia, Pennsylvania*

. . . .

CULTURED HICKORY HOLLOW CHICKEN BREASTS

■

3 chicken breasts, split and
   skinned
Vegetable oil
2 tablespoons butter
1 tablespoon unbleached all-
   purpose flour
⅓ cup chicken stock
1 cup plain yogurt
¼ cup white wine
2 teaspoons grated lemon rind
1 tablespoon chopped parsley
1 tablespoon chopped chives
Salt and pepper, to taste
½ cup sliced mushrooms

An unusual, flavorful sauce with a dazzling touch of lemon and a very enthusiastic review from our tester. Serve with rice.

Preheat oven to 350°F. In a skillet, lightly brown the chicken in oil. Transfer the chicken to a large, ungreased baking dish and bake uncovered for about 30 minutes.

In a saucepan, melt the butter, add the flour, and mix thoroughly. Add the stock and continue to cook, stirring constantly, until the sauce is thick. Remove from heat and let cool.

Stir in the yogurt, wine, lemon rind, parsley, chives, and salt and pepper. Turn the chicken in the baking dish, cover with the mushrooms, and pour the sauce on top. Cover and bake for about 15 minutes more.

Yield: 4 to 6 servings.

*Helen Shepherd
Lyndhurst, Ontario, Canada*

. . . .

141

PARMESAN YOGURT CHICKEN

∎

1 chicken, cut in pieces and skinned
2 tablespoons fresh lemon juice
Cayenne pepper or Tabasco, to taste
1 cup plain low-fat yogurt
2 tablespoons unbleached all-purpose flour
¼ cup mayonnaise
2 tablespoons Dijon mustard
¼ teaspoon Worcestershire sauce
¼ teaspoon dried thyme
¼ cup minced green onions
Paprika
2 tablespoons grated Parmesan cheese

Easy to make and very flavorful and tender. Serve with rice or rice pilaf and salad — not fancy, but excellent company fare nonetheless.

Preheat oven to 350°F. Arrange the chicken pieces in a lightly oiled baking dish. Drizzle with lemon juice and sprinkle lightly with cayenne.

In a small bowl, mix the yogurt with the flour and add the mayonnaise, mustard, Worcestershire sauce, and thyme. Spread over the chicken. Top with green onions and sprinkle with paprika. Bake uncovered for 1 hour or until fork tender.

Sprinkle the chicken with Parmesan. Broil 6 inches from heat until the cheese is light brown. Serve warm.

Yield: 6 servings.

L. Crane
Pritchard, British Columbia, Canada

. . . .

YOGURT CHICKEN SATAY

∎

3 large chicken breasts, split, skinned, and boned
2 tablespoons peanut butter
1 cup plain yogurt
1 tablespoon lemon juice
2 teaspoons grated fresh ginger
2 teaspoons ground coriander
4 shallots, chopped

Mildly spiced chicken with a complex nutty flavor. Great barbecue fare.

Cut the chicken into bite-size pieces. Mix together the peanut butter, yogurt, lemon juice, ginger, coriander, and shallots. Pour the mixture over the chicken, cover, and refrigerate overnight or for at least 2 hours.

Thread the chicken pieces onto skewers. Grill them gently until cooked and browned; turning is not necessary. Serve with rice or rice pilaf and a salad.

Yield: 4 to 6 servings.

Sandra Brown
Port Dover, Ontario, Canada

. . . .

CHICKEN BREASTS SUPREME

■

2 cups low-fat plain yogurt
¼ cup lemon juice
1 clove garlic, pressed
4 teaspoons celery salt
½ teaspoon pepper
2 teaspoons paprika
5 or 6 chicken breasts, split, skinned, and boned
1 to 1¼ cups coarse bread crumbs or rice cake crumbs
½ cup margarine or butter

Attractive and tasty enough for company, but too easy to reserve for special occasions. Definitely a hit.

Mix together the yogurt, lemon juice, garlic, celery salt, pepper, and paprika. Place the chicken in a large bowl, pour the yogurt mixture over the chicken, cover, and refrigerate overnight.

Preheat oven to 350°F. Roll the yogurt-coated chicken in the crumbs and place in a greased shallow pan. Melt the butter and spoon over the chicken. Cover with foil. Bake for 45 minutes, then uncover and baste the chicken. Leave uncovered and bake for 15 minutes more or until tender.

Yield: 8 to 10 servings.

Carol Longhurst
London, Ontario, Canada

. . . .

OVEN-FRIED CHICKEN

■

1 cup plain yogurt
½ cup toasted wheat germ
½ cup freshly grated Parmesan cheese
¼ teaspoon freshly ground pepper
½ teaspoon dried thyme
1 tablespoon toasted sesame seeds
⅛ teaspoon garlic powder
3 whole chicken breasts, split, skinned, and boned
Lemon wedges, for garnish (optional)
Fresh parsley, for garnish (optional)

An easy, healthful chicken dish with a great blend of flavors.

Preheat oven to 350°F. Pour the yogurt into a pie plate and set aside. Combine the wheat germ, cheese, pepper, thyme, sesame seeds, and garlic powder in a bowl and mix well.

Dip each chicken breast in the yogurt and then in the coating mixture. Place the coated chicken pieces in an ungreased baking pan and bake uncovered for 45 minutes or until the juices run clear when the chicken is pricked with a fork. Arrange the chicken on a warm serving platter, garnish with lemon wedges and fresh parsley if desired, and serve.

Yield: 6 servings.

Pat Sprankle
Nashua, New Hampshire

. . . .

CHICKEN ON A CLOUD

■

1¾ cups milk, divided
4 tablespoons tamari or soy
  sauce, divided
1¼ cups plain yogurt, divided
1 cup bread crumbs
1 chicken breast, split
2 tablespoons butter
5 or 6 scallions, chopped
2 cloves garlic, finely minced
Dried oregano
1 teaspoon vegetable oil

Chicken and stuffing all in one pan, plus a sauce that's creamy, mild, and very flavorful.

In a large bowl, mix together 1 cup milk, 2 tablespoons tamari, 1 cup yogurt, and the bread crumbs. Smother the chicken with the crumb mixture and set it aside.

Grease a skillet with butter, and lightly sauté the scallions and garlic with a generous pinch of oregano. Add the chicken to the skillet and sprinkle it generously with more oregano. Cook slowly over low heat.

In another bowl, mix together ¾ cup milk, 2 tablespoons tamari, ¼ cup yogurt, and oil. Gradually add this sauce to the chicken as it cooks. Serve with steamed fresh artichokes.

Yield: 2 servings.

Sarah Jane Cion
Cambridge, Massachusetts

. . . .

TURKEY TETRAZZINI

■

1 pound spaghetti
1½ cups sliced mushrooms
1 clove garlic, pressed
1 tablespoon butter
3 tablespoons white wine
2 tablespoons butter
2 tablespoons unbleached all-
  purpose flour
1 tablespoon dried oregano
1½ teaspoons dried marjoram

(continued)

A delicious casserole with a rich, flavorful sauce. The mozzarella topping enriches the flavor.

Preheat oven to 375°F. Cook the spaghetti *al dente;* rinse and drain. Meanwhile, sauté the mushrooms and garlic in 1 tablespoon butter. Add the wine, stir to blend, and remove from heat.

In a separate medium-size skillet, melt remaining 2 tablespoons butter and stir in the flour. Cook for a couple of minutes, then add the oregano, marjoram, sage, and chicken stock; stir to blend. Bring to a boil, stirring constantly with a wire whisk; continue cooking until mixture thickens. Remove from heat and add the yogurt. Combine with the mushroom mixture and turkey.

1½ teaspoons dried sage
1½ to 2 cups chicken stock
1 cup plain yogurt
2 cups chopped cooked turkey
Mozzarella cheese

Place the cooked and drained spaghetti in a large greased casserole dish and pour the turkey mixture over it. Sprinkle with mozzarella cheese. Bake for about ½ hour or until cheese melts and is golden.

Yield: 4 to 6 servings.

Marsha and Mike Stenstrom
Huntington, Massachusetts

· ·

RED MEAT

· ·

ARMENIAN SHISH KEBAB

■

2 cups plain yogurt
¼ cup red wine vinegar
3 large yellow onions, cut in
   large chunks
2 garlic cloves, crushed
Salt and pepper, to taste
2 to 3 pounds boneless lamb,
   cut into 2-inch cubes
Chunks of fresh tomato, eggplant, bell pepper, and
   mushrooms
Whole cloves of garlic, peeled

A traditional Armenian shish kebab with a great garlicky crunch. Serve with Greek Raita (see page 115) and rice pilaf or rice curry. See photo, page 131.

Mix the yogurt, vinegar, onions, garlic, and salt and pepper in a large bowl. Add the lamb. Cover the bowl and marinate the lamb for 2 hours at room temperature.

Place the lamb on skewers with chunks of tomato, eggplant, bell pepper, and mushrooms, and the cloves of garlic; place on a grill. Drain the onion chunks that were marinated and arrange them on the grill around the skewers. Cook the shish kebab over a hot grill or barbecue. Grill the onions until they are soft but have crispy edges. Serve with toasted pita or flat bread.

Yield: 6 servings.

Gilles Mesrobian
New York, New York

· ·

LAMB CURRY

■

2 tablespoons vegetable oil
2 cloves garlic, minced
1½ pounds boneless lamb, cubed
½ cup sherry
1 can (16 ounces) stewed tomatoes, drained and chopped (reserve juice)
½ teaspoon dried basil
1 cup plain yogurt
2 tablespoons curry powder
⅛ teaspoon cayenne pepper

A strong, hot, delicious curry that's easy to prepare.

In a deep skillet, heat the oil and garlic. Add the lamb and sauté for 3 to 4 minutes. Stir in the sherry and cook for another 2 minutes. Add the chopped tomatoes, basil, yogurt, curry, and pepper; stir to combine. Cover and simmer over low to medium heat, stirring occasionally, for 30 to 40 minutes or until the lamb is tender. If necessary, the sauce may be thinned with reserved tomato juice. Serve hot over rice or noodles.

Yield: 4 servings.

Emile Ferrara
Bristol, Rhode Island

. . . .

INDIAN MEATBALLS IN YOGURT SAUCE

■

MEATBALLS
½ pound ground lean lamb
1 tablespoon chopped mint leaves
¼ teaspoon ground cumin
¼ teaspoon salt
¼ cup soft bread crumbs
1 small egg white
¼ teaspoon ground coriander
¼ teaspoon cornstarch or tapioca
1 tablespoon vegetable oil

SAUCE
2 cloves garlic, chopped
(continued)

Inexpensive and easily assembled, with a distinctive spicy flavor. A great recipe for ground lamb.

In a food processor, pulse the lamb, mint, cumin, salt, bread crumbs, egg white, coriander, and cornstarch to mix thoroughly. Form the mixture into ¾-inch balls. In a heavy pan or skillet, brown the meatballs lightly in the vegetable oil. Remove with a slotted spoon and keep warm. Drain all but 1 teaspoon of fat from the pan.

To make the sauce, mince the garlic, onion, and ginger to near-paste consistency in the food processor. Sauté the mixture in the pan used to brown the meatballs. Stir in the garam masala and salt.

In a small pan, combine the yogurt and cornstarch and bring slowly to a near boil, stirring constantly. Reduce heat and continue to cook and thicken for 5 minutes. Combine the yogurt mixture with the onion mixture, add the meatballs and the bell pepper (for color), and heat through. Serve over rice or bulgur.

1 small onion, chopped
1 teaspoon minced fresh ginger
1 teaspoon garam masala or
   curry powder
½ teaspoon salt
1 cup plain yogurt
1 teaspoon cornstarch or tapioca
½ small red bell pepper, cored,
   seeded, and thinly sliced

KASHMIRI-STYLE LEG OF LAMB

∎

5-pound leg of lamb
1 tablespoon grated fresh ginger
4 cloves garlic, crushed
1 teaspoon salt
1 teaspoon ground cumin
1 teaspoon ground turmeric
½ teaspoon black pepper
½ teaspoon ground cinnamon
½ teaspoon ground cardamom
¼ teaspoon ground cloves
½ teaspoon chili powder
2 tablespoons lemon juice
1 cup plain yogurt
2 tablespoons blanched slivered
   almonds
2 tablespoons pistachios
1 tablespoon ground turmeric
1 tablespoon honey

Variation: This sauce and method work equally well with chicken breasts or lamb shoulder chops in place of the meatballs.

Yield: 2 servings.

Roger Ruth
Victoria, British Columbia, Canada

. . . .

Great full, spicy flavor, with an interesting texture from the nuts. Excellent company fare and perfect for a buffet. Best prepared two days in advance so the aromatic spices can mingle with the meat as the yogurt tenderizes it.

Remove any excess fat from the lamb. Using the point of a sharp knife, make deep slits all over the leg. Place the lamb in a glass, stainless-steel, or enamel dish. Combine the ginger, garlic, salt, cumin, turmeric, black pepper, cinnamon, cardamom, cloves, chili powder, and lemon juice. Rub this spice mixture over the lamb, pressing into each slit.

Thoroughly blend the yogurt, almonds, pistachios, and turmeric in a blender. Spread the blender mixture over the lamb. Drizzle the honey over the lamb, cover, and allow to marinate 2 days in the refrigerator, turning occasionally with wooden spoons.

Preheat oven to 450°F. Transfer the lamb to an ungreased baking dish, cover, and cook for 30 minutes. Reduce heat to 350°F and cook for another 1¾ hours. Uncover, allow to cool, and serve at room temperature.

Yield: 6 to 8 servings.

Cynthia R. Topliss
St. Stanislas de Kostka, Quebec, Canada

. . . .

NUTMEG LAMB

∎

2 tablespoons butter
2 medium onions, chopped
1½ pounds boneless lamb, cubed
1 can (16 ounces) apricot halves in heavy syrup
1 teaspoon ground nutmeg
Salt and pepper, to taste
1 cup plain yogurt
Parsley for garnish
Dash of nutmeg, for garnish

Quick and easy after a hard day's work, and perfect for unexpected company, this dish got rave reviews. The apricots and their syrup impart a light sweetness, nicely complemented by the nutmeg.

Melt the butter in a large saucepan or skillet over medium heat. Add the onions and lamb, stir together, and cook until tender. Add the apricots with their syrup, followed by the nutmeg. Cook for 10 more minutes, stirring often. Season with salt and pepper, to taste. Remove pan from burner and stir in yogurt. Serve over brown rice, garnished with parsley and nutmeg.

Yield: 2 to 4 servings.

*Kate Marker
Bethel, Connecticut*

LAMB RANI

∎

2 to 3 onions, coarsely chopped
1 tablespoon chopped fresh ginger
1 tablespoon ground coriander
1 teaspoon salt
Pinch of red pepper
1 heaping cup plain yogurt
2 pounds lean boneless lamb, cubed
⅓ cup butter
2 cloves garlic, minced
1 teaspoon ground cumin
1 teaspoon ground nutmeg
½ cup heavy cream (optional)

Lamb in a delicate, fragrant yogurt sauce. Quickly prepared since there is no sautéing involved.

In a blender or food processor, purée the onions, ginger, coriander, salt, pepper, and yogurt to make a marinade. Place the lamb in a large bowl and cover it with the marinade, coating the lamb evenly. Cover the bowl and allow the lamb to rest at room temperature for 1 to 2 hours.

Transfer the meat and the marinade to a large heavy-bottomed pan. On top of the stove, gently bring the contents of the pan to a near boil. Reduce heat, cover, and simmer, stirring occasionally, for 35 to 45 minutes or until the lamb is very tender.

Heat the butter in a small skillet. Add the garlic, cumin, and nutmeg; stir to combine. Remove from heat and pour the fragrant butter over the meat. Add the cream, if desired. Let the dish rest at room temperature for a couple of hours. Taste and add salt if needed. Reheat gently on top of the stove and serve with plain boiled rice.

Yield: 4 servings.

Rani Sarin
Lexington, Massachusetts

. . . .

MIDDLE EASTERN "TACOS"

■

1 small onion, minced
1 tablespoon vegetable oil
1 pound ground lamb (patties are fine)
2 tablespoons unbleached all-purpose flour
1 tablespoon ground cumin
¾ cup water
Salt and pepper, to taste
8 ounces mushrooms, chopped
1 tablespoon margarine
1 tablespoon ground coriander
4 large rounds oat-bran pita bread
2 cups low-fat plain yogurt

Satisfying and similar in taste to traditional beef tacos, but with the distinctive flavor of lamb.

Sauté the onion in the oil. Add the lamb and cook, stirring, until the lamb is no longer pink. Sprinkle the flour over the lamb and stir in the cumin and water. Mix thoroughly. Simmer uncovered, stirring occasionally, for about 20 to 25 minutes or until most of water has been absorbed. Season with salt and pepper, to taste.

Meanwhile, in a separate skillet, sauté the mushrooms in the margarine. Add the coriander, cover, and simmer for 10 minutes.

Warm the pita bread. Cut each piece of pita bread in half, forming 2 rounds. Layer the meat mixture, yogurt, and mushrooms in each round, as you would the ingredients of a beef taco, and wrap the pita bread around the filling. Serve with a green salad.

Yield: 8 large tacos.

Jocelyn Secker-Walker
Burlington, Vermont

. . . .

BEEF & POTATO CURRY

■

3 medium onions, chopped
5 tablespoons vegetable oil
6 peppercorns
4 cardamom seed pods
4 cloves
1 teaspoon coriander seeds
1 pound stew beef, cut into cubes
3 teaspoons ground turmeric
3 teaspoons ground cumin
2 teaspoons chili powder
3 cloves garlic, crushed
2 teaspoons grated fresh ginger
1 green chili, minced or sliced
2 cups beef broth
1 cup plain yogurt
1 tomato, sliced in wedges
4 medium potatoes, peeled and cut into quarters

Delicious! Very spicy and extremely satisfying, with tender meat and a superb gravy. Best made a day or two ahead.

Fry the onions in oil with the peppercorns, cardamom, cloves, and coriander until the coriander seeds pop. Add the beef and brown on all sides. Add the turmeric, cumin, chili powder, garlic, ginger, and chili and continue to cook, stirring constantly, for 2 minutes more. Add the broth. Stir in the yogurt and the tomato. Cover and simmer for 1½ hours.

Add the potatoes and cook for 45 minutes longer. Serve with rice and a yogurt raita (see pages 113-18) for a cooling complement to the spiciness.

Variation: Try substituting lamb for the beef.

Yield: 4 servings.

Cynthia R. Topliss
St. Stanislas de Kostka, Quebec, Canada

- -

TASTE-OF-NEW-ENGLAND SKILLET

■

1½ pounds boned and skinned chicken breasts
¾ pound pork sausage links
½ pound fully cooked ham, cut in 1-inch chunks or smaller
1 tablespoon Dijon mustard
2 cloves garlic, minced
2 cups thickly sliced fresh mushrooms

(continued)

Very hearty and rich but definitely worth the calories and cholesterol occasionally.

Cut the chicken breasts in half and then into 2 to 3 lengthwise strips; set aside. In a large covered skillet over medium-high heat, brown the sausages; remove with a slotted spoon. In the same skillet, brown the ham; remove with a slotted spoon. In the same skillet, brown the chicken strips, a few at a time; remove with a slotted spoon. Pour off all but 2 tablespoons of drippings.

Return all the browned meats to the skillet; stir in the mustard and garlic. Add the mushrooms; pour wine over all and stir to combine. Bring to a boil, then lower heat, cover, and simmer for 30 minutes or until chicken is fork-tender.

1 cup dry white wine
3 tablespoons cornstarch
3 tablespoons water
2 cups plain yogurt
2 tablespoons maple syrup
Cracked pepper, to taste

Dissolve the cornstarch in the water, and stir into the chicken mixture; cook, stirring constantly, until thickened. Stir the yogurt and maple syrup together and add to the skillet, stirring to blend. Cook until the mixture is heated through and just beginning to bubble. Sprinkle with pepper and serve over noodles.

Yield: 6 servings.

Marjorie Fortier
West Redding, Connecticut

. . . .

BEEF STROGURTOFF

■

1 large onion, chopped
5 tablespoons butter
10 fresh mushrooms, sliced
1 pound stew beef, cut into chunks
½ cup cooking sherry
1 cup plain yogurt (be sure to use the creamy layer, if available)
Cornstarch mixed with water (optional)
Salt and pepper

A rich-tasting stroganoff made with yogurt instead of sour cream.

Fry the onion slowly in a large pan with 2 tablespoons of butter until limp. Add the mushrooms to the onion with another tablespoon of butter. Stir to combine, and cook until tender.

Place the remaining 2 tablespoons butter in a separate pan, add the beef, and fry until brown. Add the beef to the onions and mushrooms. Add the sherry, then the yogurt, stirring after each addition. Heat until almost boiling, stirring all the while. If you find the sauce too thin, mix a small amount of cornstarch with water and add it to the sauce. Season to taste with salt and pepper and serve over noodles, rice, or toast.

Yield: 4 servings.

Jonathan Steiner
Durham, New Hampshire

. . . .

BONELESS VEAL WITH YOGURT DRESSING

■

2 pounds boneless veal shoulder
3 tablespoons unbleached all-
  purpose flour
¾ teaspoon salt
¼ teaspoon black pepper
¼ cup vegetable oil
2½ tablespoons minced onion
1 tablespoon paprika
2 cups chicken broth
1 can (6 ounces) tomato paste
½ teaspoon dried rosemary
½ teaspoon dried sage
½ teaspoon dried basil
2 tablespoons butter
1 tablespoon flour
1 tablespoon paprika
½ cup milk
1 cup plain yogurt
Chopped fresh parsley, for
  garnish

A good, hearty, full-flavored dish, excellent for entertaining. A bit of effort, but the taste is worth it.

Cut the veal into 1-inch cubes and sprinkle with 3 tablespoons of flour mixed with the salt and pepper. Heat the oil in a deep skillet or Dutch oven. Add the veal, onion, and 1 tablespoon paprika. Brown the veal on all sides. Add the chicken broth, tomato paste, rosemary, sage, and basil; stir to combine. Cover tightly and simmer for 45 to 60 minutes, or until tender, stirring occasionally.

Melt the butter in a small saucepan and blend in 1 tablespoon flour and 1 tablespoon paprika. Cook and stir until bubbly. Drain the remaining juice from the cooked veal and gradually stir the juice into the butter mixture. Add the milk, bring to a boil, and stir constantly until thick. Reduce heat. Gradually blend in the yogurt and mix well.

Pour the sauce over the cooked veal in the skillet; heat through but do not boil. Serve over hot broad noodles, garnished with parsley.

Yield: 4 servings.

Peg Rice
Bedford, New Hampshire

. . . .

PORK CHOPS PAPRIKA

■

1 medium onion, sliced
2 tablespoons vegetable oil
4 center-cut pork chops
2 tablespoons paprika
Juice of 2 lemons
1 cup plain yogurt
Salt and pepper, to taste

Pork chops in a creamy onion sauce. Wonderfully flavorful and easy to prepare.

Sauté the onion slices in oil until they begin to brown. Remove from pan and reserve. In the same pan, brown the chops thoroughly on both sides. Sprinkle paprika on both sides of the chops. Add the lemon juice. Return the onion to the pan and stir the sauce thoroughly. Cover the pan and bring the sauce to a boil. Turn the heat down and simmer gently for 30 minutes, turning the chops once.

Remove the chops to a warm serving dish. Stir the yogurt into the sauce in the pan and reheat to close to boiling; do not boil or the yogurt will curdle. Season with salt and pepper and pour the sauce over the chops. Serve with rice or noodles.

Yield: 2 servings.

Jocelyn Secker-Walker
Burlington, Vermont

. . . .

FRIED MEATBALLS WITH YOGURT

∎

2 pounds lean ground beef
1 small carrot, peeled and
   finely grated
4 crusts whole-wheat bread
   grated to form soft crumbs
½ teaspoon garlic powder
2 eggs, lightly beaten
6 tablespoons minced fresh
   parsley
4 sprigs mint, finely chopped
1 teaspoon ground allspice
5 tablespoons burgundy or
   other red wine
Flour
Safflower oil for frying
1 lemon, cut in wedges
2 cups plain yogurt

A hearty dish enjoyed by everyone who sampled it. The yogurt and lemon wedges are essential to the flavor; be sure not to leave them out.

In a large glass or ceramic bowl, combine the ground beef, carrot, bread crumbs, garlic, eggs, parsley, mint, allspice, and burgundy. Mix well. Cover and refrigerate for at least 1 hour.

Remove from refrigerator and pinch off pieces of the meat mixture the size of walnuts or smaller. Roll them into balls between your palms, then dredge them lightly in flour. Pour oil into a skillet to a depth of about ¼ inch and heat over medium heat; the oil should be hot but should not smoke. Fry the meatballs until crisp, turning gently. Remove and drain on a paper towel for a minute.

Serve immediately, while still very hot. Accompany each serving with a wedge of lemon and a dish of yogurt for dipping, or pour yogurt over each helping of meatballs and serve with a lemon wedge on the side.

Yield: About 2 to 3 servings.

Diane Seiler
Waltham, Massachusetts

. . . .

VEAL MEATBALLS IN YOGURT SAUCE

■

¼ cup milk
1 cup fine white bread crumbs
1 medium onion, finely
   chopped
2 teaspoons lemon juice
½ teaspoon salt
⅛ teaspoon pepper
1 egg, beaten
1 pound ground veal
1 tablespoon butter
1 cup dry white wine
1 bay leaf
¼ teaspoon dried rosemary
1 cup plain yogurt
½ cup water
1 tablespoon flour

A lovely combination of flavors, and a warm and hearty meal.

In a large bowl, combine the milk and bread crumbs. Stir in the onion, lemon juice, salt, pepper, and egg. Add the veal and mix thoroughly. Form the mixture into 12 large or 16 smaller balls.

Heat the butter in a large skillet. Over medium heat, brown the meatballs evenly. Add the wine, bay leaf, and rosemary; stir, then bring to a boil. Lower heat, cover, and simmer for 30 minutes. Remove the meatballs from the skillet and keep them warm through the next stage.

Combine the yogurt, water, and flour; stir the yogurt mixture into the liquid remaining in the skillet. Cook over low to medium heat, stirring constantly, until the sauce is thickened. Do not boil. Return the meatballs to the skillet and heat gently until hot. Remove the bay leaf and serve over hot buttered noodles or rice.

Yield: 12 to 16 meatballs.

Lynda Cohen
Concord, Massachusetts

. . . .

RABBIT WITH YOGURT

■

1 fryer-size rabbit, cut up
Vegetable oil or margarine to
   cover bottom of pan
2 onions, diced
2 to 4 cloves garlic, minced
2 cups apple cider, apple juice,
(continued)

Spooned over hot wide noodles, this is a tasty way to serve rabbit.

In a large Dutch oven, sauté the rabbit pieces in oil until browned. Add the onions and garlic and sauté briefly. Add the cider, pepper, thyme, and marjoram; stir to combine. Cover and cook over very low heat for about 1 hour or until the meat separates easily from the bones with a fork.

Remove the lid and dip ½ cup of liquid out of the stew. Dissolve the cornstarch in this liquid, then add

or white wine (or use 1 cup
cider vinegar and 1 cup
water)
Freshly ground black pepper, to
taste
Fresh or dried thyme leaves, to
taste
Fresh or dried marjoram leaves,
to taste
2 tablespoons cornstarch
2 cups plain yogurt

the mixture to the stew and allow it to come to a boil.
Stir in the yogurt just before serving. Heat through
and serve over hot wide noodles or potatoes.

Yield: 3 to 4 servings.

Martha McChesney
Afton, Nova Scotia, Canada

. . . .

FAIRVIEW FARMS CHEESE PIE

■

1 cup plain yogurt
¼ cup water
2 eggs, slightly beaten
1 cup unbleached all-purpose
flour
1 teaspoon salt
1½ teaspoons dried onion
Pinch each of dried basil,
parsley, pepper, and dried
minced garlic (optional)
2 slices Swiss cheese, broken in
pieces
Generous 1-inch cube of any
Cheddar cheese, broken into
pieces
¼ cup chopped crisp cooked
bacon
¼ to ⅓ cup chopped cooked
broccoli

*Like a quiche without the crust! Perfect for brunch
or for Sunday-night supper; we loved it.*

Preheat oven to 425°F. Thoroughly whisk together
the yogurt, water, eggs, flour, salt, onion, basil,
parsley, pepper, and garlic. Add the cheeses, bacon,
and broccoli. Mix thoroughly. Pour into a greased 9-
or 10-inch pie plate. Bake for 30 to 35 minutes or until
set. Serve hot with crusty French bread.

Variation: Use ham chunks or sweet sausage in place
of the bacon, or substitute any other vegetable for
the broccoli; leftover vegetables work well.

Yield: 4 to 5 servings.

Priscilla Fauver
Wilmot Flat, New Hampshire

. . . .

YOGURT, MUSHROOM & BACON QUICHE

∎

4 eggs, slightly beaten
1½ cups plain yogurt
⅛ teaspoon pepper
⅛ teaspoon ground nutmeg
1 small onion, diced
2 cups grated Swiss cheese
1 cup sliced mushrooms
6 slices bacon, cooked and
   crumbled
Unbaked 9-inch pie crust
2 tablespoons grated Parmesan
   cheese

A cheesy, flavorful quiche with an excellent texture.

Preheat oven to 375°F. In a large bowl, combine the eggs, yogurt, pepper, and nutmeg. Beat well. Add the onion, Swiss cheese, mushrooms, and bacon. Stir well. Pour into the pie shell and sprinkle with Parmesan cheese. Bake for 35 to 45 minutes or until cooked. Let cool for 10 minutes before serving.

Yield: 8 servings.

Amanda Tobin
Barre, Ontario, Canada

. . . .

SEAFOOD

. . . .

TARRAGON HERRING

∎

1 cup plain yogurt
1 teaspoon dried tarragon
Pinch of garlic powder
3 medium herring (2 pounds),
   or any other white fish

Moist and tender, with a delicate tarragon flavor. Easy to make, too. If herring is not available, substitute scrod or another white fish.

Preheat oven to 375°F. Mix together the yogurt, tarragon, and garlic powder. Grease a baking dish. Place the herring in the dish, skin side down, and pour the yogurt mixture over the fish. Bake for 25 to 30 minutes or until the fish flakes.

Yield: 4 servings.

Kathleen Hall
Port Coquitlam, British Columbia, Canada

. . . .

GARY'S YOGURT SAUCE FOR FISH

■

¼ cup olive oil
3 pounds fish (steak or fillets)
¼ cup balsamic vinegar
1 cup plain yogurt
¼ cup Dijon mustard
1 teaspoon garlic salt
1 teaspoon celery salt
1 teaspoon dried dill
½ teaspoon pepper
2 tablespoons lemon juice
¼ teaspoon sesame oil

Whenever Gary, president of Stonyfield Farm Yogurt, makes this recipe, people proclaim it the best fish they've ever had. It's especially wonderful made with bluefish, salmon, or swordfish. As Gary says, "Merely combine the sauce ingredients, spread on the fish, and bake. Then put on your humblest expression and wait for the acclaim that will be yours."

Preheat oven to 325°F. Grease a baking pan with some of the olive oil. Pat the rest of the oil onto both sides of the fish pieces. Combine all the remaining ingredients in a bowl; spread the mixture over the fish until each piece is thickly covered. Grill or bake the fish for about 25 minutes or until done.

Yield: 4 to 6 servings.

Gary Hirshberg
Wilton, New Hampshire

. . . .

SHRIMP-STUFFED AVOCADOS

■

1 pound medium-size shrimp, cooked, peeled, deveined, and chilled
1 cup sliced fresh mushrooms
1 cup green seedless grapes, each cut in half lengthwise
1 cup plain yogurt
1 tablespoon fresh lemon juice
½ teaspoon crushed dried rosemary
3 tablespoons minced fresh parsley
6 large Bibb lettuce leaves
3 medium avocados, cut in half and pitted
Freshly ground pepper to taste

Shrimp, mushrooms, and grapes in a tangy herb sauce. Makes a beautiful presentation.

Combine the shrimp, mushrooms, and grapes in a large mixing bowl. In another bowl, blend the yogurt, lemon juice, rosemary, and parsley; mix well. Gently fold the yogurt mixture into the shrimp combination.

Place one lettuce leaf and an avocado half on each serving plate. Fill the avocado halves with the shrimp and yogurt mixture. Top with ground pepper and serve.

Yield: 6 servings.

Pat Sprankle
Nashua, New Hampshire

. . . .

EASY GOURMET QUICHE

■

3 eggs
1 cup plain yogurt
1 tablespoon unbleached all-purpose flour
½ teaspoon baking soda
Salt and pepper, to taste
10 ounces lobster-tail meat or crabmeat (fresh, frozen, or canned)
3 scallions, chopped fine
Unbaked 9-inch pastry shell
1 cup Swiss cheese, grated
1 package (2 ounces) sliced or slivered almonds, toasted

Our all-time favorite quiche recipe — enthusiastic reviews from all who've tried it.

Preheat oven to 450°F. In a blender, mix the eggs and yogurt thoroughly. Add flour, soda, and salt and pepper. Blend again. Pour the mixture into a large bowl. If using canned lobster or crabmeat, make sure it is well drained. Add the seafood to the egg mixture. Add the scallions and stir well.

Layer the bottom of the pastry shell with the grated cheese. Pour the egg mixture over the cheese and sprinkle toasted almonds on top as a garnish. Bake for 15 minutes, then reduce heat to 350°F and bake for 30 minutes longer. Allow the quiche to set for 5 minutes before serving.

Yield: 8 pieces.

Laurel Kluge
Boston, Massachusetts

. . . .

BAKED FISH WITH DILL

■

2 tablespoons butter
1 shallot, diced
Juice of 1 large lime
¼ cup finely chopped fresh dill or 2 tablespoons dried dill
⅛ teaspoon freshly ground white pepper
1 cup plain yogurt
2 pounds fresh bluefish fillets (3 pieces)
1 pound lemon sole or grey sole fillets

The bluefish and sole offer a pleasing contrast of flavors, and there's just the right hint of lime. Yogurt keeps the fish moist and fresh tasting. Serve with potato salad and steamed spinach, and with sliced fresh tomatoes in the summertime.

Melt the butter, add the diced shallot, and sauté until translucent. Lower the heat and add the lime juice, dill, and pepper; stir to combine. Stir in the yogurt and bring to a simmer; *do not boil.* Lay one bluefish fillet along one side of an ungreased baking dish or shallow casserole. Overlap it with sole fillets so they half cover the bluefish. Place a second bluefish fillet so that its edge slightly overlaps the inside edge of the first one. Repeat the process with the remaining sole and the last piece of bluefish. The overlapped fish should be somewhat over 1 inch thick and very little of the bottom of the pan should show; the pan should fit the fish layers snugly.

Pour the hot yogurt mixture over the fish, lifting the fillets to allow all the fish to be covered with sauce and allowing some sauce to flow underneath the fish. Let sit at room temperature for 30 minutes before baking. (The dish can be prepared ahead of time to this point and kept refrigerated, uncooked, for a longer period of time.)

Preheat oven to 350°F. Bake the fish, uncovered, for 30 minutes or until the fish flakes easily with a fork. Serve hot, immediately after baking, or chill until it sets and serve cold as a terrine.

Yield: 8 servings.

Michael Frishman
Andover, Massachusetts

. . . .

HICKORY HOLLOW FISH PUFFS

■

¾ cup unbleached all-purpose flour
¼ cup oat bran
1½ teaspoons baking powder
½ teaspoon baking soda
1 teaspoon kelp powder (optional)
1 clove garlic, minced
½ teaspoon ground ginger
¼ cup butter
1 cup flaked cooked fish
½ cup grated Monterey Jack cheese
½ cup grated Cheddar cheese
1 small onion, minced
½ cup plain yogurt

Quick, tasty, and nutritious, these are a wonderful way to use up leftover fish. Serve as an appetizer or a light lunch with salad and fresh whole-grain bread.

Preheat oven to 425°F. Combine the flour, oat bran, baking powder, soda, optional kelp powder, garlic, and ginger. Cut in the butter until the mixture is crumbly. Add the fish, cheeses, and onion. Fold in the yogurt. Drop by spoonfuls onto a lightly oiled cookie sheet. Bake for 15 to 20 minutes.

Yield: 20 fish puffs.

Helen Shepherd
Lyndhurst, Ontario, Canada

. . . .

BLENDER SALMON MOUSSE WITH TANGY YOGURT DILL SAUCE

■

MOUSSE

1 large can (15½ ounces) plus 1
    small can (7½ ounces)
    salmon
1 small onion, sliced
Juice of 1½ large lemons
1 envelope (¼ ounce) plus 1
    tablespoon unflavored gelatin
½ cup boiling water
¾ cup plain yogurt
¾ cup mayonnaise
1½ teaspoons paprika
5 tablespoons minced fresh dill
    or 2 teaspoons dried dill

SAUCE

¾ cup plain yogurt
¼ cup mayonnaise
½ teaspoon prepared mustard
2 tablespoons minced fresh dill

A creamy mousse with a smooth flavor and soft pink color. The sauce adds just the right tang. See photo, page 130.

Drain the liquid from the canned salmon into a 1½-quart fish-shaped mold; coat the mold thoroughly with the liquid to oil it, then discard the liquid.

Place in a blender or food processor the sliced onion and the lemon juice, and sprinkle the dry gelatin over this. Add ¼ cup boiling water and purée. Pour in the remaining boiling water slowly while running the blender at purée speed. Stop the blender and add the yogurt, mayonnaise, and paprika; purée for 15 to 20 seconds more.

Break the salmon into small chunks and combine with the yogurt mixture in the blender; blend on the purée setting for 1½ minutes or a little more, if necessary, until all ingredients are thoroughly blended. Add the dill and blend briefly until mixed. Pour the mixture into the fish mold and refrigerate until firm (2 to 3 hours or overnight).

Thoroughly mix all the sauce ingredients by hand; refrigerate for at least 1 hour.

Half an hour before serving, remove the mousse and sauce from the refrigerator. Spread the sauce on a large serving platter. Loosen the mousse from the mold by running the point of a sharp knife all around the edge of the mousse. Invert the mold on top of the sauce and allow the mousse to slide naturally out of the mold. Serve with crackers or cut-up raw vegetables.

Yield: 1 large mold.

*Helen Flores
Norwalk, Connecticut*

CURRIED SHRIMP & BABY VEGETABLES

■

3 cloves garlic, chopped fine
1 teaspoon finely chopped fresh ginger
1 teaspoon mustard seeds
¼ cup unsalted butter
1 teaspoon salt, or to taste
1 teaspoon ground cumin
1 teaspoon ground coriander
1 teaspoon turmeric
¼ teaspoon cayenne pepper
2 small red onions, sliced
16 baby carrots (or finger-size pieces)
1 red bell pepper, cored, seeded, and sliced into thin strips
1 yellow bell pepper, cored, seeded, and sliced into thin strips
8 baby zucchini, halved lengthwise (or larger zucchini sliced into finger-size pieces)
1 pound shrimp, skinned and deveined
Juice of 2 Valencia oranges
1 cup plain yogurt

A gourmet treat, well worth the preparation time. See photo, page 129.

In a large skillet, sauté the garlic, ginger, and mustard seeds in butter for 3 minutes over medium heat. Add the salt, cumin, coriander, turmeric, cayenne, onions, carrots, bell peppers, zucchini, and shrimp. Sauté, stirring constantly, for 5 to 7 minutes or until the shrimp just begins to change color. Add the orange juice. Continue cooking for 2 minutes more over medium heat to reduce the liquid. Remove from heat and stir in the yogurt. Serve immediately with rice.

Yield: 4 servings.

Steven Lyons
Boston, Massachusetts

. . . .

SCROD IN YOGURT SAUCE

∎

2 pounds scrod fillets
½ pound fresh mushrooms, stems removed and reserved, caps sliced
1 onion, sliced
1 bay leaf
½ cup water
½ cup vermouth
½ lemon, sliced
1 tablespoon butter
½ yellow bell pepper, seeded and thinly sliced
1 bunch scallions, sliced
1 tomato, peeled, seeded, and diced
3 to 4 sprigs fresh thyme, chopped
¼ cup chopped fresh parsley
1 tablespoon capers
1 cup plain yogurt
Freshly ground pepper, to taste
Parsley, for garnish

Simple but elegant.

Preheat oven to 325°F. Place fillets in an ungreased 13x9-inch baking pan. Add the mushroom stems, sliced onion, bay leaf, water, vermouth, and lemon. Cover with parchment paper. Bake for 10 to 15 minutes or until the fillets are opaque. Remove the fish to a hot platter and keep warm.

Strain the cooking juices into a small saucepan and cook until the liquid is reduced to ½ cup. Melt the butter in a skillet; sauté the bell pepper and mushroom caps for 5 minutes. Add the scallions, tomato, thyme, parsley, capers, and reduced stock; stir to combine. Simmer until the vegetables are of the desired tenderness. Add the yogurt and pepper, stir, and heat through. Pour over the fillets. Garnish with parsley and serve with rice or noodles and lemon slices.

Yield: 4 to 6 servings.

Martin Smith
Sandwich, Massachusetts

LING COD STEAKS IN YOGURT

∎

2 ling cod steaks (14 to 16 ounces each)
¼ teaspoon ground turmeric
¼ teaspoon salt
1 cup plain yogurt
1 teaspoon cornstarch

(continued)

Try this with shark steaks, too, for a delicious stove-top fish dinner.

Debone and skin the fish steaks, dividing each in half. Sprinkle with turmeric and ¼ teaspoon salt; set aside.

In the blender, combine the yogurt, cornstarch, 1 onion, garlic, cumin, coriander, chili, and remaining salt to make a smooth paste.

In a skillet, lightly brown the fish in oil; remove with a slotted spoon. Sauté the second onion and the bell pepper until the onion is limp. Add the yogurt paste and simmer for 10 minutes. Remove half the sauce.

1 medium onion, chopped into
large chunks
2 cloves garlic
½ teaspoon ground cumin
½ teaspoon ground coriander
¼ teaspoon powdered red chili
¼ teaspoon salt
2 tablespoons vegetable oil
1 medium onion, chopped
½ red bell pepper, seeded and
chopped

Return the fish steaks to the pan, cover them with
the removed sauce, and simmer for 10 minutes before
serving.

Yield: 4 servings.

Roger Ruth
Victoria, British Columbia, Canada

. . . .

SNAPPY SEAFOOD SHELLS

■

PASTA & GARNISH
18 giant pasta shells
Sprigs of fresh dill

STUFFING
1 small yellow bell pepper,
cored and seeded
1 small red bell pepper, cored
and seeded
1 pound sealegs or crabmeat,
chopped
1 cup chopped unpeeled
cucumber
½ cup minced scallion

DRESSING
1 cup plain yogurt
½ cup mayonnaise
½ cup chopped fresh dill
2 tablespoons grated horseradish
2 tablespoons lemon juice
1 tablespoon Dijon mustard
Freshly ground pepper

*A colorful dish of seafood shells with a delicious, full-
flavored dressing. Try serving with garlic bread.*

Cook the shells according to package directions. Rinse
with cool water, drain well, and pat dry with paper
towels.

Reserve a few thin slices of each bell pepper for garnish; chop the rest. In a large bowl, mix the seafood,
cucumber, chopped peppers, and scallion.

For the dressing, in another bowl combine the yogurt,
mayonnaise, dill, horseradish, lemon juice, and
mustard; mix well. Season to taste with pepper.

Add 1 cup of the dressing to the seafood mixture and
toss thoroughly; refrigerate the remaining dressing.
Fill each pasta shell evenly with seafood mixture and
refrigerate until ready to serve.

To serve, arrange 3 filled shells on each of 6 small
plates. Spoon the remaining dressing over the shells
and garnish each with a fresh dill sprig and thin slices
of pepper.

Yield: 6 servings.

Elizabeth March
Concord, New Hampshire

. . . .

ORZO SALAD

▪

1½ cups orzo
2 cups flaked tuna
1 cup finely chopped green
   onions
1 cup thinly sliced celery
¼ cup minced fresh parsley
½ cup plain yogurt
½ cup mayonnaise
¼ teaspoon hot-pepper sauce
1 teaspoon black pepper

Orzo is a rice-shaped pasta. This recipe makes a creamy, flavorful salad with a touch of piquancy from the hot pepper.

Cook, drain, and cool the orzo according to package directions. Using a wooden spoon, combine the cooked orzo with all the remaining ingredients and toss well. To allow the flavors to blend, let the salad rest in the refrigerator for at least 2 hours before serving.

Variation: In place of the tuna, try crabmeat, shrimp, or cooked and diced ham or chicken.

Yield: About 6 servings.

Gayle Stevens
Oakville, Ontario, Canada

VEGETARIAN

FETTUCINI

▪

1 package (12 ounces) regular
   or spinach fettucini
½ cup butter or margarine
1 cup grated Parmesan cheese
   (preferably fresh)
⅔ cup plain yogurt
Dash of pepper
½ cup chopped fresh parsley
1 cup chopped broccoli,
   steamed (optional)

Easy to make, with a fine, cheesy flavor and creamy texture. Kids enjoy this one, too.

Cook the fettucini according to package directions. Meanwhile, melt the butter in a medium-size saucepan; add the cheese, yogurt, and pepper. Cook over low heat, stirring constantly, until mixture is well blended. Drain the noodles, add them to the yogurt mixture, and toss until well coated. Add the parsley and optional broccoli; toss lightly. Serve immediately.

Yield: 4 servings.

Marty and Renata Earles
Grass Valley, California

SUNNY TORTELLINI

■

2 cups plain yogurt
¼ cup finely chopped sun-dried tomatoes
2 scallions, chopped
½ teaspoon dried thyme
Freshly ground black pepper, to taste
Dash of tamari or soy sauce
1 pound cheese-filled spinach tortellini
1 large onion, chopped
2 shallots, chopped
2 cloves garlic, crushed
3 to 5 tablespoons vegetable oil
1½ pounds mushrooms, sliced

A terrific dish that got rave reviews. An unusual combination of strong but delightful flavors, and quite easy to prepare once all the chopping is done. Serve with a tossed green salad and warm Italian bread.

Boil water for the tortellini. Combine the yogurt, tomatoes, scallions, thyme, pepper, and tamari. Mix well and set aside. Cook the tortellini according to package directions.

While the tortellini are cooking, sauté the onion, shallots, and garlic in oil. Add the mushrooms and continue cooking, stirring occasionally, for 15 to 20 minutes or until wilted.

When the tortellini are done, drain them and return them to the pot. Add the mushroom mixture immediately and toss. Add the yogurt mixture, stirring to coat the pasta and mushrooms. Serve immediately.

Yield: 4 servings.

Lise Stern
Cambridge, Massachusetts

. . . .

CREAMY BEANS

■

4 cups green beans cut into 1-inch pieces
½ cup minced onion
2 tablespoons flour
¼ teaspoon garlic salt
1 teaspoon honey
1 cup plain yogurt
2 cups grated Swiss cheese
1 cup toasted crushed sesame seeds

So easy, with a simple, satisfying flavor. A great dish for potluck suppers.

Preheat oven to 325°F. Steam the beans for 3 to 5 minutes. Mix the beans, onion, and flour together. Add the garlic salt, honey, and yogurt. Place in a deep ungreased 2-quart baking dish. Combine the cheese and sesame seeds and spread the mixture over the beans. Bake for 30 minutes or until toasty brown.

Yield: 4 servings.

Joanie LeViness
Winsted, Connecticut

. . . .

LENTILS & BARLEY WITH MINTED YOGURT

■

1 cup lentils
1 cup barley
4 cups vegetable or chicken bouillon
1 tablespoon margarine
¾ cup slivered almonds
½ cup raisins
½ cup minced fresh mint
¾ cup plain yogurt

Wholesome and easy, this dish is satisfying warm or cold. Ideal for a summer picnic.

Wash and drain the lentils. Cook them with the barley in the bouillon for about 40 minutes or until tender.

Melt the margarine in a frying pan over medium heat. Add the almonds and raisins, stir, and heat until the raisins puff. Stir the almond-raisin mixture into the lentils and barley. Combine the mint and the yogurt and blend gently with the lentil-barley mixture. Serve warm or cold.

Yield: 6 to 8 servings.

Sara Fielder
Brownsville, Oregon

· ·

VEGETABLE PASTA YOGURT TOSS

■

2 tablespoons olive oil
3 cloves garlic, minced
3 to 4 carrots, peeled and cut diagonally
1 medium onion, sliced
¼ head red cabbage, shredded
1 red bell pepper, cored, seeded, and chopped
1 teaspoon caraway seeds
¼ cup water
1 teaspoon cider vinegar
1 pound spinach pasta (any kind)
¾ cup sliced mushrooms
1 teaspoon dried dill
¼ teaspoon white pepper

A surprising combination of vegetables and spices that's colorful, nutritious, and tasty. Try serving with freshly grated Parmesan cheese.

Heat 2 tablespoons olive oil over medium-high heat in a large skillet. Add the garlic and cook until softened. Add the carrots and sauté for 2 to 3 minutes. Add the onion, red cabbage, chopped bell pepper, and caraway seeds. Sauté for 1 minute. Add the water and vinegar; stir to combine. Continue cooking; when steaming is evident, cover the pan and reduce the heat to medium-low. Cook for 10 minutes. Meanwhile, start the pasta cooking according to package directions.

Add the mushrooms, dill, and white pepper to the cabbage mixture. Cover and cook for 5 more minutes.

To make the sauce, combine the olive oil, butter, yogurt, and cornstarch in a small saucepan. Stir constantly over medium-low heat. Add the cheese gradually while continuing to stir. Simmer gently for 1 minute.

SAUCE
1 tablespoon olive oil
1 tablespoon butter
1 cup plain yogurt
1 tablespoon cornstarch
1 cup grated sharp Cheddar
  cheese

When the pasta is done, drain it and return it to the cooking pot. Add the vegetables and toss. Add the yogurt sauce and toss again. Serve immediately.

Yield: 4 large portions.

David Niedel-Gresh
Providence, Rhode Island

. . . .

SHEPHERD'S FALL VEGETABLE PIE

■

¾ cup cubed tofu
1 tablespoon soy sauce
1 tablespoon cornstarch
1½ cups plain yogurt
2 cups peeled carrots, cut in
  large dice
1 cup unpeeled parsnips, cut in
  large dice
2 cups winter squash, cut in
  large dice
1 tablespoon butter
2 cups sliced mushrooms
1 small red pepper, sweet or
  hot, diced
1 clove garlic, minced
1 teaspoon ground ginger
½ teaspoon salt
2 tablespoons cornstarch
¼ teaspoon kelp powder
  (optional)
⅛ teaspoon cayenne pepper
1 cup milk
¾ cup grated Jarlsberg or Swiss
  cheese
Unbaked 10-inch pie crust

Ideal for warming body and spirit on a cold winter night. Serve with tossed greens and crusty bread. See photo, page 135.

Preheat oven to 375°F. Combine the tofu and soy sauce; set aside. Add 1 tablespoon cornstarch to the yogurt and set aside. Steam the carrots, parsnips, and squash until tender.

Melt the butter in a skillet; add the mushrooms, red pepper, garlic, ginger, and salt and sauté until the mushrooms and pepper are tender. Do not brown. Combine 2 tablespoons cornstarch, optional kelp powder, cayenne, and milk, and add to the mushroom mixture. Bring to a boil, stirring constantly, and boil for 1 minute.

Remove from heat and stir in the cheese. Fold in the tofu, then stir in the yogurt mixture. Add the steamed vegetables and transfer the mixture to an ungreased 10-inch deep-dish pie plate. Top with the unbaked crust, and slash the crust to let steam escape. Bake for 35 to 40 minutes or until crust is lightly browned.

Yield: 4 to 6 servings.

Helen Shepherd
Lyndhurst, Ontario, Canada

. . . .

HERB BULGUR & GARBANZOS

■

½ cup dry garbanzos
5 cups water
3 cloves garlic
3 tablespoons olive oil
2 medium onions, coarsely chopped
8 to 12 mushrooms, sliced
1¼ cups bulgur
1 teaspoon dried dill
3 bay leaves
1 tablespoon tamari or soy sauce
1 cup plain yogurt

A healthful dish that's easy to prepare and has an earthy, mellow flavor, though not at all bland.

Soak the garbanzos in water overnight. Add the garlic to the garbanzos and water and cook for 2 to 3 hours or until the garbanzos are tender. Reserve cooking liquid and discard the garlic.

Heat the oil in a large skillet. Add onions, mushrooms, and bulgur. Sauté until onions are just tender but not browned. Carefully add 2½ cups reserved cooking liquid, along with dill, bay leaves, and tamari; stir to combine. Bring to a boil, then reduce heat and simmer until liquid is absorbed.

While bulgur is cooking, lightly brown the cooked garbanzos in a small amount of oil in a skillet, stirring occasionally, until they are slightly browned. Add the garbanzos to the bulgur mixture along with the yogurt. Stir to combine, remove bay leaves, and serve.

Note: If portions are reheated, or if you prefer the dish more moist and creamy, add more yogurt.

Yield: 4 servings.

Pamela Jarvi
Fitchburg, Massachusetts

• •

MEATISH SWEET BALLS

■

1 cup bread crumbs
1 cup cooked brown rice
1 cup chopped walnuts or almonds, or a combination
2 eggs, beaten
Scant ½ cup sour cream
Scant ½ cup plain yogurt
(continued)

Tender little "meatballs" with a rich gravy. The rice tastes like ground meat! Delicious over noodles.

To make the sweet balls, mix the bread crumbs, brown rice, nuts, eggs, sour cream, yogurt, salt, and thyme together until thoroughly blended. Shape into about 18 balls, adding crumbs to thicken if needed. Sauté the balls in oil until brown. Remove with a slotted spoon and keep warm. Reserve the pan drippings.

To make the sauce, using the same pan in which the sweet balls were cooked, sauté the garlic, onion, and

Pinch of salt
1 teaspoon dried thyme
Additional bread crumbs
2 tablespoons vegetable oil

SAUCE
1 clove garlic, minced
½ cup chopped onion
1 cup thinly sliced mushrooms
1 teaspoon Worcestershire sauce
~ tomato paste

SAUCE

■

Butter or oil for frying
1 small onion, chopped
1 clove garlic, finely chopped
½ cup sliced mushrooms
½ cup peeled and diced carrots
1 ear of corn, sliced off the cob
  (or ¾ cup frozen corn)
1 cup diced cooked turkey
  and/or ham (optional)
Tamari or soy sauce, to taste
2 cups plain yogurt, at room
  temperature
1 package (12 ounces) egg
  noodles
Butter
Paprika
Thinly sliced zucchini, for garnish (optional)

mushrooms until soft. Stir in the Worcestershire sauce and tomato paste. Blend in the yogurt and sour cream. To thicken the sauce, add the pan drippings mixed with flour to the consistency of heavy cream. Stir the mixture over medium heat until thoroughly blended and of the desired consistency; do not allow the mixture to boil. Pour the sauce over the sweet balls and serve.

Yield: 18 sweet balls.

Dawn P. Ramage
Acton, Massachusetts

. . . .

*An easy vegetable stroganoff, with meat as an op-
tional addition.*

Heat the butter in a skillet. Working with one ingredient at a time and stirring after each addition, add the onion, garlic, mushrooms, carrots, and corn. Sprinkle in a small amount of water as the vegetables cook so they don't become too dry. Add the meat if desired and stir in. Add the tamari and stir again. When the vegetables are tender, remove from heat, add the yogurt, and stir to blend. Then place the pan of vegetables in a warm oven to blend the flavors while you cook the noodles.

Cook the egg noodles according to package directions. Drain, place in a serving dish, and dot with butter. Cover with the yogurt-vegetable sauce and sprinkle with paprika. Garnish with zucchini if desired.

Yield: 2 to 3 servings.

Ann Arnold
Watertown, Massachusetts

. . . .

169

LAYERED QUICHE

■

3 to 4 tablespoons butter
4 chippatis or 6 tortillas
½ cup chopped leeks
½ cup chopped scallions
1 cup peeled and sliced zucchini or summer squash
1 cup plain yogurt
1 pound silken (smooth) tofu, cubed
1 pound cottage cheese or ricotta
¾ cup grated Parmesan cheese
6 eggs, slightly beaten
1 teaspoon dried tarragon
1 tomato, diced
1 green bell pepper, cored, seeded, and diced

A terrific, fresh-tasting dish, with great flavor and texture.

Preheat oven to 350°F. Lightly grease a large casserole with 1 teaspoon of the butter. Pan-fry the chippatis or tortillas on both sides, using ¼ teaspoon butter per patty. Set aside.

Sauté the leeks and scallions with 1 tablespoon butter for 3 to 5 minutes; set aside. Sauté the zucchini with 1 tablespoon butter for 3 to 5 minutes and set aside.

In a bowl, blend the yogurt, tofu, cheeses, eggs, tarragon, tomato, and bell pepper.

Layer the ingredients in the greased casserole dish as follows: Place 1 chippati or tortilla (or enough to cover 1 layer) in the bottom of the dish. Add one-third of the tofu-cheese mixture, then a layer consisting of all the leeks and scallions. Cover with another chippati or tortilla, then another third of the tofu-cheese mixture. Add a layer of all the zucchini. Top with another chippati or tortilla and the remaining tofu-cheese mixture. Bake for about 45 minutes or until firm.

Yield: 4 servings.

David Liberty
Allston, Massachusetts

. . . .

POTATO PEPPER BAKE

■

3 large russet potatoes
1 small red potato
2 large carrots
4 cups boiling water
2 tablespoons butter
1 large onion
1 small onion
4 large eggs
¼ cup plain yogurt
1 teaspoon salt
¼ teaspoon freshly ground black pepper, or to taste
2 tablespoons unbleached all-purpose flour
1 red bell pepper, cored, seeded, and grated
1 cup plain yogurt
½ teaspoon ground cumin

A very hearty and satisfying dish that's also quite attractive. We loved it the next morning for breakfast, too.

Peel the potatoes and carrots. Cut them all into thirds, add to boiling water, and cook for 10 minutes. Drain the potatoes and carrots in a colander, running cold water over them until they are cool. Put the butter in a 9-inch square pan and place it in the oven. Heat oven to 350°F. Grate the large onion and set aside. Grate the small onion and the partially cooked potatoes and carrots and mix together.

In a separate bowl, beat the eggs until thick and lemon-yellow. Add ¼ cup yogurt, salt, and ground pepper and stir for 1 minute. Add the potato mixture and mix well. Sprinkle 1 tablespoon flour over the mixture and stir; repeat with the remaining flour. Set aside.

In a bowl, stir together the bell pepper, yogurt, and cumin. Remove the pan with the butter from the oven; the melted butter should be brown. Turn the pan to coat the sides with the butter. Spoon in the grated large onion, stir to coat it with butter, then spread the onion evenly over the bottom of the pan. Pour in the potato mixture, smoothing the top. Pour on the bell pepper and yogurt mixture, smoothing it to cover the potato layer completely. Return the pan to the oven and bake for 1 to 1½ hours, until the edges are golden brown.

Yield: 4 servings.

*Lise Stern
Cambridge, Massachusetts*

. . . .

DESSERTS

■

Yogurt is the perfect basis for wonderful desserts — witness the large number of desserts in this book! Yogurt makes pies that are creamy and rich tasting, and frozen desserts that are terrific substitutes for ice cream. The custards are light, the tarts not overly sweet. And after you try these extra-moist cakes, their non-yogurt counterparts will begin to seem dry, chalky, and unappealing. You won't go back!

The recipes in this chapter range from the humble New England Yogurt Bread Pudding to the positively elegant Strawberry Mocha Parfait — one of our all-time favorites for both taste and appearance. Again and again as these dessert recipes were tested, the reports that came back were of scrumptious treats that were quick and easy to make, not too sweet, and extra special enough for company.

Rare is the delectable dessert that can be truly described as being good for you. But these yogurt treats are delicate and satisfying, yet have far fewer calories than the cream, cream cheese, ice cream, and sour cream alternatives. So go ahead and indulge!

CAKES & COOKIES

YOGURT CHOCOLATE-CHIP CAKE

■

½ cup butter or margarine, softened
1 cup sugar
2 eggs
1¼ cups plain yogurt
1 teaspoon vanilla
1 cup unbleached all-purpose flour
1 cup whole-wheat flour
1 teaspoon baking soda
1 teaspoon baking powder
⅓ cup semi-sweet chocolate chips

TOPPING
¼ cup butter or margarine, softened
½ cup brown sugar
½ cup unbleached all-purpose flour
1½ teaspoons cocoa
¼ cup semi-sweet chocolate chips

A whole-wheat dessert with the consistency of a pound cake and the flavor of a coffee cake. Tastes rich and buttery but not overly sweet.

Preheat oven to 350°F. Cream together the butter and sugar. Add the eggs one at a time, beating well after each addition. Stir in the yogurt and vanilla. In a separate bowl, sift together flours, soda, and baking powder. Add the dry ingredients to the yogurt mixture and stir to mix. Stir in the chocolate chips. Pour into a greased 9x13-inch pan.

For the topping, cream the butter, brown sugar, flour, and cocoa until well blended; stir in the chocolate chips. Sprinkle the topping over the cake batter. Bake for 35 to 45 minutes or until a toothpick inserted in the middle comes out clean.

Yield: One 9x13-inch cake.

Lisa Grant
Oakbank, Manitoba, Canada

APRICOT SNACK CAKE

■

¾ cup butter, softened
1 cup sugar
3 eggs
1 cup plain yogurt
1 teaspoon vanilla
2 cups unbleached all-purpose flour
2 teaspoons baking powder
½ teaspoon nutmeg
1 cup peeled and chopped fresh apricots
1 cup chopped pecans

An easy, fruit-and-nutty cake that makes a fine snack. Keeps well, too. Canned apricots can be substituted for the fresh ones, but be sure to drain them before measuring.

Preheat oven to 350°F. Cream the butter and sugar until light and fluffy. Add the eggs one at a time, beating well after each addition. Mix in the yogurt and vanilla. Sift in the flour, baking powder, and nutmeg and mix again. Stir in the apricots and pecans. Spread batter in a well-greased 13x9-inch baking pan and bake for 30 to 40 minutes, or until a toothpick inserted in the center comes out clean.

Yield: 10 to 12 servings.

Carol Forcum
Marion, Illinois

. . . .

BLUEBERRY CAKE

■

½ cup shortening
½ cup granulated sugar
½ cup brown sugar
2 eggs, beaten
1 cup blueberry yogurt
1½ cups blueberries (drained if frozen)
3 cups unbleached all-purpose flour
½ teaspoon baking soda
4 teaspoons baking powder
¾ cup milk
1 teaspoon vanilla
Confectioners' sugar (optional)

A tasty, light cake, best made with fresh blueberries.

Preheat oven to 325°F. Cream the shortening, add the sugars, and beat until fluffy. Add the eggs and yogurt to the sugar mixture and beat until smooth. Fold in the berries. In a separate bowl, sift together the flour, soda, and baking powder. Add the dry ingredients alternately with the milk and vanilla to the yogurt mixture, beating well after each addition. Pour into a greased 10-inch tube pan and bake for 50 minutes or until a toothpick inserted in the center comes out clean.

Cool the cake in the pan on a rack for 10 minutes, then turn it out of the pan to cool completely. Before serving, sprinkle with confectioners' sugar if desired.

Yield: About 12 slices.

Louise Seekins
Sudbury, Massachusetts

. . . .

175

APPLE CAKE

■

4 large tart apples, such as
  Granny Smith
1 teaspoon vanilla
1 cup plain yogurt
1 cup sugar
4 large eggs
2¼ cups unbleached all-
  purpose flour
1 teaspoon salt
2 teaspoons baking powder
1 teaspoon baking soda
1 teaspoon sugar

Very moist and heavy with apples. Good for snacks or for dessert with coffee.

Preheat oven to 350°F. Core, peel, and slice the apples; place them in a small bowl and sprinkle with the vanilla. In a large bowl, combine the yogurt, 1 cup sugar, and eggs; beat well. In another small bowl, whisk together the flour, salt, baking powder, and soda. Stir this mixture into the egg mixture.

Butter and flour a 10-inch Bundt pan or two 8x4-inch loaf pans. Spread a thin layer of batter in the pan(s), then a layer of apple. Repeat and then top with a final (third) layer of batter. (You now have 3 layers of batter alternating with 2 layers of apple.) Sprinkle 1 teaspoon sugar over the top. Bake for about 50 minutes to 1 hour.

Yield: 2 loaves or 1 Bundt cake.

Helen Campbell
Loughborough Inlet, British Columbia, Canada

• •

LEMON YOGURT CAKE

■

1 cup butter or margarine,
  softened
1 cup sugar
4 eggs
1 tablespoon grated lemon peel
1 teaspoon vanilla
2½ cups unbleached all-
  purpose flour
1 teaspoon baking powder
1 teaspoon baking soda
½ teaspoon salt
1 cup plain yogurt
¾ cup ground blanched
  almonds

A dense lemony cake with a golden shell and moist interior. It keeps well and is great toasted and served with frozen yogurt. Our tester especially liked the strong lemon flavor of the sauce.

Preheat oven to 350°F. Cream the butter and sugar. Beat in the eggs one at a time until smooth. Stir in the lemon peel and vanilla. In a separate bowl, sift together the flour, baking powder, soda, and salt. Stir the flour mixture and the yogurt alternately into the butter mixture, mixing well after each addition. Fold in the almonds. Spoon the batter into a greased 9-inch tube pan and bake for about 1 hour. Cool in pan for 5 minutes.

While the cake is cooling, heat together the lemon juice and sugar for the sauce. Bring to a boil, reduce heat, and simmer for 5 minutes. Spoon the lemon mixture over the slightly cooled cake, allowing the

SAUCE
½ cup fresh lemon juice
½ cup sugar

syrup to soak down the sides of the pan and into the cake. Cool the cake completely and invert it onto a serving plate.

Variation: For a delicious change of pace, substitute grated orange rind for the lemon rind in the cake, and use orange juice rather than lemon juice in the sauce.

Yield: One 9-inch tube cake.

Shirley Vandor
Ormstown, Quebec, Canada

. . . .

CARROT CAKE

■

3 cups grated carrots
⅓ cup raisins
½ cup grated coconut
1 cup chopped walnuts or
  pecans
2 cups unbleached all-purpose
  flour
2 teaspoons baking soda
½ teaspoon baking powder
1 teaspoon ground cinnamon
½ cup maple syrup
½ cup maple sugar, raw sugar,
  or granulated sugar
3 eggs
½ cup safflower oil
1 cup plain yogurt
1 teaspoon vanilla

A moist, light treat that stays fresh tasting for days. Loaded with healthful ingredients, it's good for lunch boxes.

Preheat oven to 350°F. Mix together the carrots, raisins, coconut, and walnuts. In a separate bowl, sift together the flour, soda, baking powder, and cinnamon. In a blender, mix the maple syrup, sugar, eggs, oil, yogurt, and vanilla. Add the blender mixture to the sifted dry ingredients and beat until smooth. Add the carrot mixture and stir to combine. Turn the batter out into a greased 9x13-inch pan and bake for 45 minutes or until a toothpick inserted in the center comes out clean.

Frost with your favorite confectioners' sugar glaze. Or use softened cream cheese, beaten together with maple syrup or honey until it reaches spreading consistency. Garnish with sprinkles of granola if you wish.

Yield: One 9x13-inch cake.

Donna Schmidt
Walpole, New Hampshire

. . . .

CREAMY BANANA CAKE

■

¾ cup butter, softened
¾ cup sugar
3 eggs
1 teaspoon vanilla
2 large ripe bananas, mashed
1 cup unbleached all-purpose flour
1 cup whole-wheat flour
1 teaspoon baking powder
1 teaspoon baking soda
1½ cups plain yogurt

FROSTING
1 package (8 ounces) cream cheese, at room temperature
6 tablespoons unsalted butter, at room temperature
1 cup confectioners' sugar
1 teaspoon vanilla

A simple, satisfying banana cake.

Preheat oven to 350°F. Cream the butter and sugar in a large bowl. Add the eggs and vanilla and beat in. Add the bananas and mix. Sift the flours, baking powder, and soda into the banana mixture; stir to combine. Add the yogurt and mix well. Pour the batter into 2 buttered and floured 9-inch cake pans or 8x4-inch loaf pans. Bake for about 40 minutes or until golden brown.

For the frosting, cream together the cream cheese and butter. Slowly sift in the confectioners' sugar; beat until fully incorporated. The mixture should be free of lumps. Stir in the vanilla and spread over the cooled cake.

Yield: One 9-inch layer cake or 2 loaves.

Jane Vercelli
Thompson, Connecticut

. . . .

LITTLE BIRD'S PEAR CAKE

■

CAKE
1¼ cups whole-wheat pastry flour
¼ teaspoon baking soda
1¾ teaspoons baking powder
¼ teaspoon salt
⅓ cup butter, softened
¾ cup honey
(continued)

A rich and luscious treat with a delectable frosting. The perfect birthday cake.

Preheat oven to 375°F. Sift together the flour, soda, baking powder, and salt. In a separate bowl, cream the butter and add the honey, beating until smooth. Beat in the egg yolks and rum. Add the dry ingredients to the butter mixture in three portions, alternating with the yogurt. Fold in the pears and chocolate chips. Beat the egg whites with a pinch of salt until stiff but not dry. Gently fold into the pear mixture. Bake in 2 greased 8-inch round pans for 25 to 30 minutes. Cool before removing from pans.

2 eggs, separated
1 teaspoon rum or vanilla
1 cup plain yogurt
2 cups pears in ½-inch cubes
½ cup semi-sweet chocolate or
  carob chips
Pinch of salt

FROSTING
½ cup cream from top of
  yogurt, if available, or ½ cup
  plain yogurt
1 package (8 ounces) soft or
  whipped cream cheese
¼ cup maple syrup
½ teaspoon rum or vanilla

For frosting, beat together the cream from the top of the yogurt, cream cheese, maple syrup, and vanilla. Spread between the layers and on the top and sides of the cooled cake.

Yield: 8 to 10 servings.

*Shlomit Auciello
North Billerica, Massachusetts*

. . . .

FRUIT SHORTCAKE

■

2 cups unbleached all-purpose
  flour
1 tablespoon baking powder
½ cup butter or margarine,
  softened
½ cup maple syrup
½ cup maple sugar or plain
  sugar
2 eggs
1 cup plain yogurt
Strawberries, blueberries,
  peaches, or bananas
Yogurt or whipped cream,
  sweetened to taste, for
  topping

We enjoyed the moistness and maple flavor of these shortcakes. Wonderful with cling peaches topped with slightly sweetened plain yogurt. One consumer called them "wicked good."

Preheat oven to 350°F. In a large bowl, sift the flour and baking powder together. In a separate bowl, cream the margarine, maple syrup, and sugar. Slightly beat the eggs and add them to the butter mixture. Add the yogurt and the sifted dry ingredients alternately to the butter mixture. Mix well. Grease Mary Jane pans or muffin tins and spoon ⅓ cup of batter into each cup. Bake for 20 to 25 minutes, then allow to cool.

Remove all stems and pits from the fruit and slice the fruit if appropriate. Top the shortcakes with fruit and then top each cake with slightly sweetened yogurt or whipped cream.

Yield: 12 shortcakes.

*Donna Schmidt
Walpole, New Hampshire*

. . . .

LUSCIOUS POUND CAKE

■

6 ounces cream cheese, softened
1 cup butter or margarine,
   softened
1 cup sugar
2½ cups unbleached all-
   purpose flour
Pinch of salt
4 teaspoons baking powder
½ cup milk
1 cup plain yogurt
1 teaspoon vanilla
4 eggs

A very dense, moist version of a pound cake. It has a delicate flavor and is not overly sweet.

Preheat oven to 350°F. Using an electric mixer, mix together the cream cheese and butter until well blended. Blend in the sugar. In a separate bowl, sift the flour, salt, and baking powder together. Add to the creamed mixture and mix until well blended. Stir in the milk. Mix for about 1 minute, then stir in the yogurt, vanilla, and eggs. Blend for 1 to 2 minutes.

Grease and flour a 10-inch Bundt pan. Pour the batter into the pan, and bake for 1 hour or until the cake is golden brown and a toothpick inserted in the center comes out clean. The cake should spring back when touched. Let the cake cool before removing from pan.

Yield: One 10-inch Bundt cake.

Debra McPhee
Stamford, Connecticut

RICOTTA YOGURT CAKE

■

4 cups ricotta cheese
4 eggs
1 cup plain yogurt
⅓ cup honey or sugar, or to
   taste
2 teaspoons vanilla
Juice and grated rind of ½
   lemon
¼ teaspoon salt
Fresh fruit or preserves for
   topping (optional)

A home-style Italian cheesecake, with great flavor.

Preheat oven to 375°F. Cream the cheese in a bowl. Add the eggs and beat. Add the yogurt, honey, vanilla, lemon juice, rind, and salt, and beat until the mixture is smooth and fluffy. (A food processor with a steel blade can be used to speed up this process.) Pour into a lightly buttered 8-inch spring-form pan.

Place the cheesecake on the middle rack of the oven and a pan of water on the bottom rack. Bake for 45 to 50 minutes. Cool completely and spread with fruit or preserves if desired. Chill before serving.

Yield: 8 to 10 servings.

Maria Sperduti
Cranston, Rhode Island

TRACY'S CHEESECAKE

∎

FILLING

3 eggs at room temperature
¾ cup sugar
2 packages (8 ounces each)
    cream cheese, softened at
    room temperature
Pinch of salt (optional)
2 teaspoons vanilla
½ teaspoon almond extract
2 cups sour cream
1 cup plain yogurt

GLAZE (optional)

1 pint fresh strawberries, hulled
⅔ cup water
1½ tablespoons cornstarch
⅓ cup sugar
⅓ cup water

Try this filling with the crust from Sally Ogden's Maple Yogurt Cheesecake (see page 182).

Make the crumb crust from the Maple Yogurt Cheesecake and chill for 15 minutes.

Preheat oven to 425°F. Beat the eggs and set aside. In a separate bowl, cream the sugar with the cream cheese. Add the beaten eggs, optional salt, vanilla, and almond extract and beat until smooth. Fold in the sour cream and yogurt; pour the batter into the crust.

Bake for 10 to 15 minutes, then reduce oven temperature to 250°F and continue baking for 45 to 60 minutes more. Turn off oven; let the cake cool in oven with the door ajar.

To make the glaze, crush 1 cup of berries with ⅔ cup water. Cook for 2 minutes over medium heat, then press through a sieve. Mix the cornstarch, sugar, and ⅓ cup water until there are no lumps, then stir into the hot berry liquid. Bring to a low boil and cook until thickened. Remove from heat and let cool. Slice the remaining berries and stir them into the glaze, then spoon the glaze over the cheesecake. Serve either at room temperature or chilled.

Yield: One 10-inch cake.

Tracy Grundland
Milford, Connecticut

. . . .

Maple Yogurt Cheesecake

■

CRUST
1 cup graham-cracker crumbs
½ cup ginger-snap crumbs
⅓ cup ground walnuts
⅓ cup butter, melted
½ teaspoon ground cinnamon
½ teaspoon ground ginger

FILLING
4 eggs
3 packages (8 ounces each)
  cream cheese
½ cup maple syrup
1 cup plain yogurt
2 teaspoons vanilla
¼ teaspoon almond extract

Our tester vows she'll throw away her old cheesecake recipe and use this one from now on.

Preheat oven to 325°F. Be sure all ingredients are at room temperature.

Combine the crust ingredients and mix thoroughly. Press into a 10-inch pie plate and chill for 15 minutes.

For the filling, beat the eggs until creamy. In a separate bowl, cream the cream cheese. Add the maple syrup to the cream cheese and stir until well blended. Add the yogurt, vanilla, and almond extract and stir until thoroughly combined. (A food processor with a steel blade can be used to speed up this process.) Pour this mixture into the chilled crumb shell. Bake for 50 to 55 minutes. Remove from oven and cool for 30 minutes, then place in the refrigerator for at least 3 hours before serving.

Yield: One 10-inch cake.

Sally Ogden
Landgrove, Vermont

. . . .

Chocolate Yogurt Cheesecake

■

CRUST
16 chocolate wafers (each 2¼
  inches), crumbled
¼ cup butter, melted

FILLING
2 packages (8 ounces each)
  cream cheese, softened at
  room temperature

(continued)

Rich and creamy, with a delectable chocolate flavor. See photo, page 136.

For the crust, mix the chocolate wafer crumbs and butter together. Press the mixture onto the bottom and against the sides of an 8- or 9-inch spring-form pan. Chill.

Preheat oven to 300°F. For filling, cream together the cream cheese and sugar. Stir in the eggs, then add the vanilla, melted chocolate, and yogurt, and stir until all the ingredients are combined. Spoon the mixture into the crust.

Place the cheesecake on the middle rack of the oven and place a pan of water on the bottom rack. Bake for 50 to 60 minutes. (Do not open the oven door

1 cup sugar

3 eggs at room temperature

1½ teaspoons vanilla

6 squares semi-sweet chocolate, melted and cooled

1 cup plain yogurt

GLAZE (optional)

2 squares semi-sweet chocolate, melted

2 tablespoons butter, melted

1 tablespoon corn syrup

½ teaspoon vanilla

2 ounces white chocolate

while the cheesecake is baking.) Turn off the oven; allow the cake to cool in the oven with the door ajar.

For the glaze, mix the chocolate, butter, corn syrup, and vanilla together while the chocolate and butter are still warm. Allow the glaze to cool, then spread on top of the slightly cooled cheesecake. For a decorative feathered effect, melt the white chocolate. Using a pastry tube, pipe lines of white chocolate across the still-warm glaze, and then drag a knife across the lines to create a pattern (see photo).

Yield: One 8- or 9-inch cake.

Shirley M. Weber
Richfield, Connecticut

. . . .

GRANOLA-CRUST YOGURT CHEESECAKE

■

CRUST

2 cups granola

½ cup walnuts

¼ cup butter, melted

½ teaspoon ground cinnamon

2 teaspoons sesame seeds (optional)

FILLING

2 packages (8 ounces each) cream cheese, softened at room temperature

1 cup plain yogurt

¼ cup honey

1½ teaspoons vanilla

Grated rind of 1 lemon

A tasty, simple cheesecake with a wonderful crust. For a more delicate flavor, substitute yogurt cheese (see page 87) for the cream cheese.

To make the crust, blend the granola and walnuts to a medium-fine consistency in a food processor. Pulse in the butter, cinnamon, and optional sesame seeds. Reserving some crumbs for topping, press the crust mixture onto the bottom and sides of a greased 9-inch pie plate.

For the filling, cream the softened cream cheese in a bowl. Add the yogurt, honey, vanilla, and lemon rind; beat thoroughly. (A food processor with a steel blade can be used to speed up this process.) Spoon the filling into the pie shell. Top with the remaining crumbs and chill for 3 hours before serving.

Yield: One 9-inch cake.

Marcia Appleton
North Conway, New Hampshire

. . . .

BLUEBERRY YOGURT BUCKLE

■

½ cup butter or margarine, softened
½ cup honey
2 eggs
1 teaspoon vanilla
1 cup plain yogurt
1 cup unbleached all-purpose flour
1 cup whole-wheat flour
1¾ teaspoons baking powder
1 teaspoon baking soda
⅛ teaspoon salt

TOPPING
½ cup brown sugar
2 tablespoons unbleached all-purpose flour
2 teaspoons ground cinnamon
2 tablespoons butter, melted
½ cup walnuts, chopped (optional)
2 cups fresh or frozen blueberries

Sweet, nutty, and wet with berries. Very easy and very good.

Preheat oven to 350°F. In a large bowl, cream the butter and honey together thoroughly. Add the eggs and vanilla; beat well. Blend in the yogurt. In a smaller bowl, sift together the flours, baking powder, soda, and salt. Add the flour mixture to the butter mixture and stir together until well combined.

In another small bowl, prepare the topping by combining the brown sugar, flour, cinnamon, butter, and optional nuts.

Spread half the batter in a greased 9-inch square pan. Sprinkle with half the blueberries, then with half the topping. Spoon on the remaining batter. Cover with the remaining blueberries, then add the last of the topping. Bake for 40 to 45 minutes or until a toothpick inserted in the center comes out clean. Cut into squares and serve warm.

Yield: 6 to 8 servings.

Maurine Weaver
Hampton Beach, New Hampshire

. . . .

GREAT GINGERBREAD

■

½ cup butter, softened
½ cup sugar
¾ cup molasses
1 cup plain yogurt
2 cups unbleached all-purpose
  flour
2 teaspoons baking soda
2 teaspoons ground ginger
¾ teaspoon ground cinnamon
4 eggs, beaten

Some of the best gingerbread we've ever tasted — so moist, with the perfect blend of sweetness and spice. Serve it with freshly whipped cream, ice cream, or frozen yogurt.

Preheat oven to 425°F. In a large bowl, cream the butter and sugar together. Add the molasses and mix well. Stir in the yogurt. Sift together the flour, soda, ginger, and cinnamon and stir into the yogurt mixture. Stir in the eggs. Pour into a well-greased 9x13-inch pan. Bake for 40 minutes, or until a toothpick inserted in the center comes out clean.

Yield: 24 small pieces.

Barbara Horowitz
Needham, Massachusetts

• •

YOGURT LEMON COOKIES

■

¾ cup granulated sugar
¼ cup confectioners' sugar
1 cup shortening, cold
1 large egg
1 cup lemon or plain yogurt
3 cups unbleached all-purpose
  flour
½ teaspoon baking powder
½ teaspoon baking soda
¼ teaspoon salt, slightly
  rounded
Grated rind of 1 lemon
Granulated sugar for topping
  (optional)

Like a melt-in-your-mouth sugar cookie. Easy to prepare, and a real treat for lemon lovers.

Preheat oven to 350°F. Lightly grease the cookie sheets. In a large bowl, mix the sugars, shortening, and egg with an electric beater until mixture is light and fluffy. Add the yogurt and beat until combined. In another bowl, whisk together the flour, baking powder, soda, salt, and lemon rind. Stir the dry ingredients into the yogurt mixture and combine well.

Drop by rounded tablespoons onto the cookie sheets. Bake for 15 minutes. Remove from oven and, while cookies are still hot, sprinkle granulated sugar on top of each, if desired.

Yield: 2 dozen.

Irene Prince
Farmington Hills, Michigan

• •

185

BUTTER COOKIES

■

1½ cups butter, softened
3 cups sifted unbleached all-
   purpose flour
2 egg yolks
1¼ cups plain yogurt
1½ cups sugar
4½ teaspoons ground cinnamon
½ cup chopped walnuts

Sweet cookies that look as if they were baked by a French pastry chef. A sure sell-out at any bake sale.

Cut the butter into the flour with your fingertips until the mixture resembles cornmeal. Add the egg yolks and yogurt. Shape the dough into a ball and sprinkle with additional flour. Wrap well in waxed paper (or place in a glass bowl and cover tightly with plastic wrap); chill for at least 2 hours.

Preheat oven to 375°F. In a small bowl, combine the sugar, cinnamon, and walnuts. Sprinkle a bread-board or pastry cloth lightly with flour. Divide the dough into 4 portions. Roll one part into a large circle about ⅛ to ¼ inch thick. (Cut around the edge of a dinner plate to get the edge perfect.) Sprinkle with the nut and cinnamon mixture, and press any large nut pieces into the dough with the rolling pin.

Cut the circle into 6 or 8 pie-shaped wedges. Roll up each wedge starting at the widest end; if you like, curl the outside edges to make them resemble croissants. Place on a greased cookie sheet. Repeat with the remaining 3 portions.

Bake for 25 minutes, then remove the cookies to a rack to cool. Store in a tightly closed container; they taste even better the next day.

Yield: 2 to 3 dozen.

Barbara Remboski
Northborough, Massachusetts

. . . .

FROZEN DESSERTS

YOGURT ICE CREAM

■

2 cups unsweetened straw-
   berries, raspberries, peaches,
   blueberries, or any mixture
   (fresh or frozen)
2 cups plain yogurt
½ cup honey
1 tablespoon vanilla
1 cup heavy cream, whipped

Cool and sweet, this will refresh on a summer day or melt your winter blues. Kids love it, too.

Mash the fruit by hand or blend in a blender. In a bowl, combine the yogurt, honey, and vanilla and mix well. Add the fruit and blend. Fold in the whipped cream. Pour into a covered freezer container. Freeze for 4 to 5 hours before using. (If frozen for a longer period of time, allow the ice cream to sit at room temperature for 5 to 10 minutes before serving. It freezes very hard.)

Yield: 1 quart.

Marilyn Magnus
Barnet, Vermont

CHEESE FREEZE

■

1 cup plain yogurt
1 cup cottage cheese
¼ cup honey
¾ cup chopped fresh fruit

Quick and easy to prepare, and an excellent low-calorie treat. It's fun to be creative with this one; try adding shredded coconut, nutmeg, or anything else that complements the fruit.

Purée all the ingredients in a blender until smooth. Freeze in a covered pan for about 2 hours or until half-frozen. Turn out into a chilled bowl and whip with an electric mixer until fluffy. Return to pan. Cover and freeze solid. Let soften at room temperature for 10 minutes before serving.

Yield: 1 quart.

Joanie LeViness
Winsted, Connecticut

187

BERRY GOOD FROZEN YOGURT

■

1 cup raspberry or blueberry
  yogurt
1 cup whipped cream
1½ teaspoons lemon juice
1 teaspoon vanilla
1 cup fresh or frozen raspberries
  or blueberries
1 can (8 ounces) crushed
  pineapple, drained
2 medium bananas, chopped
2 medium unpeeled apples,
  cored and chopped (optional)
½ cup chopped walnuts
Lettuce

A creamy yogurt concoction that tastes like real ice cream. Absolutely delicious even when not frozen.

Combine the yogurt, whipped cream, lemon juice, and vanilla in a bowl; blend well. Reserve a few berries for garnish, then fold into the mixture the remaining berries and the pineapple, bananas, optional apples, and nuts. Spoon the mixture into a 4½-cup ring mold and freeze for several hours. Unmold onto a lettuce-lined serving plate. Let stand for 10 minutes at room temperature before serving, or for 15 to 20 minutes if it has been frozen overnight. Garnish with the additional berries.

Note: To make unmolding easier, first place the ring mold in a pan of warm water for about 2 minutes or until the frozen yogurt falls out of the mold when inverted and gently tapped.

Yield: 4 to 6 servings.

*Sandy Brodie
Chelmsford, Massachusetts*

. . . .

FROZEN RASPBERRY YOGURT CREAM

■

1 package (12 ounces) frozen
  raspberries without sugar,
  thawed
¾ cup sugar (or more to taste)
Squeeze of fresh lemon juice
2 cups plain yogurt
¾ cup heavy cream
2 to 3 tablespoons Framboise
  (optional)

A smooth and (as the name indicates) creamy raspberry dessert that tastes like a cross between ice cream and sherbet. Light and delicious — a real winner! See photo, page 56.

Purée the thawed raspberries in a food processor, using the steel blade. Transfer to a sieve and press the mixture through the sieve into a bowl. Discard the seeds. Mix the sugar, lemon juice, yogurt, cream, and optional Framboise into the raspberry juice. Place in the container of an ice cream maker, and freeze according to manufacturer's instructions.

This dessert can be eaten right away or transferred to a freezer container and stored in the freezer until you're ready to serve it. If the mixture becomes too hard in the freezer, let it soften in the refrigerator before serving.

Yield: About 1 quart.

Anne S. Dehman
Sharon, Massachusetts

. . . .

PEACH PRESERVE & HONEY FROZEN YOGURT

■

¾ **cup canned, drained peaches**
1½ **cups plain yogurt**
⅓ **cup honey**

Simple and very peachy-creamy.

Purée the peaches in a blender. Add the yogurt and honey and blend until thoroughly mixed. Freeze in an ice cream maker, following manufacturer's instructions. If you don't use this dessert immediately, it can be stored in the freezer but must be allowed to soften before serving.

Note: If you don't have an ice cream maker, the following method works very well. Transfer the mixture to a square baking dish and cover with plastic wrap. Freeze overnight or for at least 6 hours. Let the mixture thaw slightly, then return it to the blender and mix once more before serving.

Variation for pineapple lovers: Substitute 2 cups diced pineapple (fresh or canned unsweetened) for the peaches and ⅓ cup sugar for the honey.

Yield: 2½ cups.

Debra Fitzsimmons
Deep Cove, North Vancouver, British Columbia, Canada

. . . .

FROZEN FRUIT YOGURT

■

2 cups fresh raspberries,
  blueberries, or other fruit
1 banana, mashed
¾ cup sugar
½ cup frozen orange juice
  concentrate
2 cups plain yogurt
1 teaspoon vanilla

A simple and refreshing treat that's also delicious with canned fruit. Scoop it over fresh berries, mold it into popsicles, or serve it in parfait glasses with a helping of chocolate sauce.

Mash all the fruit; if using berries, run them through a sieve to remove large seeds. Mix all the ingredients together with a wire whisk; freeze in any suitable container for about 6 hours or until hard. Remove from freezer and allow to sit at room temperature for 20 minutes before serving.

Variation: Use peaches for the fruit and substitute brown sugar for the granulated sugar. Delicious!

Yield: 6 to 8 servings.

Sara Fielder
Brownsville, Oregon

. . . .

YUMMY YOGURT TORTONI

■

1 cup plain yogurt
¾ cup confectioners' sugar
1 teaspoon vanilla
1 teaspoon rum or rum
  flavoring
1 cup heavy cream
1 cup fresh strawberries, rinsed,
  drained, and hulled (or use
  frozen)
⅓ cup crumbs made from crisp
  macaroons

A rich, dreamy dessert that tastes like a frozen mousse. Elegant, yet easy to prepare.

In a bowl, stir together the yogurt, sugar, vanilla, and rum flavoring. Whip the heavy cream until peaks form, then fold it into the yogurt mixture. Reserve a few strawberries for garnish; fold in the remaining berries and one-fourth of the crumbs.

Fill 4 demitasse cups with the mixture; sprinkle with the remaining crumbs. Freeze hard, then cover with plastic wrap and store in freezer until needed. Just before serving, decorate with reserved berries. Serve in demitasse cups set on saucers.

Yield: 4 servings.

Barbara Horowitz
Needham, Massachusetts

. . . .

KIWI PECAN MOUSSE

■

2 cups plain yogurt
¾ cup maple syrup
6 egg yolks, well beaten
Pinch of salt
2 to 3 kiwis, peeled and sliced
½ cup ground or chopped pecans
Whole pecans for garnish

Light, refreshing, and unusual. Especially pretty when made in a large glass bowl.

Stir the yogurt until smooth. In a double boiler, heat the maple syrup until just warm. Slowly add the egg yolks, stirring constantly. Add the salt and stir over low heat for 3 to 4 minutes or until the mixture thickens. Remove from heat and stir until cool. Fold in the yogurt.

Line a large bowl or individual small bowls with sliced kiwi; sprinkle with chopped pecans. Pour the yogurt mixture over the kiwi-pecan layer, garnish with whole pecans, and freeze. Let soften at room temperature for 10 minutes before serving. If there are leftovers, be sure to refreeze them.

Yield: 6 to 8 servings.

Wendy Guyer
Charlottesville, Virginia

. . . .

STRAWBERRY DESSERT

■

2 cups low-fat plain yogurt
¼ cup powdered milk
1 pint fresh ripe strawberries, hulled and mashed

Quick and low in calories, but very good anyway!

Mix all the ingredients together. Spread in an 8-inch square pan or glass dish, cover, and freeze until hard. Before serving, remove from freezer and let stand at room temperature for about 30 minutes or until the dessert can be cut. Cut into squares and serve plain or with shaved maple sugar or brown sugar.

Variation: To satisfy a sweet tooth, stir 2 or more tablespoons of honey into the mixture before freezing.

Yield: 6 to 8 servings.

Sharon L. Marshall
Boston, Massachusetts

. . . .

ROCKY PASTURE PIE

■

FILLING
2 cups plain yogurt
3 tablespoons maple syrup
2 tablespoons sugar
1 teaspoon instant coffee granules
3 tablespoons boiling water
⅓ cup semi-sweet chocolate chips
1 banana, sliced in rounds
½ cup chopped walnuts

CHOCOLATE GRAHAM-CRACKER CRUST
½ cup butter
⅓ cup semi-sweet chocolate chips
2 cups graham-cracker crumbs

Freshly assembled, this is a delicious "ice cream" pie. If frozen and served the next day, allow it to soften in the refrigerator for half an hour before serving.

To make the filling, stir together the yogurt, maple syrup, and sugar in a bowl. In a coffee mug, combine the coffee granules and hot water. Add the chocolate chips to the coffee and mix until most of the chips are melted. Stir the coffee mixture into the yogurt. Pour the mixture into an ice-cream maker and stir constantly for about 30 minutes or until thick.

Preheat oven to 300°F. To make the crust, melt the butter and chocolate chips in a saucepan. Pour the mixture into the crumbs and stir together. Pat the mixture into a buttered 9-inch pie plate or individual custard cups. Bake for 10 minutes or until crisp. Cool.

Layer the cooled crust with the sliced banana and sprinkle with chopped walnuts. Smooth the yogurt ice cream over the top. Serve immediately or freeze.

Yield: 8 to 10 pieces.

Connie Fischer
Durham, New Hampshire

· ·

BELLA'S BEST POPSICLES

■

1 cup fresh peaches, apricots, strawberries, raspberries, or bananas
1 cup plain yogurt
Sugar

Easily made and blissfully cooling. A wonderful creamy treat for kids.

Peel all the fruit and remove seeds, stems, and pits. Mash the fruit; if using berries, run them through a sieve to remove the seeds. Blend the yogurt with the fruit. Sweeten with sugar, to taste. Place in popsicle molds and freeze.

Yield: 6 popsicles.

Arabella Campbell
Loughborough Inlet, British Columbia, Canada

· ·

YOGURT POPSICLES

■

1 cup plain yogurt
1 cup frozen orange juice concentrate, or mashed mango pulp

A nutritious, simple snack the kids can make by themselves. But they won't be the only ones eating them!

Mix the yogurt and the orange juice concentrate. Put into a popsicle mold, insert sticks, and freeze.

Variation: For a change of pace, use any fruit concentrate in place of the orange juice or mango pulp.

Yield: 6 popsicles.

Zana M. Lutfiyya
Syracuse, New York

. . . .

CARA'S DELIGHT

■

18 Nabisco Famous Chocolate Wafers (do not substitute) rolled into crumbs
3 tablespoons butter, melted
1 cup plain yogurt, well mixed
2 teaspoons vanilla
3 large strawberries, hulled and chopped
Sliced strawberries for garnish

A chocolate lover's dream, with a deliciously rich, buttery chocolate wafer crust. Best served when texture is semi-frozen.

Set aside about one-third of the crumbs; mix the remaining crumbs in the melted butter. Press the buttered crumbs into two 6-ounce custard dishes to form crusts. Mix together the yogurt, vanilla, chopped strawberries, and remaining crumbs. Pour the mixture into the crusts and freeze. Remove from the freezer and let thaw somewhat before serving. Top with sliced strawberries and serve.

Yield: 2 servings.

J. J. Costanzo
Nashua, New Hampshire

. . . .

193

YOGURT BARS

∎

2 cups fruited yogurt (any
flavor)
1 cup peeled and chopped fresh
fruit (or substitute frozen
fruit that's been thawed)
⅔ cup nonfat dry milk
1⅓ cups Grape-Nuts cereal
⅔ cup oat bran

*A crunchy, healthful, flavorful snack, and a good way
to serve roughage. Kids love them.*

Blend the yogurt, fruit, and dry milk in a food processor or by hand. In a separate bowl, combine the Grape-Nuts and oat bran. Fold into the yogurt mixture. Pour into an 8-inch square pan and freeze. Cut into bars before completely frozen, and wrap individually. Store in freezer.

Yield: 15 medium-size bars.

*Susan Risse
Fairbanks, Alaska*

FROZEN YOGURT SANDWICH

∎

1 teaspoon unflavored gelatin
¼ cup cold water
2 cups flavored yogurt
¼ cup sugar or honey
½ cup chopped nuts
18 graham crackers

*A new and delicious ice cream sandwich that keeps
well in the freezer. Our tester, who used raspberry
yogurt and honey, reported that her children couldn't
get enough.*

In a small saucepan, soften the gelatin in the water. Cook over low heat, stirring frequently, until gelatin is dissolved. In a large bowl, combine the gelatin, yogurt, sugar, and nuts. Arrange half the graham crackers on the bottom of a 9x13-inch pan. Spread the yogurt mixture on top, then cover with the remaining crackers. Cover with foil and freeze until firm. Cut between the crackers and serve.

Yield: 9 bars.

*Wilma VanHerk
Morinville, Alberta, Canada*

PIES, PUDDINGS & OTHER DESSERTS

PEACHES & CREAM PIE

■

CRUST
½ cup butter, softened
1½ cups unbleached all-
  purpose flour
½ teaspoon salt

FILLING
4 cups peeled and sliced fresh
  peaches
¾ cup sugar, divided
2 tablespoons tapioca
1 egg
¼ teaspoon salt
½ teaspoon vanilla
1 cup plain yogurt

TOPPING
⅓ cup brown sugar
¼ cup butter
⅓ cup unbleached all-purpose
  flour
1 teaspoon ground cinnamon

A sublime dessert, not overly sweet, that takes no time to make for unexpected company.

Preheat oven to 400°F. To make the crust, cut the butter into the flour and salt. Press the dough into a 9- or 10-inch deep-dish pie plate.

To make the filling, place the peaches in a bowl, sprinkle with ¼ cup sugar, and let stand. In a separate bowl, combine ½ cup sugar with the tapioca, egg, salt, and vanilla. Fold in the yogurt. Pour the mixture over the peaches and stir to combine. Pour the filling into the crust. Bake for 15 minutes, then reduce heat to 350°F and bake for 20 minutes longer.

Combine all the topping ingredients. Sprinkle the topping evenly over the filling, then bake 5 to 10 minutes more. Serve warm or cold.

Note: If you use sweetened canned peaches rather than fresh ones, reduce the amount of sugar in the rest of the recipe. Omit the step of sprinkling sugar over the sliced peaches and use just ¼ cup sugar with the tapioca.

Yield: One 9- or 10-inch deep-dish pie (6 to 8 servings).

Gillian Richardson
Regina, Saskatchewan, Canada

YOGURT STRAWBERRY PIE

■

1 pint whipping cream
1 teaspoon vanilla
1 teaspoon sugar
2 cups strawberry yogurt
1 pint fresh strawberries, hulled and quartered
1 large ripe banana, sliced
9-inch graham-cracker pie shell
Whole fresh, hulled strawberries, for garnish

Fluffy, pink, creamy, and fit for company. If you're making the crust yourself, prepare that first, because the filling will thin out if it sits too long.

Whip the cream with the vanilla and sugar until peaks form. Fold in the yogurt, strawberries, and banana. Pour the filling into the pie shell. Chill for 2 hours before serving. Garnish with fresh strawberries if desired.

Variation: In place of the strawberries and strawberry yogurt, try fresh peaches and peach yogurt — or any other fruit and yogurt combination.

Yield: One 9-inch pie (6 to 8 servings).

Debra Herron
Buzzards Bay, Massachusetts

APPLE HONEY CUSTARD PIE

■

2½ cups cored, peeled, and sliced apples
1 unbaked 9-inch pie shell
4 large eggs
¾ cup honey
1 cup plain yogurt
1 teaspoon vanilla
½ teaspoon ground cinnamon
¼ teaspoon salt
Sliced almonds
Ground nutmeg

Simple, quick, smooth, and good.

Preheat oven to 375°F. Spread the apple slices in the pie shell. In the bowl of an electric mixer, combine the eggs, honey, yogurt, vanilla, cinnamon, and salt; beat on high speed until well mixed. Pour the mixture over the apples. Top with almonds and sprinkle lightly with nutmeg. Bake for about 45 minutes or until the pie looks solid when jiggled. Do not overbake.

Yield: One 9-inch pie (6 to 8 servings).

Ann Lutz
Black Mountain, North Carolina

YOGURT-CREAM APPLE PIE

■

CRUST
2 cups unbleached all-purpose
flour
½ teaspoon salt
1 teaspoon ground cinnamon
¾ cup butter or margarine
5 to 6 tablespoons cold water

FILLING
2 cups plain yogurt
⅓ cup whole-wheat flour
½ cup barley malt
2 teaspoons vanilla
½ teaspoon salt
1 egg, or substitute 1 teaspoon
baking powder, 1½ table-
spoons vegetable oil, and 1½
tablespoons apple juice
8 sweet cooking apples such as
Cortlands or Winesaps, cored,
peeled, and thinly sliced

TOPPING
6 tablespoons butter, softened
½ cup unbleached all-purpose
flour
½ cup date sugar (available at
most natural-foods stores)
1 tablespoon blackstrap molasses
1 tablespoon ground cinnamon
Pinch of salt
1 cup walnuts or pecans,
chopped

A pleasing, simple pie, not overly sweet. Serve with vanilla ice cream for that extra indulgence.

To make the crust, combine the flour, salt, and cinnamon. Cut in the butter with a fork. Stir in the water 1 tablespoon at a time until the dough begins to stick together. Roll out on a floured breadboard, then place in a 10-inch deep-dish pie plate.

Preheat oven to 450°F. For the filling, combine the yogurt, flour, barley malt, vanilla, and salt. Beat the egg well and stir it quickly into the yogurt mixture. Place the apple slices in a separate bowl, pour the yogurt mixture over them, and stir until the apples are thoroughly coated. Spoon the filling into the crust and bake for 10 minutes. Reduce heat to 350°F and bake for 40 minutes more or until the pie is lightly browned and puffed up.

For topping, mix the butter, flour, sugar, molasses, cinnamon, and salt together until crumbly. Mix in the nuts and stir to coat them. Spoon the topping over the pie and bake 15 to 20 minutes longer. Let sit until cooled before serving.

Yield: One 10-inch pie (8 to 10 servings).

Cherie Sisti
Scarborough, Maine

PEACH YOGURT CUSTARD PIE

■

⅓ cup butter, softened
¾ cup maple syrup
3 eggs
1½ cups plain yogurt
2 teaspoons lemon juice
1 teaspoon grated lemon rind
8 to 10 peach halves, canned or
  fresh, peeled

A light, delicious custard that's quickly prepared. There's no crust, which is a boon to those who are cutting calories.

Preheat oven to 325°F. Cream the butter and syrup; add the eggs, yogurt, lemon juice, and rind. Beat well. Place the peach halves in an ungreased 9-inch pie plate, flat side down, until the plate is full. Pour the batter over the peaches. Bake for 45 minutes or until set.

Yield: 8 generous servings.

Jane Dwinell
Irasburg, Vermont

BANANA MINT YOGURT PIE

■

YOGURT CHEESE
2 quarts plain yogurt

CRUST
¾ cup finely crushed graham
  crackers
¾ cup finely chopped pecans
  or walnuts
¼ cup light brown sugar
⅓ cup butter or margarine,
  melted
¼ teaspoon ground cinnamon

FILLING
1 teaspoon unflavored gelatin
⅓ cup water
¼ cup honey
1 cup mashed banana (about 2
  medium bananas)
10 fresh mint leaves, finely
  chopped

A creamy yogurt pie with the fresh taste of mint. Be sure to prepare the yogurt cheese a day ahead, and allow plenty of time for chilling the pie; the results are well worth it.

Drain the yogurt for 8 to 10 hours to make yogurt cheese; see instructions on page 87.

Mix all the crust ingredients in a bowl until well blended. Using the back of a spoon, press the mixture to the bottom and sides of a well-greased 9-inch pie plate. Chill for at least 2 hours. This is important; if the crust is not chilled, the yogurt mixture will make the crust soggy.

To prepare the filling, sprinkle the gelatin over the water in a small saucepan; let stand for 5 minutes to soften. Heat the gelatin mixture over very low heat until it clears and dissolves; set aside to cool.

Combine the honey and mashed banana in a bowl; add the gelatin mixture slowly, stirring until smooth. Measure 2¾ cups of the yogurt cheese and stir into the banana mixture until thoroughly blended; save any remaining yogurt cheese for another use. Fold the mint leaves into the mixture. Pour the filling into the

TOPPING
2 bananas, sliced
2 tablespoons lemon juice
Fresh mint sprigs, for garnish

prepared crust; chill for at least 3 hours.

Brush the banana slices with lemon juice and arrange them on top of the pie. Garnish with mint sprigs.

Variation I: Drain 9 cups of yogurt to make yogurt cheese. Prepare the gelatin as directed above. Combine ⅓ cup honey with 1 tablespoon grated orange rind and ¼ cup orange juice. Add the gelatin. Measure 3 cups yogurt cheese and stir into the mixture. Pour into the prepared crust; chill for 5 hours or overnight. Garnish with 2 cups halved seedless green grapes and 1 orange cut into sections.

Variation II: Drain 9 cups of yogurt to make yogurt cheese. Prepare the gelatin as directed above. Combine the gelatin with ⅓ cup honey, 1 teaspoon vanilla, and 3 cups yogurt cheese. Pour into the prepared crust and chill for 5 hours. Garnish with 1 pint hulled and halved strawberries, mint leaves, and chopped nuts.

Yield: One 9-inch pie (6 to 8 servings).

Christine Taylor
Norbertville, Quebec, Canada

. . . .

LEMON PIE

■

1 cup sugar
3½ tablespoons cornstarch
1 tablespoon lemon rind
½ cup freshly squeezed lemon juice
3 egg yolks
1 cup milk
¼ cup butter
1 cup plain yogurt
1 baked 9-inch pie shell
1 cup heavy cream, whipped
Lemon rind, for garnish

Easy, creamy, and elegant.

In a large saucepan, mix together the sugar, cornstarch, lemon rind, lemon juice, egg yolks, and milk over medium heat until thick. Add the butter and stir until melted. Allow the mixture to cool, then stir in the yogurt. Pour into the pie shell. Cover with the whipped cream and add the lemon rind for garnish. Chill for 1 hour before serving.

Yield: One 9-inch pie (6 to 8 servings).

Elaine Park
Williston, Vermont

. . . .

MAPLE STRAWBERRY CRUMBLE

■

1 cup Grape-Nuts cereal
¼ cup butter, melted
1 tablespoon honey
1 quart plain yogurt
8 teaspoons maple syrup
1½ cups sliced fresh strawberries (or any fresh fruit)

A delicious crunchy crust with sweet maple filling.

Preheat oven to 350°F. Combine the Grape-Nuts, butter, and honey and press the mixture into a 9-inch pie plate to form a bottom crust. Bake for 6 to 8 minutes. Cool.

Thoroughly combine the yogurt and the maple syrup and spoon the mixture into the cool pie crust; top with strawberries. Don't attempt to serve this crumble like a pie but spoon it out into individual glass dessert dishes. The flavors will mingle nicely.

Yield: 4 to 6 servings.

Katie Jarvis
Rye, New Hampshire

. . . .

MOCK SOUR CREAM PIE

■

CRUST
1 cup plus 1 tablespoon
  unbleached all-purpose flour
Sprinkle of salt
⅓ cup sunflower oil, scant
2 to 3 tablespoons cold water

FILLING
1 cup brown sugar
2 tablespoons unbleached all-
  purpose flour or cornstarch
3 eggs, separated
1 cup plain yogurt
1 cup raisins, rinsed in hot
  water if not moist
¼ cup granulated sugar

Tastes like an old-fashioned raisin pie, with a pleasant mix of sweet and tart.

Preheat oven to 400°F. To make the crust, mix the flour and salt in a bowl. Add the oil, mixing it in with a fork, or combine the ingredients in a food processor until the mixture is crumbly. Add the cold water and mix. Work the dough into a ball with your hands. Roll it out on floured waxed paper. (Note: you can roll out this dough only once or twice.)

Use the dough to form a bottom crust in an 8- or 9-inch pie plate. Prick it and let it brown in the oven for 15 to 20 minutes. When done, the crust will be dry and opaque.

For the filling, combine the sugar and flour. In a separate bowl, stir the egg yolks into the yogurt. Blend the yogurt mixture into the sugar mixture. Stirring constantly, cook in a saucepan over medium heat until simmering. Cook 1 minute more. Beat with a whisk if necessary to remove lumps. Stir in the raisins. Remove from heat and let rest 3 to 5 minutes, stirring occasionally. Pour into the cooked pie shell.

Preheat oven to 350°F. Whip the egg whites until soft peaks form. Gradually add the granulated sugar while continuing to whip. Pile this meringue on top of the filling; be sure the meringue completely covers the filling and overlaps the crust. Bake for 15 minutes or until lightly browned. Cool before serving.

Yield: One 8- or 9-inch pie (6 to 8 servings).

Bonnie Vanni
Hagersville, Ontario, Canada

. . . .

BANANA YOGURT PIE

■

FILLING
1 large ripe banana
3 eggs
2 cups plain yogurt
2 tablespoons maple syrup
¼ cup unsweetened coconut

CRUST
1 cup walnut pieces
1 package (⅓ of 16-ounce box)
   all-natural graham crackers
¼ cup raisins
¼ cup wheat germ
¼ cup butter
¼ cup maple syrup

A refreshing variation on the typical banana cream pie. The crust is particularly flavorful.

Preheat oven to 350°F. For the filling, mash the banana and eggs together until smooth. Stir in the yogurt, maple syrup, and coconut. Set aside.

For the crust, blend the walnuts and graham crackers together in a food processor until fine. Pulse in the raisins and wheat germ. Melt the butter and pulse it into the dry mixture with the maple syrup. Press the crust into a lightly greased 9-inch pie plate. Add the filling and bake for 40 to 55 minutes or until firm. After cooling to room temperature, refrigerate. Serve cold.

Yield: One 9-inch pie (6 to 8 servings).

Cheryl Magoveny
Boston, Massachusetts

. . . .

YOGURT & CREAM CHEESE PIE

■

CRUST
1¾ cups graham-cracker crumbs
¼ cup sugar
⅓ cup butter or margarine, melted

FILLING
1 package (8 ounces) cream cheese, softened at room temperature
½ cup sugar
3 eggs
2 teaspoons vanilla (or substitute 2 teaspoons lemon juice plus 2 teaspoons grated lemon rind)
¼ teaspoon salt
2 cups plain yogurt

A smooth, custardlike cheese pie, with a sweet and crunchy graham-cracker crust. Try serving it with berries on the side.

Preheat oven to 350°F. To make the crust, combine the crumbs, sugar, and margarine. Press the mixture over the bottom and sides of a 10-inch pie plate. Bake for 5 minutes. Let cool, then refrigerate for 1 hour.

For the filling, combine the cream cheese and sugar in the bowl of an electric mixer. Beat in the eggs one at a time. Add the vanilla and salt and beat at medium speed until light. Using low speed, blend in the yogurt. Pour into the crumb-lined pan. Bake for 40 to 45 minutes or until the filling feels dry when lightly touched. Cool on counter, then chill before serving.

Yield: One 10-inch pie (6 to 8 servings).

Helen F. Weissman
Palm Springs, California

. . . .

GREEK-STYLE BLUEBERRY PIE

■

Unbaked pastry for a 9-inch pie shell (not rolled out)
½ cup finely chopped walnuts
3 tablespoons honey
1 package (8 ounces) cream cheese, softened at room temperature
2 tablespoons lemon juice
1 tablespoon grated lemon rind
¼ teaspoon ground allspice
1 cup plain yogurt
1½ cups blueberries

An easy-to-make blueberry delight.

Preheat oven to 450°F. Add the nuts to the pie-crust dough. Roll out the dough, place in a 9-inch pie plate, and bake for 10 to 12 minutes or until lightly browned. Cool.

Cream the honey and cheese together. Add the lemon juice, rind, and allspice and blend. Fold in the yogurt gradually. Fold in the blueberries. Pour the filling into the crust and chill for 24 hours before serving.

Yield: One 9-inch pie (6 to 8 servings).

Cheryl Veitch
Quesnel, British Columbia, Canada

. . . .

Blueberry Cream Dessert

■

CRUST

1¼ cups graham-cracker crumbs

¼ cup sugar

6 tablespoons butter or margarine, melted

FILLING

½ cup sugar

1 package (¼ ounce) unflavored gelatin

¾ cup cold water

1 cup sour cream

1 cup blueberry yogurt

½ teaspoon vanilla

½ cup whipping cream

1 cup fresh or frozen blueberries

Wonderful! Smooth, great tasting, impressive looking, and easy to prepare. But not for you if you're counting calories!

For the crust, mix together the graham-cracker crumbs, sugar, and butter. Reserve ¼ cup of the crumb mixture to sprinkle over the top of the pie; press the remainder into an 8- or 9-inch spring-form pan.

For the filling, heat the sugar, gelatin, and water in a small saucepan, stirring until the sugar and gelatin are dissolved. Remove from heat and set aside to cool while preparing the other ingredients.

Stir together the sour cream and yogurt. Gradually blend in the gelatin mixture, then add the vanilla and stir. In a separate bowl, whip the cream; fold it into the yogurt mixture. Fold in the berries.

Spread the filling on the crust and sprinkle the reserved crumbs over the top. Chill for at least 4 hours or until well set. Set out half an hour before serving.

Yield: One 8- or 9-inch dessert (8 servings).

Beverly Butcher
Williams Lake, British Columbia, Canada

. . . .

BLUEBERRY YOGURT PIE

■

CRUST
1¾ cups graham-cracker
    crumbs
6 tablespoons butter, melted
¼ cup sugar

FILLING
3 large eggs
¾ cup sugar
1 cup plain yogurt
2 cups fresh blueberries

Delicious, simple, and attractive, too. Wonderfully fruity and not overly sweet. If you really want to indulge, top with a little whipped cream or vanilla ice cream.

Preheat oven to 325°F. For the crust, mix the graham-cracker crumbs, butter, and sugar until well blended. Use the back of a spoon to press the mixture to the bottom and sides of a well-greased 10-inch pie plate. Refrigerate while preparing the filling.

For the filling, stir together the eggs, sugar, and yogurt until well blended. Fold in the blueberries. Pour the filling into the crust and bake for 45 to 55 minutes. Cool and refrigerate until firm.

Yield: One 10-inch pie (8 to 10 servings).

Ann Lutz
Black Mountain, North Carolina

• •

KEY LIME PIE

■

2½ quarts plain yogurt
2 envelopes (¼ ounce each)
    unflavored gelatin
1 cup boiling water
¾ cup fresh lime juice
1 tablespoon grated lime rind
½ cup sugar, or more to taste

A tangy, crustless custard pie that's a lime lover's dream. Also good in a graham-cracker or chocolate-cookie crumb crust.

The day before serving, drain the yogurt for 8 to 10 hours to make yogurt cheese (see directions on page 87).

In a large bowl, dissolve the gelatin in the boiling water. Add the lime juice, rind, and sugar. Stir well. Add 3 cups of the yogurt cheese to the gelatin mixture, stirring until smooth; reserve any remaining yogurt cheese for another use. Pour the mixture into an ungreased 9-inch pie pan and chill until firm.

Yield: One 9-inch pie (6 to 8 servings).

Cathy Malcolmson
Thornhill, Ontario, Canada

• •

ABC (Almond Banana Custard) Pie

■

CRUST
1⅓ cups unbleached all-
  purpose flour
¾ teaspoon baking powder
¾ cup sugar
¼ cup cocoa
1 teaspoon almond extract
⅓ cup vegetable oil
½ cup orange juice
½ cup sliced almonds
½ cup semi-sweet chocolate
  chips

FILLING
½ cup apricot or raspberry
  preserves

CUSTARD
2 cups plain yogurt
1 egg
½ cup sugar
1 teaspoon vanilla
1 tablespoon cornstarch
1 medium banana, broken into
  large chunks
3 teaspoons sugar
1 teaspoon cocoa

A rich, very special dessert. The delicious chocolate-almond crust has just a hint of orange.

Preheat oven to 350°F. To make the crust, combine and mix well the flour, baking powder, sugar, cocoa, almond extract, oil, and juice. Add the almonds and chocolate chips. Press the dough on the bottom of a well oiled 10-inch glass pie plate. Spread the preserves on top of the dough.

To make the custard, blend the yogurt, egg, ½ cup sugar, vanilla, cornstarch, and banana in a blender; pour the custard mixture on top of the preserves. Combine 3 teaspoons sugar with 1 teaspoon cocoa and sprinkle on top of the custard. Bake for at least 30 to 40 minutes or until done. Allow to cool before serving. Store leftovers in the refrigerator.

Yield: One 10-inch pie (6 to 8 servings).

Barbara Turesky
Chestnut Hill, Massachusetts

COCONUT TARTS

■

3 cups plain yogurt
¼ cup margarine or butter, softened
½ cup sugar
2 eggs, beaten
1 teaspoon almond extract (optional)
2 cups unsweetened flaked coconut
Unbaked pastry for 2-crust pie

Wonderful, beautifully golden little tarts with a sweet, nutty flavor and creamy centers. Well worth the extra effort.

The day before serving, drain the yogurt for 8 to 10 hours to make yogurt cheese (see directions on page 87).

Preheat oven to 425°F. To make the filling, cream together the margarine and sugar. Add 1 cup of the yogurt cheese to the creamed mixture along with the beaten eggs and optional almond extract; reserve any leftover yogurt cheese for another use. Stir. Blend in the coconut.

Line 24 greased tart or muffin tins with the pie pastry. Pour in the filling and bake for 10 minutes. Reduce temperature to 350°F and bake for 5 to 10 minutes more or until the tarts are light gold and just firm to the touch.

Note: To satisfy a very sweet tooth, place a little jam in the pastry shells before adding the filling.

Yield: 22 to 24 tarts.

Audrey Reeves
Hornby Island, British Columbia, Canada

• •

YOGURT CHEESE TARTS

■

3 cups plain yogurt
½ cup raisins
¼ cup hot water
Unbaked pastry for 2-crust pie
¼ cup margarine or butter
½ cup sugar
2 beaten eggs

Golden brown crusts with soft melt-in-your-mouth filling. Wonderful dessert pastries.

The day before serving, drain yogurt for 8 to 10 hours to make yogurt cheese (see directions on page 87).

Preheat oven to 425°F. Soak the raisins in the hot water. Line 24 greased tart or muffin tins with pastry. For the filling, cream together the margarine and sugar. Add the beaten eggs and 1 cup of the yogurt cheese; reserve any leftover yogurt cheese for another use. Stir to combine. Add the raisins and stir again.

206

(If the yogurt cheese is very firm, the water that the raisins soaked in can be added, too.) Fill the tart shells and bake for 10 minutes. Reduce heat to 350°F and bake for 10 minutes more or until filling is just firm.

Yield: 24 tarts.

Audrey Reeves
Hornby Island, British Columbia, Canada

. . . .

STRAWBERRY MAPLE YOGURT TART

■

CRUST
1 cup finely ground pecans
1 cup unbleached all-purpose flour
½ cup sugar
6 tablespoons butter, softened
1 egg
Grated rind of 1 orange

FILLING
2 cups plain yogurt
3 eggs
½ cup maple syrup
⅓ cup unbleached all-purpose flour

TOPPING
1 quart strawberries, hulled and sliced

A flavorful custard dressed with fresh strawberries for a fancy and beautiful dessert.

Preheat oven to 375°F. To make the crust, blend the nuts, flour, and sugar. Cut in the butter. Mix in the egg and rind. (If using a food processor, blend the nuts, flour, sugar, butter, and rind, then quickly pulse in the egg.) You may need to add a teaspoon or two of water to make a workable dough. Press the dough into a 9-inch pie plate, using only enough dough to make a crust ¼ inch thick. Bake for 10 minutes.

While the crust is starting to bake, whisk all of the filling ingredients together until the mixture is smooth. Remove the tart shell from the oven and reduce the temperature to 350°F. Pour the filling into the shell. Bake the filled tart for about 35 minutes, or until the filling is set. Place on a wire rack to cool.

Once the tart has cooled, arrange the sliced strawberries on top. Chill before serving.

Variation: Virtually any other fruit can be substituted for the strawberries.

Yield: One 9-inch pie (6 to 8 servings).

Helaine Selin
Amherst, Massachusetts

. . . .

YOGURT BERRY FLAN

■

CRUST
½ cup shortening
2 tablespoons brown sugar
1 cup quick-cooking oats
2 tablespoons oat bran
¼ cup water
½ cup unbleached all-purpose flour
½ cup whole-wheat pastry flour
½ teaspoon salt
1½ teaspoons baking powder
1 teaspoon ground cinnamon

FILLING
1 cup mashed strawberries, raspberries, or blackberries, or pitted cherries
1 tablespoon orange juice, or orange liqueur
2 envelopes (¼ ounce each) unflavored gelatin
⅓ cup hot water
3 cups plain yogurt
2 tablespoons sugar

Pretty to look at and great to eat. A good dessert for company.

Preheat oven to 350°F. To make the crust, cream the shortening and brown sugar together, then mix in the oats and oat bran. Beat in the water. In a separate bowl, combine the flours, salt, baking powder, and cinnamon, then stir into the oat mixture. Press the dough into a 9-inch flan pan or deep-dish pie plate, forming a 1-inch-high rim. Bake for 20 to 25 minutes or until golden brown. Cool.

To make the filling, combine the mashed berries and orange juice, or liquefy them in a blender. Sprinkle the gelatin over the hot water in a saucepan and heat to dissolve. Set aside to cool.

Place the yogurt in a bowl, stir the cooled gelatin mixture into the yogurt, and add the sugar and three-fourths of the berry mixture. Stir to combine. Pour the filling into the cooled crust and chill for at least 30 minutes. Drizzle the remaining berry mixture over the yogurt layer and chill until served.

Yield: One 9-inch flan (6 servings).

Helen Shepherd
Lyndhurst, Ontario, Canada

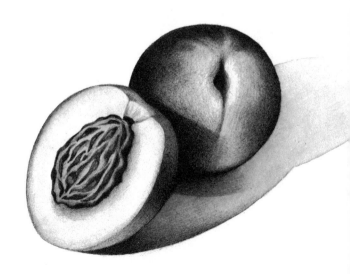

FRUIT YOGURT MOUSSE

■

1 cup water
2 tablespoons unflavored gelatin
3 tablespoons honey or sugar
1 can (12 ounces) frozen juice concentrate (orange, raspberry, or apple)
2 teaspoons vanilla
1 cup water
4 cups plain yogurt

A simple, nutritious treat that is quite easy to make. Try serving with chopped fresh fruit.

In a large saucepan, bring 1 cup water to a boil. Remove from heat and sprinkle gelatin over the top; let stand for 10 minutes, then beat gently to dissolve. Stir the honey into the saucepan mixture. Add the juice concentrate and the vanilla; stir well. In a separate bowl, blend 1 cup of water into the yogurt until smooth. Stir the yogurt mixture into the juice mixture, blending well. Pour into individual serving dishes, cover, and chill until set.

Yield: 6 to 8 servings.

Mary Miller
Vancouver, British Columbia, Canada

. . . .

PEACHY CREAM YOGURT MOUSSE

■

1 package (¼ ounce) unflavored gelatin
¼ cup water at room temperature
½ cup boiling water
6 tablespoons frozen orange juice concentrate
3 tablespoons frozen apple juice concentrate
2 tablespoons peach schnapps (peach liqueur)
1 cup whipping cream
1 cup plain yogurt

An easy dessert but one sure to impress those last-minute guests.

In a blender, soften the gelatin in ¼ cup water. Add ½ cup boiling water and let stand for several minutes until the gelatin dissolves. Blend until frothy. Add the orange juice, apple juice, and peach schnapps to the frothy gelatin and blend. Pour into a bowl. Fold the whipping cream and the yogurt together and fold them into the gelatin mixture. Pour into individual serving dishes. Chill for 20 minutes before serving.

Yield: 5 servings.

Janet Getler
Manchester, New Hampshire

. . . .

MOCHA PUDDING

∎

1 cup plain yogurt
1 package (8 ounces) cream cheese, softened
¼ cup maple syrup
2 teaspoons cocoa
1½ teaspoons coffee powder
½ teaspoon vanilla
Pinch of ground cinnamon, for garnish
Chopped walnuts, for garnish

A simple but elegant dessert with a full mocha taste and a very creamy texture. A food processor makes it especially easy. For the coffee powder, use finely ground decaffeinated coffee beans or the powder from which you make instant coffee.

Blend together the yogurt, cream cheese, maple syrup, cocoa, coffee powder, and vanilla in a blender. Pour into sherbet glasses and chill for 3 to 5 hours. Serve cold, sprinkled with cinnamon and walnuts.

Yield: 3 to 4 small servings.

Laura and Maurio Geilen
Arlington, Massachusetts

• •

NEW ENGLAND YOGURT BREAD PUDDING

∎

1 cup vanilla yogurt
1 cup milk
¼ cup butter or margarine
3 cups soft whole-wheat bread crumbs (easy to make in food processor) or bread cubes
½ cup honey
1 teaspoon ground cinnamon
¼ teaspoon ground nutmeg
Dash of salt
2 eggs, slightly beaten
½ cup raisins
1 cup unpeeled, cored, and diced apples

A delightful version of an old favorite.

Preheat oven to 350°F. Heat the yogurt, milk, and butter over medium heat, stirring constantly with a wire whisk, until the butter melts. Mix all the remaining ingredients in a 2-quart casserole. Add the yogurt mixture and stir. Place the casserole in a large pan; then pour boiling water into the large pan halfway up the sides of the casserole. Bake for 40 to 50 minutes or until a knife inserted in the center comes out clean.

Yield: 6 servings.

Lisa Mack
Boston, Massachusetts

• •

STRAWBERRY RHUBARB PUDDING

∎

1½ pounds fresh rhubarb
3 medium apples
1 pint fresh strawberries
2 cups water
½ to ¾ cup maple syrup
1 teaspoon vanilla
1 to 2 cups plain yogurt

Tastes like strawberry rhubarb pie without the crust.

Rinse the fruit. Cut the tough ends off the rhubarb; peel and core the apples; hull the strawberries. Chop all the fruit into ½-inch pieces. In a large saucepan, bring the fruit to a boil with the water. Lower heat and add the maple syrup and vanilla. Stir to combine. After about 15 minutes, begin to mash the softened fruit. Continue to simmer about 1 hour more, mashing occasionally until the sauce is fairly smooth. Remove from heat. Refrigerate and chill at least 3 hours. Just before serving, stir in the yogurt.

Yield: 4 servings.

Janice Convoy-Hellman
Burlington, Vermont

. . . .

BAKED FRUIT CUSTARD

∎

2 to 3 cups fresh peaches, strawberries, or a mixture — or 1 can (16 ounces) of un-sweetened fruit, drained
¼ cup unbleached all-purpose flour
¼ cup honey or sugar
1 cup plain yogurt
1 teaspoon vanilla
3 eggs

TOPPING
½ cup unbleached all-purpose flour
⅓ cup honey or brown sugar
1 teaspoon ground cinnamon
3 tablespoons butter, softened

Delicious all year long, served warm or cold, with or without whipped cream or ice cream. If you use canned fruit, try to get fruit packed in its natural juice so the custard does not become too sweet.

Preheat oven to 350°F. Remove any hulls, pits, seeds, or peels from the fruit; cut the fruit into bite-size pieces and place in the bottom of an ungreased soufflé dish or 8-inch square pan. In a medium-size bowl, mix the flour, honey, yogurt, vanilla, and eggs thoroughly and pour over the fruit. Mix the topping ingredients in the same bowl already used, and place dollops of topping on the fruit-custard mixture. Bake for 35 minutes.

Note: Substituting brown sugar for the honey in the topping gives it a more crumbly texture.

Yield: 6 servings.

Sarah Gloudemans
Dublin, New Hampshire

. . . .

AUNT ELEANOR'S YOGURT PUDDING

■

1 quart fresh raspberries or strawberries
1 cup whipping cream
1 cup plain yogurt
Turbinado or Demerara sugar (available at natural-foods stores)

An elegant and creamy dish that migrated to North America from Portsmouth, England. The crunchy sugar topping is a delicate treat.

Rinse and pick over the berries (if you're using strawberries, slice them) and place them in a wide glass bowl. Whip the cream with an electric mixer until stiff. At slow speed, quickly blend in the yogurt. Do not overbeat; the mixture should be loose but not runny. Spread evenly over the fruit. Sprinkle on sugar until the mixture is thoroughly covered (the sugar should be about ⅛ inch deep). Using the back of a spoon, press down the sugar lightly on the top of the pudding. Refrigerate for at least 4 hours before serving.

Yield: 4 servings.

Susan Joyner
Belleville, Ontario, Canada

. . . .

YOGURT CHEESE PARFAIT

■

1½ quarts plain yogurt, generously measured
1 cup sugar
1 tablespoon finely grated lemon rind
2 cups fresh raspberries, blueberries, or hulled and sliced strawberries

A simple but delectable summer dessert, elegant when served in parfait glasses. Start the yogurt cheese early on the day you plan to serve the parfait. See photo, page 53.

The day before serving, stir the plain yogurt and sugar together. Let this mixture drain for 4 hours to make yogurt cheese (see directions on page 87).

The next day, add the grated lemon rind to the yogurt cheese and mix well. Spoon the yogurt cheese into parfait glasses, alternating with layers of fresh berries. If the yogurt cheese is too thick, it can be thinned slightly with additional yogurt.

Yield: 4 servings.

Katie Herzog
Newton, Massachusetts

. . . .

STRAWBERRY MOCHA PARFAIT

∎

2 packages (8 ounces each) cream cheese, softened

2 cups plain yogurt

½ cup maple syrup or honey

2 teaspoons unsweetened cocoa powder

2 teaspoons instant coffee powder

2 cups hulled and sliced strawberries

1 cup crushed all-natural graham crackers

6 whole strawberries, for garnish

1 square semi-sweet chocolate, shaved

6 whole graham crackers, for garnish

An absolutely delicious layered parfait. Elegant, simple to prepare, and very special.

With an electric mixer, blend together the cream cheese and yogurt. Add the maple syrup and blend. Divide the mixture in half. Into one half, mix the cocoa and coffee; fold the strawberries into the other half. Mix each portion thoroughly.

In parfait glasses, layer as follows: Divide half the mocha mixture among the glasses. Sprinkle one-third of the crushed graham crackers on top. Add half the strawberry mixture, followed by another third of the graham crackers. Add the remaining mocha mixture, then the remaining graham crackers, and finally the last of the strawberry mixture. Top each glass with a whole strawberry, chocolate shavings, and one graham cracker tipped into the parfait. Chill for 3 to 5 hours, then serve cold with long-handled spoons.

Yield: 4 to 6 servings.

Laura Geilen
Arlington, Massachusetts

. . . .

HEAVENLY YOGURT DESSERT

∎

4 cups plain yogurt

1 tablespoon lemon juice

4 to 6 teaspoons brown sugar

½ cup orange marmalade, diced candied ginger, or jam or marmalade of your choice

A light, delicate, no-fuss finale for a dinner party. Heavenly with the candied ginger.

Blend all the ingredients. Chill for at least 2 hours to blend the flavors, then serve in stemmed dessert glasses.

Yield: 4 to 6 servings.

Connie Dingman
Hannon, Ontario, Canada

. . . .

PEARS ELEGANZA

■

5 large pears, peeled with
  stems on
2 cups water
½ cup sugar
1 cinnamon stick
1 inch fresh ginger, peeled
¾ cup Grand Marnier
¾ cup heavy cream, divided
1 tablespoon confectioners'
  sugar
1 tablespoon Grand Marnier
1 cup plain yogurt, divided
½ pound carob chips

A recipe true to its name. It even wowed a non-carob lover to whom we served it. Start this the day before you want to serve it. See photo, page 133.

Core the pears from the bottom, keeping the stems in place and leaving walls about ½ inch thick. Reserve the cores. Place the pears upright in a large saucepan with the water, sugar, cinnamon stick, ginger, and ½ cup Grand Marnier. Cook the pears until they are tender but not mushy—anywhere from 3 to 15 minutes, depending on the variety and ripeness. Cool, then add another ¼ cup Grand Marnier. Let stand in refrigerator overnight.

Just before serving, whip together ½ cup heavy cream, the confectioners' sugar, and 1 tablespoon Grand Marnier in an electric mixer until stiff. On slow speed, beat in ½ cup yogurt. Fill the cavities of the pears with this semi-stiff mixture. Trim a ½-inch-thick piece from each reserved pear core and plug the pear cavities. Place the pears on individual serving plates. To make the pears easy to eat, slice them horizontally at the point where the base narrows into the neck (see photo).

Melt the carob chips in a double boiler. Slowly add ¼ cup heavy cream and ½ cup yogurt, beating until smooth. Heat just until warmed through; do not allow to simmer. Pour the sauce over the pears and serve. Any additional whipped-cream mixture may be served separately on the side.

Note: The poaching liquid can be stored in the refrigerator and used to make this special dessert again.

Yield: 5 servings.

Susan Mess
Cambridge, Massachusetts

. . . .

YOGURT CHEESE CUSTARD

∎

1½ quarts plain yogurt
1 cup light cream
3 large eggs, separated
¼ cup sugar
¼ teaspoon almond extract
½ teaspoon grated lemon rind
¼ cup sliced almonds
3 cups hulled and sliced
  strawberries

A creamy, sweet strawberry custard with a pleasant almond crunch.

The day before serving, drain the yogurt for 8 to 10 hours to make yogurt cheese (see directions on page 87).

Preheat oven to 350°F. In a blender, combine 2 cups of the yogurt cheese with the cream, egg yolks, sugar, and almond extract; reserve any leftover yogurt cheese for another use. Blend the mixture until smooth. Stir in the lemon rind. In a bowl, beat the egg whites until stiff peaks form. Fold the egg whites into the yogurt mixture.

Pour the custard into a buttered 2-quart shallow baking dish. Set this dish in a larger shallow baking dish. Pour boiling water into the outer dish to a depth of 1 inch and place the pair of dishes in the oven. Bake for 20 minutes, then top with the nuts. Bake 10 to 15 minutes longer or until the custard sets. Serve warm or cool, topped with the berries.

Yield: 8 servings.

Roxanne E. Chan
Albany, California

YOGURT CREAM MOLD WITH RASPBERRY SAUCE

■

YOGURT CREAM MOLD
4 teaspoons unflavored gelatin
¼ cup cold water
1½ cups heavy cream
½ cup sugar
2¼ cups plain yogurt
1 teaspoon vanilla

RASPBERRY SAUCE
2 packages (10 ounces each)
    frozen raspberries in syrup,
    thawed
2 tablespoons sugar
1 tablespoon lemon juice
Kiwi or orange slices, for
    garnish (optional)

A dessert that everyone loves. Simple to prepare, and eye catching if made in the proper mold. See cover photo.

In a small bowl, soften the gelatin in the cold water for about 10 minutes. In a saucepan, combine the cream and sugar, then cook over moderate heat, stirring constantly, for 5 minutes or until the sugar is dissolved. Remove from heat. Add the gelatin mixture and stir until the gelatin is dissolved. Transfer to a bowl. Let the mixture cool for about 5 minutes, then whisk in the yogurt and vanilla. Mix well.

Rinse a pretty 1-quart mold or individual molds with cold water; shake the mold(s) but don't dry. Pour in the yogurt mixture; chill for 2 hours.

Dip a knife in warm water and run the blade around the edge of the mold. Invert the mold and rap on it to loosen the yogurt cream. Just before serving, top with sauce of combined raspberries, sugar, and lemon juice. Garnish with kiwi or orange slices if desired.

Yield: 6 servings.

Mimi Powell
Westport, Massachusetts

. . . .

HONEY SHRIKAND WITH YOGURT

■

1 quart plain yogurt
3 to 5 tablespoons honey
½ teaspoon ground cardamom
3 to 4 drops rose essence (optional)
Unsalted roasted pistachio nuts
    (optional)

A traditional dessert often served at weddings and on other special occasions in India. The more customary version is made from clabbered milk (raw milk left to thicken on its own enzymes), saffron, and sugar. Because this is an exceedingly delicate and delectable dish, it's best to keep the portions small.

The day before serving, drain the yogurt for no more than 8 hours to make yogurt cheese (see directions on page 87).

Add the honey, cardamom, and optional rose essence to 1½ to 2 cups of yogurt cheese and combine everything thoroughly while pushing the mixture through a wire strainer. Scrape the outside of the strainer to gather any of the mixture that sticks there. Spoon the dessert into small bowls and garnish with pistachio nuts if desired.

Yield: 4 to 6 servings.

Kamala Diwan
North Windham, Connecticut

. . . .

ALMOND KUGEL

■

1 package (8 ounces) cream cheese, softened at room temperature
½ cup butter, softened at room temperature
1 cup plain yogurt
6 eggs, slightly beaten
2 cups hot milk
⅓ cup sugar
1 teaspoon almond extract
1 package (16 ounces) egg noodles (fine or wide), cooked *al dente*

TOPPING
¼ cup sugar
1 teaspoon ground cinnamon
½ cup finely chopped almonds
2 tablespoons wheat germ

Served warm, a real treat for kugel devotees, and a pleasant alternative to the more common fruit or raisin version.

Preheat oven to 325°F. Cream together the cream cheese and butter, then stir in the yogurt. Add the eggs and mix well. Add the milk and mix well. Add the sugar and almond extract and mix again. Fold in the cooked noodles. Spoon the mixture into either a well-greased 9x13-inch pan or 2 well-greased 8-inch square pans.

For the topping, mix together the sugar, cinnamon, chopped almonds, and wheat germ; sprinkle over the kugel. Bake for 40 minutes to 1 hour.

Yield: 12 to 24 servings.

Edna Stohn
Malden, Massachusetts

. . . .

INDEX

■

A

■

ABC (Almond Banana Custard) Pie, 205
Almond Kugel, 217
Apples
    Apple & Yogurt Coffee Cake, 48
    Apple Cake, 176
    Apple Cranberry Muffins, 44
    Apple Honey Custard Pie, 196
    German Apple Cake, 60-61
    Yogurt-Cream Apple Pie, 197
Apricots
    Apricot Snack Cake, 175
    Oat Bran, Apricot & Yogurt Bread, 36
Arabic Cold Yogurt Soup, 103
Armenian Shish Kebab, 145
    (*photograph*, 131)
Artichoke Chicken, 138-39
    (*photograph*, 54)
Aunt Eleanor's Yogurt Pudding, 212
Austrian Alps Yogurt Dip, 82
Avocados
    Avocado Salad Dressing, 95
    Guacamole, 83
    Shrimp-Stuffed Avocados, 157

B

■

Baba Ghanooj, 86
Bagels, Yogurt & Oat Bran, 64
Baked Fish with Dill, 158-59
Baked Fruit Custard, 211
Bananas
    ABC (Almond Banana Custard)
      Pie, 205
    Banana & Coconut Raita, 117
    Banana Mint Yogurt Pie, 198-99
    Banana Raita, 118
    Banana Yogurt Pie, 201
    Basic Nutritious Frappe, 76
    Breakfast Bananas for Two, 24
    Creamy Banana Cake, 178
    Frosty Shake, 77
    Fruit Smoothie, 76

    Strawberry Yogurt Shake, 75
Barbecued Spicy Chicken, 139
Basic Nutritious Frappe, 76
Beans, Creamy, 165
Beef
    Beef & Potato Curry, 150
    Beef Strogurtoff, 151
    Fried Meatballs with Yogurt, 153
Beets
    Beet Koshumbir, 118
    Creamy Yogurt Beet Soup, 102
Bella's Best Popsicles, 192
Berry Good Frozen Yogurt, 188
Berry Patch Potato Salad, 111
Berry Walnut Bread, 34
Best-Ever Shake, 78
Black-Currant Muffins, 40
Blender Salmon Mousse with Tangy
    Yogurt Dill Sauce, 160
    (*photograph*, 130)
Blue Cheese Dunk, 84
Blue Cheese Salad Dressing, 95
Blueberries
    Berry Walnut Bread, 34
    Blueberry Cake, 175
    Blueberry Cream Dessert, 203
    Blueberry Yogurt Buckle, 184
    Blueberry Yogurt Pie, 204
    Bran Blueberry Muffins, 42
    Creamy Blueberry Bisque, 99
    Greek-Style Blueberry Pie, 202
    Very Blueberry Muffins, 43
      (*photograph*, 51)
    Wildcat Cafe Blueberry Pancakes, 20
    Yogurt Blender Pancakes, 21
Bobbie's Balanced Breakfast, 25
Boneless Veal with Yogurt Dressing, 152
Bran
    Bran Blueberry Muffins, 42
    Oatmeal Bran Muffins, 43
    Yogurt Bran Muffins, 44
Bread Pudding, New England Yogurt,
    210
Breads. *See* Coffee cakes; Muffins; Quick
    breads; Rolls; Yeast breads
Breakfasts and brunches, 19-25
    Bobbie's Balanced Breakfast, 25

    Breakfast Bananas for Two, 24
    Creamy Peach Melba Breakfast
      Bread, 23
    Maple Wheat & Raisin Pancakes, 21
    Muesli Pancakes, 20
    New England Breakfast Muesli, 25
    Wheat Berry Porridge, 22
    Whole-Grain Waffles, 22
    Wildcat Cafe Blueberry Pancakes, 20
    Wow! Waffles, 24 (*photograph*, 49)
    Yogurt Blender Pancakes, 21
    Yogurt Waffles, 23
Brunch Biscuit, 32-33
Brunches. *See* Breakfasts and brunches
Butter Cookies, 186
Buying yogurt, 15

C

■

Cakes & Cookies, 174-86. *See also* Coffee
    cakes
    Apple Cake, 176
    Apricot Snack Cake, 175
    Blueberry Cake, 175
    Blueberry Yogurt Buckle, 184
    Butter Cookies, 186
    Carrot Cake, 177
    Chocolate Yogurt Cheesecake, 182-83
      (*photograph*, 136)
    Creamy Banana Cake, 178
    Fruit Shortcake, 179
    Granola-Crust Yogurt Cheesecake, 183
    Great Gingerbread, 185
    Lemon Yogurt Cake, 176-77
    Little Bird's Pear Cake, 178-79
    Luscious Pound Cake, 180
    Maple Yogurt Cheesecake, 182
    Ricotta Yogurt Cake, 180
    Tracy's Cheesecake, 181
    Yogurt Chocolate-Chip Cake, 174
    Yogurt Lemon Cookies, 185
Cara's Delight, 193
Carrots
    Carrot Cake, 177
    Carrot Raita, 116

Grandmother's Carrot Salad, 109
Yogurt Carrot Soup, 104
Cheese Freeze, 187
Cheese, Yogurt. *See* **Yogurt Cheese**
Cheesecakes
Chocolate Yogurt Cheesecake, 182-83
(*photograph*, 136)
Granola-Crust Yogurt Cheesecake, 183
Maple Yogurt Cheesecake, 182
Ricotta Yogurt Cake, 180
Tracy's Cheesecake, 181
Chicken
Artichoke Chicken, 138-39
(*photograph*, 54)
Barbecued Spicy Chicken, 139
Chicken & Barley Salad, 126
Chicken Breasts Supreme, 143
Chicken Enchiladas, 140-41
Chicken in Curried Yogurt, 138
Chicken Karma, 128
Chicken on a Cloud, 144
Cold Chicken Curry, 126
Cultured Hickory Hollow Chicken
Breasts, 141
Indian Chicken, 127
Low-Cal Yogurt Baked Chicken, 128
Mandarin Chicken Salad, 125
(*photograph*, 52)
Mediterranean Chicken Salad, 124
Oven-Fried Chicken, 143
Parmesan Yogurt Chicken, 142
Sitoo (Grandmother's) Chicken, 129
Summer Chicken Curry, 127
Yogurt Chicken Satay, 142
Chicken Livers Stroganoff with Snow
Peas, 140
Chocolate
Cara's Delight, 193
Chocolate Raspberry Muffins, 45
Chocolate Yogurt Cheesecake, 182-83
(*photograph*, 136)
Cholesterol, 11
Citrus Yogurt Sauce, 91
Coconut Tarts, 206
Coffee cakes
Apple & Yogurt Coffee Cake, 48
Cranberry Pecan Coffee Cake, 60
Fruity Coffee Cake, 46-47
Honey Almond Coffee Cake, 57
Pecan Orange Coffee Cake, 58
Yogurt Spice Coffee Cake, 59
Yogurt Streusel Coffee Cake, 58-59
(*photograph*, 51)
Yummy Honey & Yogurt Coffee
Cake, 47
Cold Chicken Curry, 126
Cold Tomato Dill Soup, 100
Cookies
Butter Cookies, 186
Yogurt Lemon Cookies, 185
Cooking tips, 16-17

Corn & Barley Muffins, 39
Cornbreads
Country Cornbread, 36
Hearty Cornbread, 38
Spicy Cornbread, 37
Yogurt Cornbread, 37
Cranberries
Apple Cranberry Muffins, 44
Cranberry Almond Muffins, 41
Cranberry Pecan Coffee Cake, 60
Cream of Asparagus Soup, 105
Creamy Banana Cake, 178
Creamy Beans, 165
Creamy Blueberry Bisque, 99
Creamy Cucumber Dip, 83
Creamy Fruit Topping, 73
Creamy Mustard Salad Dressing, 93
Creamy Peach Melba Breakfast Bread, 23
Creamy Yogurt Beet Soup, 102
Crunchy Curried Yogurt Sauce, 91
Cucumbers
Arabic Cold Yogurt Soup, 103
Creamy Cucumber Dip, 83
Cucumber & Blue Cheese Dressing, 94
Cucumber & Tomato Raita, 116
Cucumber Mint Soup, 103
Cucumber Soup, 100
Cucumber Yogurt Soup, 101
Cucumbers & Fennel, 112
Greek Cucumber Dip, 85
Persian Yogurt Soup, 101
Yogurt-Dill Marinated Cucumbers
Raita, 113
Cultured Hickory Hollow Chicken
Breasts, 141
Currant Corn Muffins, 38
Curries
Beef & Potato Curry, 150
Chicken in Curried Yogurt, 138
Chicken Karma, 128
Cold Chicken Curry, 126
Curried Shrimp & Baby Vegetables,
161 (*photograph*, 129)
Indian Chicken, 127
Lamb Curry, 146
Rice Curry, 121
Summer Chicken Curry, 127
Curry Dip, 86
Custards
Baked Fruit Custard, 211
Yogurt Cheese Custard, 215

D

■

Desserts. *See* **Cakes & Cookies; Frozen**
Desserts; Pies, Puddings & Other
Desserts
Dips
Austrian Alps Yogurt Dip, 82

Baba Ghanooj, 86
Blue Cheese Dunk, 84
Creamy Cucumber Dip, 83
Curry Dip, 86
Greek Cucumber Dip, 85
Guacamole, 83
Hummus with a Difference, 84
Yogurt Dip, 83
Yogurt Vegetable Dip, 82
Zucchini Coriander Dip, 85
Dips, Spreads, Sauces & Dressings. *See*
Dips; Salad dressings; Sauces;
Spreads
Dressings. *See* **Salad dressings**
Dried Fruit & Yogurt Brown Bread, 35

E

■

Easy Gourmet Quiche, 158
Easy Nifty Dressing, 94-95
Egg Noodles with Yogurt-Vegetable
Sauce, 169
Egg Salad with Yogurt Dressing, 108
Eggplants
Baba Ghanooj, 86
Eggplant Salad with Chili Bites, 119
Emerald Salad with Yogurt Dressing, 71
Enchiladas, Chicken, 140-41
English Muffins, Honey Whole-Wheat,
62-63

F

■

Fairview Farms Cheese Pie, 155
Fantastic Fruit Salad, 70
Fast & Easy Yogurt Bread, 33
Fettucini, 164
Fish. *See* **Seafood**
Frappes. *See* **Smoothies**
Fresh Fruit & Yogurt Delight, 69
Fresh Fruit & Yogurt. *See* **Fruit &**
Yogurt, Fresh
Fresh Fruit with Yogurt Dressing, 72
(*photograph*, 51)
Fried Meatballs with Yogurt, 153
Frosty Shake, 77
Frozen Desserts, 187-94
Bella's Best Popsicles, 192
Berry Good Frozen Yogurt, 188
Cara's Delight, 193
Cheese Freeze, 187
Frozen Fruit Yogurt, 190
Frozen Raspberry Yogurt Cream,
188-89 (*photograph*, 56)
Frozen Yogurt Sandwich, 194
Kiwi Pecan Mousse, 191

Peach Preserve & Honey Frozen
Yogurt, 189
Rocky Pasture Pie, 192
Strawberry Dessert, 191
Yogurt Bars, 194
Yogurt Ice Cream, 187
Yogurt Popsicles, 193
Yummy Yogurt Tortoni, 190
Fruit & Nut Slaw, 108
Fruit & Yogurt, Fresh, 67-79
Basic Nutritious Frappe, 76
Best-Ever Shake, 78
Creamy Fruit Topping, 73
Emerald Salad with Yogurt
Dressing, 71
Fantastic Fruit Salad, 70
Fresh Fruit & Yogurt Delight, 69
Fresh Fruit with Yogurt Dressing, 72
(photograph, 51)
Frosty Shake, 77
Fruit Cream, 74
Fruit Smoothie, 76
Grand Marnier Fruit Salad, 68
Hawaiian Papaya Cooler, 79
Layered Fruit Salad, 71
Orange Yogurt Cooler, 79
Peach Colada, 78 (photograph, 50)
Pineapple Yogurt Ambrosia, 70
Scrumptious Sundae, 69
Simple, Creamy Yogurt Sauce, 73
Strawberries in Yogurt, 68
Strawberry Fruit Frappe, 76
Strawberry Yogurt Shake, 75
Summer Fruit Delight, 75
Sunflower Seed & Strawberry
Salad, 72
Tropical Fruit Frappe, 77
Walnut Raisin Yogurt, 73
Yogurt with Curried Fruit, 74
Fruit salads
Emerald Salad with Yogurt
Dressing, 71
Grand Marnier Fruit Salad, 68
Layered Fruit Salad, 71
Sunflower Seed & Strawberry
Salad, 72
Fruit Shortcake, 179
Fruit Smoothie, 76
Fruit Yogurt Mousse, 209
Fruity Coffee Cake, 46-47

G
■

Gary's Yogurt Sauce for Fish, 157
German Apple Cake, 60-61
Gingerbread, Great, 185
Grand Marnier Fruit Salad, 68
Grandmother's Carrot Salad, 109

Granola-Crust Yogurt Cheesecake, 183
Great Gingerbread, 185
Greek Cucumber Dip, 85
Greek Raita, 115 (photograph, 131)
Greek-Style Blueberry Pie, 202
Green Sauce, 89
Guacamole, 83

H
■

Ham & Cheese Muffins, 39
Hawaiian Papaya Cooler, 79
Healthy Salad Dressing with Yogurt, 93
Hearty Cornbread, 38
Heavenly Yogurt Dessert, 213
Herb Bulgur & Garbanzos, 168
Herb Rolls, 31
Herring, Tarragon, 156
Hickory Hollow Fish Puffs, 159
Homogenization, 15
Honey Almond Coffee Cake, 57
Honey Shrikand with Yogurt, 216-17
Honey Whole-Wheat English Muffins,
62-63
Hors d'Oeuvres, Yogurt Cheese, 89
How to buy yogurt, 15
Hummus with a Difference, 84

I
■

Indian Chicken, 127
Indian Meatballs in Yogurt Sauce, 146-47
Indian Potatoes, Cabbage & Green
Peppers, 120

K
■

Kashmiri-Style Leg of Lamb, 147
Key Lime Pie, 204
Kiwi Pecan Mousse, 191
Kugel, Almond, 217

L
■

Lactobacillus acidophilus, 12-13, 15
Lactose intolerance, 12
Lamb
Armenian Shish Kebab, 145
(photograph, 131)
Indian Meatballs in Yogurt Sauce,
146-47
Kashmiri-Style Leg of Lamb, 147

Lamb Curry, 146
Lamb Rani, 148-49
Middle Eastern Tacos, 149
Nutmeg Lamb, 148
Layered Fruit Salad, 71
Layered Quiche, 170
Lemon Pie, 199
Lemon Yogurt Cake, 176-77
Lemon Yogurt Muffins, 46
Lentils & Barley with Minted Yogurt, 166
Ling Cod Steaks in Yogurt, 162-63
Little Bird's Pear Cake, 178-79
Louise's Cucumber & Yogurt Raita, 114
Low-Cal Yogurt Baked Chicken, 128
Luscious Pound Cake, 180

M
■

Main Dishes, Poultry. See Poultry
Main Dishes, Red Meat. See Meat, Red
Main Dishes, Seafood. See Seafood
Main Dishes, Vegetarian. See Vegetarian
dishes
Mandarin Chicken Salad, 125
(photograph, 52)
Maple
Maple Strawberry Crumble, 200
Maple Wheat & Raisin Pancakes, 21
Maple Yogurt Cheesecake, 182
Strawberry Maple Yogurt Tart, 207
Masto-Khiar Raita, 114
Meat, Red
Armenian Shish Kebab, 145
(photograph, 131)
Beef & Potato Curry, 150
Beef Strogurtoff, 151
Boneless Veal with Yogurt Dressing, 152
Fairview Farms Cheese Pie, 155
Fried Meatballs with Yogurt, 153
Indian Meatballs in Yogurt
Sauce, 146-47
Kashmiri-Style Leg of Lamb, 147
Lamb Curry, 146
Lamb Rani, 148-49
Middle Eastern Tacos, 149
Nutmeg Lamb, 148
Pork Chops Paprika, 152-53
Rabbit with Yogurt, 154-55
Taste-of-New-England Skillet, 150-51
Veal Meatballs in Yogurt Sauce, 154
Yogurt, Mushroom & Bacon
Quiche, 156
Meatballs
Fried Meatballs with Yogurt, 153
Indian Meatballs in Yogurt
Sauce, 146-47
Veal Meatballs in Yogurt Sauce, 154
Meatish Sweet Balls, 168-69

Mediterranean Chicken Salad, 124
Middle Eastern Tacos, 149
Mint, Onion & Hot-Chili Raita, 117
Mocha Pudding, 210
Mock Sour Cream, 91
Mock Sour Cream Pie, 200-01
Mousses
    Blender Salmon Mousse with Tangy
      Yogurt Dill Sauce, 160
      (*photograph*, 130)
    Fruit Yogurt Mousse, 209
    Kiwi Pecan Mousse, 191
    Peachy Cream Yogurt Mousse, 209
Muesli Pancakes, 20
Muffins
    Apple Cranberry Muffins, 44
    Black-Currant Muffins, 40
    Bran Blueberry Muffins, 42
    Chocolate Raspberry Muffins, 45
    Corn & Barley Muffins, 39
    Cranberry Almond Muffins, 41
    Currant Corn Muffins, 38
    Ham & Cheese Muffins, 39
    Lemon Yogurt Muffins, 46
    Oatmeal Bran Muffins, 43
    Poppy-Seed Muffins, 41
    Salmon Muffins, 40
    Strawberry Yogurt Muffins, 45
    Very Blueberry Muffins, 43
      (*photograph*, 51)
    Yogurt Bran Muffins, 44
    Zucchini Date Muffins, 42

N

Natural Garlic Dressing, 92-93
New England Breakfast Muesli, 25
New England Yogurt Bread Pudding, 210
Nutmeg Lamb, 148
Nutritional value of yogurt, 10-13

O

Oat Bran
    Oat Bran, Apricot & Yogurt
      Bread, 36
    Yogurt & Oat Bran Bagels, 64
Oatmeal Bran Muffins, 43
Orange Yogurt Cooler, 79
Orzo Salad, 164
Oven-Fried Chicken, 143

P

Pancakes
    Maple Wheat & Raisin Pancakes, 21
    Muesli Pancakes, 20
    Wildcat Cafe Blueberry Pancakes, 20
    Yogurt Blender Pancakes, 21
Papaya Cooler, Hawaiian, 79
Parfaits
    Strawberry Mocha Parfait, 213
    Yogurt Cheese Parfait, 212
      (*photograph*, 53)
Parmesan Yogurt Chicken, 142
Pasta
    Egg Noodles with Yogurt-Vegetable
      Sauce, 169
    Fettucini, 164
    Orzo Salad, 164
    Snappy Seafood Shells, 163
    Sunny Tortellini, 165
    Vegetable Pasta Yogurt Toss, 166-67
Peaches
    Peach Colada, 78 (*photograph*, 50)
    Peaches & Cream Pie, 195
    Peach Preserve & Honey Frozen
      Yogurt, 189
    Peachy Cream Yogurt Mousse, 209
    Peach Yogurt Custard Pie, 198
Pears
    Little Bird's Pear Cake, 178-79
    Pears Eleganza, 214 (*photograph*, 133)
Pecan Orange Coffee Cake, 58
Peppers
    Indian Potatoes, Cabbage & Green
      Peppers, 120
    Potato Pepper Bake, 171
    Roasted Pepper & Yogurt Soup, 98
      (*photograph*, 55)
Persian Yogurt Soup, 101
Pies, Puddings & Other Desserts, 195-217
    ABC (Almond Banana Custard)
      Pie, 205
    Almond Kugel, 217
    Apple Honey Custard Pie, 196
    Aunt Eleanor's Yogurt Pudding, 212
    Baked Fruit Custard, 211
    Banana Mint Yogurt Pie, 198-99
    Banana Yogurt Pie, 201
    Blueberry Cream Dessert, 203
    Blueberry Yogurt Pie, 204
    Coconut Tarts, 206
    Fruit Yogurt Mousse, 209
    Greek-Style Blueberry Pie, 202
    Heavenly Yogurt Dessert, 213
    Honey Shrikand with Yogurt, 216-17
    Key Lime Pie, 204
    Lemon Pie, 199
    Maple Strawberry Crumble, 200
    Mocha Pudding, 210
    Mock Sour Cream Pie, 200-01
    New England Yogurt Bread
      Pudding, 210
    Peaches & Cream Pie, 195

Peachy Cream Yogurt Mousse, 209
Peach Yogurt Custard Pie, 198
Pears Eleganza, 214
    (*photograph*, 133)
Strawberry Maple Yogurt Tart, 207
Strawberry Mocha Parfait, 213
Strawberry Pie, 196
Strawberry Rhubarb Pudding, 211
Yogurt & Cream Cheese Pie, 202
Yogurt Berry Flan, 208
Yogurt Cheese Custard, 215
Yogurt Cheese Parfait, 212
    (*photograph*, 53)
Yogurt Cheese Tarts, 206-07
Yogurt-Cream Apple Pie, 197
Yogurt Cream Mold with Raspberry
    Sauce, 216 (*photograph*, 134)
Pineapple Yogurt Ambrosia, 70
Poppy-Seed Muffins, 41
Popsicles
    Bella's Best Popsicles, 192
    Yogurt Popsicles, 193
Pork Chops Paprika, 152-53
Potato salads
    Berry Patch Potato Salad, 111
    Potato Salad with Yogurt, 110
    Zesty Potato Salad, 110
Potatoes
    Beef & Potato Curry, 150
    Indian Potatoes, Cabbage & Green
      Peppers, 120
    Potato Pepper Bake, 171
    Stuffed Baked Potatoes, 121
Poultry, 124-28, 137-45
    Artichoke Chicken, 138-39
      (*photograph*, 54)
    Barbecued Spicy Chicken, 139
    Chicken & Barley Salad, 126
    Chicken Breasts Supreme, 143
    Chicken Enchiladas, 140-41
    Chicken in Curried Yogurt, 138
    Chicken Karma, 128
    Chicken Livers Stroganoff with
      Snow Peas, 140
    Chicken on a Cloud, 144
    Cold Chicken Curry, 126
    Cultured Hickory Hollow Chicken
      Breasts, 141
    Indian Chicken, 127
    Low-Cal Yogurt Baked Chicken, 128
    Mandarin Chicken Salad, 125
      (*photograph*, 52)
    Mediterranean Chicken Salad, 124
    Oven-Fried Chicken, 143
    Parmesan Yogurt Chicken, 142
    Sitoo (Grandmother's) Chicken, 129
    Summer Chicken Curry, 127
    Turkey Tetrazzini, 144-45
    Yogurt Chicken Satay, 142
Pound Cake, Luscious, 180
Puddings

Mocha Pudding, 210
New England Yogurt Bread
    Pudding, 210
Strawberry Rhubarb Pudding, 211

Q

Quiches
    Easy Gourmet Quiche, 158
    Layered Quiche, 170
    Yogurt, Mushroom & Bacon
      Quiche, 156
Quick breads. *See also* **Coffee cakes; Corn-**
    breads; Muffins
    Berry Walnut Bread, 34
    Dried Fruit & Yogurt Brown Bread, 35
    Oat Bran, Apricot & Yogurt Bread, 36
    Yogurt Herb Quick Bread, 34
Quick Yogurt Yeast Rolls, 32

R

Rabbit with Yogurt, 154-55
Raitas
    Banana & Coconut Raita, 117
    Banana Raita, 118
    Carrot Raita, 116
    Greek Raita, 115 (*photograph*, 131)
    Louise's Cucumber & Yogurt Raita, 114
    Masto-Khiar Raita, 114
    Mint, Onion & Hot-Chili Raita, 117
    Spiced Yogurt & Zucchini Raita, 115
    Yogurt-Dill Marinated Cucumbers
      Raita, 113
Raspberries
    Frozen Raspberry Yogurt Cream,
      188-89 (*photograph*, 56)
    Yogurt Cream Mold with Raspberry
      Sauce, 216 (*photograph*, 134)
Refreshing Spinach, 120
Rice Curry, 121
Rich Yogurt Bread, 30
Ricotta Yogurt Cake, 180
Roasted Pepper & Yogurt Soup, 98
    (*photograph*, 55)
Rocky Pasture Pie, 192
Rolls
    Herb Rolls, 31
    Quick Yogurt Yeast Rolls, 32

S

Salad dressings
    Avocado Salad Dressing, 95
Blue Cheese Salad Dressing, 95
Creamy Mustard Salad Dressing, 93
Cucumber & Blue Cheese Dressing, 94
Easy Nifty Dressing, 94-95
Egg Salad with Yogurt Dressing, 108
Fresh Fruit with Yogurt Dressing, 72
    (*photograph*, 51)
Healthy Salad Dressing with Yogurt, 93
Natural Garlic Dressing, 92-93
Yogurt Dijon Salad Dressing, 92
    (*photograph*, 135)
Yogurt, Radish & Mint Salad
    Dressing, 94
Salads & Side Dishes, 107-21. *See also*
    Fruit salads
Banana & Coconut Raita, 117
Banana Raita, 118
Beet Koshumbir, 118
Carrot Raita, 116
Cucumber & Tomato Raita, 116
Cucumbers & Fennel, 112
Egg Salad with Yogurt Dressing, 108
Eggplant Salad with Chili Bites, 119
Fruit & Nut Slaw, 108
Grandmother's Carrot Salad, 109
Greek Raita, 115 (*photograph*, 131)
Indian Potatoes, Cabbage & Green
    Peppers, 120
Louise's Cucumber & Yogurt
    Raita, 114
Masto-Khiar Riata, 114
Mint, Onion & Hot-Chili Raita, 117
Potato Salad with Yogurt, 110
Refreshing Spinach, 120
Rice Curry, 121
Spiced Yogurt & Zucchini Raita, 115
Stuffed Baked Potatoes, 121
Super Slim Salad, 113
Tangy Cabbage Salad, 109
Yogurt Coconut Rice, 112
Yogurt-Dill Marinated Cucumbers
    Raita, 113
Zesty Potato Salad, 110
Salads, main dish
Chicken & Barley Salad, 126
Mandarin Chicken Salad, 125
    (*photograph*, 52)
Mediterranean Chicken Salad, 124
Salmon
Blender Salmon Mousse with Tangy
    Yogurt Dill Sauce, 160
    (*photograph*, 130)
Salmon Muffins, 40
Salmon Spread, 88
Sauces
Blender Salmon Mousse with Tangy
    Yogurt Dill Sauce, 160
    (*photograph*, 130)
Citrus Yogurt Sauce, 91
Crunchy Curried Yogurt Sauce, 91
Gary's Yogurt Sauce for Fish, 157
Green Sauce, 89
Sesame Yogurt Sauce, 90
    (*photograph*, 132)
Simple, Creamy Yogurt Sauce, 73
Steven's Simple Sensational Sauce, 90
Scones
Scones, 63
Yogurt Scones with Lemon, 65
Scrod in Yogurt Sauce, 162
Scrumptious Sundae, 69
Seafood, 156-64
Baked Fish with Dill, 158-59
Blender Salmon Mousse with Tangy
    Yogurt Dill Sauce, 160
    (*photograph*, 130)
Curried Shrimp & Baby Vegetables,
    161 (*photograph*, 129)
Easy Gourmet Quiche, 158
Gary's Yogurt Sauce for Fish, 157
Hickory Hollow Fish Puffs, 159
Ling Cod Steaks in Yogurt, 162-63
Orzo Salad, 164
Scrod in Yogurt Sauce, 162
Shrimp-Stuffed Avocados, 157
Snappy Seafood Shells, 163
Tarragon Herring, 156
Sesame Yogurt Sauce, 90
    (*photograph*, 132)
Shakes. See Smoothies
Shepherd's Fall Vegetable Pie, 167
    (*photograph*, 135)
Shish Kebab, Armenian, 145
    (*photograph*, 131)
Shrimp
Curried Shrimp & Baby Vegetables,
    161 (*photograph*, 129)
Shrimp-Stuffed Avocados, 157
Side dishes. See Salads & Side Dishes
Simple, Creamy Yogurt Sauce, 73
Sitoo (Grandmother's) Chicken, 129
Smoked Bluefish Spread, 88
Smoothies
Basic Nutritious Frappe, 76
Best-Ever Shake, 78
Frosty Shake, 77
Fruit Smoothie, 76
Hawaiian Papaya Cooler, 79
Orange Yogurt Cooler, 79
Peach Colada, 78 (*photograph*, 50)
Strawberry Fruit Frappe, 76
Strawberry Yogurt Shake, 75
Tropical Fruit Frappe, 77
Snappy Seafood Shells, 163
Soups, 97-105
Arabic Cold Yogurt Soup, 103
Cold Tomato Dill Soup, 100
Cream of Asparagus Soup, 105
Creamy Blueberry Bisque, 99
Creamy Yogurt Beet Soup, 102
Cucumber Mint Soup, 103

Cucumber Mint Soup, 103
Cucumber Soup, 100
Cucumber Yogurt Soup, 101
Persian Yogurt Soup, 101
Roasted Pepper & Yogurt Soup, 98
    (*photograph*, 55)
Strawberry Soup, 99
Summer Yogurt Soup, 102
Turkish Yogurt Soup, 104
Yogurt Carrot Soup, 104
Sour Cream, Mock, 91
Sour Cream Pie, Mock, 200-01
Spiced Yogurt & Zucchini Raita, 115
Spicy Cornbread, 37
Spreads
    Baba Ghanooj, 86
    Hummus with a Difference, 84
    Salmon Spread, 88
    Smoked Bluefish Spread, 88
    Yogurt Cheese, 87
Steven's Simple Sensational Sauce, 90
Stonyfield Farm Yogurt, 8-10
Strawberries
    Maple Strawberry Crumble, 200
    Strawberries in Yogurt, 68
    Strawberry Dessert, 191
    Strawberry Fruit Frappe, 76
    Strawberry Maple Yogurt Tart, 207
    Strawberry Mocha Parfait, 213
    Strawberry Pie, 196
    Strawberry Rhubarb Pudding, 211
    Strawberry Soup, 99
    Strawberry Yogurt Muffins, 45
    Strawberry Yogurt Shake, 75
    Sunflower Seed & Strawberry Salad, 72
    Yogurt Cheese Custard, 215
    Yummy Yogurt Tortoni, 190
Stuffed Baked Potatoes, 121
Summer Chicken Curry, 127
Summer Fruit Delight, 75
Summer Yogurt Soup, 102
Sunflower Seed & Strawberry Salad, 72
Sunny Tortellini, 165
Super Slim Salad, 113

T
∎

"Tacos," Middle Eastern, 149
Tangy Cabbage Salad, 109
Tarragon Herring, 156
Tarts
    Coconut Tarts, 206
    Strawberry Maple Yogurt Tart, 207
    Yogurt Cheese Tarts, 206-07
Taste-of-New-England Skillet, 150-51
Tomatoes
    Cold Tomato Dill Soup, 100
    Cucumber & Tomato Raita, 116

Tortellini, Sunny, 165
Tracy's Cheesecake, 181
Tropical Fruit Frappe, 77
Turkey Tetrazzini, 144-45
Turkish Yogurt Soup, 104

V
∎

Veal
    Boneless Veal with Yogurt
        Dressing, 152
    Veal Meatballs in Yogurt Sauce, 154
Vegetable Pasta Yogurt Toss, 166-67
Vegetarian dishes, 164-71
    Creamy Beans, 165
    Egg Noodles with Yogurt-Vegetable
        Sauce, 169
    Fettucini, 164
    Herb Bulgur & Garbanzos, 168
    Layered Quiche, 170
    Lentils & Barley with Minted
        Yogurt, 166
    Meatish Sweet Balls, 168-69
    Potato Pepper Bake, 171
    Shepherd's Fall Vegetable Pie, 167
        (*photograph*, 135)
    Sunny Tortellini, 165
    Vegetable Pasta Yogurt Toss, 166-67
Very Blueberry Muffins, 43
    (*photograph*, 51)

W
∎

Waffles
    Whole-Grain Waffles, 22
    Wow! Waffles, 24 (*photograph*, 49)
    Yogurt Waffles, 23
Walnut Raisin Yogurt, 73
Wheat Berry Porridge, 22
Whole-Grain Waffles, 22
Whole-Wheat Bread, 29
Whole-Wheat Raisin Bread, 28-29
    (*photograph*, 51)
Wildcat Cafe Blueberry Pancakes, 20
Wow! Waffles, 24 (*photograph*, 49)

Y
∎

Yeast breads. *See also* **Rolls**
    Fast & Easy Yogurt Bread, 33
    Rich Yogurt Bread, 30
    Whole-Wheat Bread, 29
    Whole-Wheat Raisin Bread, 28-29
        (*photograph*, 51)

Yogurt & Cream Cheese Pie, 202
Yogurt & Oat Bran Bagels, 64
Yogurt Bars, 194
Yogurt Berry Flan, 208
Yogurt Blender Pancakes, 21
Yogurt Bran Muffins, 44
Yogurt Carrot Soup, 104
Yogurt Cheese, 87
    Banana Mint Yogurt Pie, 198-99
    Coconut Tarts, 206
    Yogurt Cheese Custard, 215
    Honey Shrikand with Yogurt, 216-17
    Key Lime Pie, 204
    Salmon Spread, 88
    Smoked Bluefish Spread, 88
    Summer Fruit Delight, 75
    Yogurt Cheese Custard, 215
    Yogurt Cheese Hors d'Oeuvres, 89
    Yogurt Cheese Parfait, 212
        (*photograph*, 53)
    Yogurt Cheese Tarts, 206-07
Yogurt Chicken Satay, 142
Yogurt Chocolate-Chip Cake, 174
Yogurt Coconut Rice, 112
Yogurt Cornbread, 37
Yogurt-Cream Apple Pie, 197
**Yogurt Cream Mold with Raspberry
    Sauce, 216 (*photograph*, 134)**
Yogurt Cream Topping, 92
Yogurt Dijon Salad Dressing, 92
    (*photograph*, 135)
**Yogurt-Dill Marinated Cucumbers Raita,
    113**
Yogurt Dip, 83
Yogurt Herb Quick Bread, 34
Yogurt Ice Cream, 187
Yogurt Lemon Cookies, 185
Yogurt, Mushroom & Bacon Quiche, 156
Yogurt Popsicles, 193
**Yogurt, Radish & Mint Salad
    Dressing, 94**
Yogurt Scones with Lemon, 65
Yogurt Spice Coffee Cake, 59
Yogurt Streusel Coffee Cake, 58-59
    (*photograph*, 51)
Yogurt Vegetable Dip, 82
Yogurt Waffles, 23
Yogurt with Curried Fruit, 74
Yummy Honey & Yogurt Coffee Cake, 47
Yummy Yogurt Tortoni, 190

Z
∎

Zesty Potato Salad, 110
Zucchini
    Spiced Yogurt & Zucchini Raita, 115
    Zucchini Coriander Dip, 85
    Zucchini Date Muffins, 42

Meg Cadoux Hirshberg lives in Wilton, New Hampshire, with her husband, Stonyfield Farm Yogurt president Gary Hirshberg, and two children. Her interest in healthful cooking, which began while she was manager of an organic vegetable farm, has been further enriched by her years of experience cooking with yogurt.